UNCOVERING RACE

Uncovering Race

A Black Journalist's Story of
Reporting and Reinvention

Amy Alexander

BEACON PRESS
BOSTON

Beacon Press
Boston, Massachusetts
www.beacon.org

Beacon Press books
are published under the auspices of
the Unitarian Universalist Association of Congregations.

18 17 16 15   8 7 6 5 4 3 2 1

This book is printed on acid-free paper that meets the uncoated paper
ANSI/NISO specifications for permanence as revised in 1992.

Text design and composition by Wilsted & Taylor Publishing Services

Library of Congress Cataloging-in-Publication Data
Alexander, Amy.
Uncovering race : a black journalist's story of reporting and reinvention /
Amy Alexander.
p. cm.
Includes index.
ISBN 978-0-8070-6102-2 (paperback : alk. paper)
1. Alexander, Amy, 1963– 2. African American women journalists—Biography.
3. Journalists—United States—Biography. 4. United States—Race relations—
Press coverage. 5. Minorities—Press coverage—United States. I. Title.
PN4874.A34A3 2011
070.92—dc22
[B]   2011012344

CONTENTS

April 29, 1992—Southbound on U.S. Interstate Highway 5

We hurtled out of the Tehachapi Mountains as dusk deepened to blue night, the Chevrolet Lumina moving swiftly toward South Central Los Angeles. Once out of the San Fernando Valley on the San Diego Freeway, we saw splashes of flames between buildings. I was in the car with two others, a female reporter riding shotgun and a male photographer behind the wheel. Two hours earlier we had sat in a fluorescent-lit newsroom 250 miles north of Los Angeles. Now I rode in the backseat of a silvery-blue sedan speeding south from Fresno toward disaster. Radio antennas bobbed on the car. It crossed my mind that our midsize Chevy looked like an unmarked police vehicle.

This could be a problem.

Four white Los Angeles cops had been acquitted of criminal charges in the 1991 beating of an unarmed black motorist named Rodney King. The jury in Simi Valley had returned the verdict at 3:15 p.m. on that Wednesday. Ten minutes later, through an electronic in-house message, I flippantly told my editor at the *Fresno Bee* newspaper that I'd volunteer for "riot duty." Seated twenty feet away, he read my message on the big, bulky computer atop his city desk, and by early evening the flat San Joaquin Valley and the silent Tehachapi Mountains stretched between me and the largest civil disturbance in the nation's history.

Not far from LA, we realized we needed to spread out. My reporting colleague—a white Los Angeles native—parted ways with us just north of the sprawling city. Taking one of the two large, first-generation cellular phones we'd brought, she set out for the Civic

Center driving a rented white Chrysler LeBaron. The photographer, a Chinese American man I'd known since college, steered our car toward South Central. Emergency sirens sounded. Loose knots of people formed every few miles. The radio announcer's voice rattling from the Chevy dashboard reported looting at downtown stores.

I had covered disasters before, natural and social, in cities across America. The rush that always preceded covering calamity wasn't new, and the urgency of this story was unmistakable. Yet as we neared the University of Southern California exit off the freeway, something less recognizable spiked the familiar adrenalin high. The idea of confronting a full-scale urban uprising brought queasy twitching to my stomach.

I wondered whether there would be shootings, firebombings, or mobs of rioters clubbing bystanders at random. But it was more than that. Something else cranked up the anxiety, turning it into a prickly pear I didn't want to handle. This denial troubled me further. Finally, my concentration drifting away from the map opened across my lap, I owned up to what troubled me.

What if I became suddenly incapable of separating my feelings as a liberal, African American woman from those of my objective, professional self? Could I agree with the crowd's anger without endorsing its actions? Is this what's referred to in those laborious newspaper seminars as an "ethical dilemma"? I was allowing my mind to drift toward the future, though I also knew better; staying in the moment was crucial, not only for my ability to report and write on deadline but also for staying safe if things heated up around me.

The photographer turned up the volume of the car radio; we listened more closely to a local news program. Every few moments, breathless correspondents from Simi Valley to Long Beach filed urgent-sounding reports describing small crowds of people gathering in streets. A *Los Angeles Times* satellite office was hit, and the culprits made off with a few computers, according to the radio broadcast. In the three or four hours since the verdict had come in, the Civic Center in downtown Los Angeles had drawn hundreds of angry, chanting people.

From above South Central, a reporter aboard a news helicopter described watching black and brown residents yanking white-looking motorists from their cars and beating them at the intersection of Florence and Normandie Avenues in South Central Los Angeles. The local news station also reported that a city firefighter riding an engine toward a burning building had been shot. All this sounded like mayhem.

The ethical questions bubbled once again in my chest. I struggled to swallow them. We had only about an hour to get to the action in South Central; interview residents, police, and fire officials; and then roll out to the Associated Press offices at Second and Figueroa Streets in downtown LA. From there, we would transmit our stories and photographs to the newsroom in Fresno.

After pulling the Chevrolet off the freeway and into the intersection of Normandie and La Salle Avenues, we saw we had missed our mark, Florence and Normandie, by a few miles. Turning back wasn't an option. We watched a crowd gathering along a commercial strip nearby.

A furniture store and adjacent apartment building were ablaze, their broken windows framing angry lashes of yellow-orange flame that whipped up into the dark sky. Firefighters, evidently stunned by reports that they were being shot at, had positioned their trucks between themselves and the crowd in order to work the fire. We parked half a block away on La Salle, locked the car, and stood for a moment looking toward the intersection at Normandie Avenue.

The photographer, like me, was a native San Franciscan. We had gone to the same university, circulated in the same tight circle of twenty-something Bay Area print journalists. During and after college, on the streets of Berkeley, San Francisco, and Oakland, boisterous public demonstrations, protests, and marches had been regular assignments for us. We had both recorded—and experienced—the sweeping momentum that often overtakes public protests.

The photographer buckled the clasp of a small canvas pack tightly around his waist, its generous pocket fitting snugly against the small of his back. Then he slid the pocket around his body to rest below his abdomen. Inside were a heavy black lens and a few rolls of film. A 35-mm camera, weighted with a flash and lens, hung over his left shoulder. I knew that he would keep an elbow or fingertip discreetly pressing the camera's nylon strap to his side whenever he was not shooting.

I slipped a narrow reporter's notebook into the back pocket of my Levis and gripped a black ballpoint pen in the sweating palm of my right hand. I swiveled the bill of my black San Francisco Giants baseball cap forward, pulling it tightly around my short, curly hairdo. The night air was warm, but I snapped shut the windbreaker I'd thrown on.

Looking up at the sky to the south, I watched the horizon take on a peach-colored glow. Firelight. It was getting late, and we had to file soon. The sounds of scattered yells and sharp concussions of breaking glass grew louder as we ran-walked out of the residential street toward the commercial strip of Normandie Avenue. Los Angeles was on fire, a disaster in the making. We were primed to chronicle the calamity.

It seems odd to say, but the LA riots couldn't have happened at a better time. Before that moment, midway through my second year as a staff writer on the metro desk of the *Fresno Bee*, I was becoming restless, gripped by impatience and a persistent worry that I would never work my way out of the Central Valley.

Even before I'd flung myself into the major blowup in LA, my professional persona had been forged by disaster coverage. My byline had appeared on stories about big forest fires in the Sierra Nevada mountains, the gargantuan Loma Prieta earthquake that had creased Northern California in October 1989, massive street protests over inadequate federal funding for AIDS and HIV research, and any number of high-profile murders and crimes in San Francisco and Fresno. Yet my modest treasure trove of "war stories" derived from the escapades that lay beneath those bylines was puny compared to that of older newsroom veterans.

Nevertheless, my portfolio had filled out nicely by the time I arrived in Los Angeles in 1992 to cover the riots for the McClatchy Company's newspapers. I saw a long career ahead in the news business; I just didn't want it to play out entirely in the dusty, hot, politically conservative "Bible Belt" region of my home state.

I didn't know yet how much I didn't know about reporting and writing—but I had the feeling that the professional experience the photographer and I were obtaining was preparing me to work on the larger journalistic stage. We had successfully performed in conditions that were akin to war, covering the massive urban and political turmoil of that week-long riot for McClatchy, which published newspapers across the western United States. I returned to Fresno after five days on the streets in LA and felt exhilarated. But the initial sense of pride and accomplishment dropped like a sack of rocks after I looked at the copies of the daily *Bee* that a news aide had arranged on my desk in the newsroom. (In the days before the Internet, reporters working on hot stories in remote locations often didn't see their published stories until they returned to home base.)

When I picked up the *Fresno Bee* daily editions that held my stories detailing the riots and aftermath, my heart sank. An editor back in Fresno, who had received the stories I'd transmitted by the clunky portable computers we'd traveled with, had inserted language in some of the stories that was troubling. To realize that I had risked life and limb amid the shooting and burning that had transpired in LA and had managed to deliver compelling, unbiased stories about the angry residents, the frustrated business owners who lost property, and other aspects of the conflagration, only to have a white male editor sitting safely in the newsroom hundreds of miles away muck up my reporting with words like "savage" and "rampaging," well . . . I was deflated.

But not deterred.

And the LA riots, it seemed to me, might be just the story to propel me up to the next level of news organizations: the *Los Angeles Times* or one of the big East Coast newspapers. After that, who knew where the work might lead?

My name on a news story—my byline—had become a defining part of my professional identity, and I wanted it to represent good work, not the work of a hack or a partisan or a dilettante. I wanted readers to know that when they saw my name above a news story or a feature, they could rest assured that they were receiving accurate information that was delivered in compelling language. Above all, I wanted readers to trust that when they saw my name on a story, they would walk away with information that helped them better navigate their world—or at least gave meaningful context to their lives.

My life before I became a journalist had been positively informed and enriched by good bylines. Even before I knew what it took to deliver high-quality reporting and writing, day in and day out, I recognized that some reporters in my hometown newspapers always seemed to produce stories that were satisfying, while some others just seemed to be phoning it in. I wanted to be a reporter who delivered substance, consistently.

Coming of age in Northern California had been ideal preparation for this line of work, especially the genus known as "run-and-gun" journalism. By the time I parachuted into the thick of the looting, shooting, and burning of South Central Los Angeles in late April 1992, I had already witnessed plenty of strange, harrowing events.

Growing up during the 1960s and '70s, I came to see journalists, like cops and teachers, as professionals who fulfilled sacred civic duties in cities across the United States: preserving and protecting democracy.

Was I naive in this understanding?

Idealistic?

Oh, yes.

But consider this partial list of events that I watched unfold during my formative years in San Francisco. I was born there in 1963, and by the age of five, I was absorbing the news events around me:

- 1968–1974: The DayGlo rise and slow death of hippie culture in Haight-Ashbury; student anti–Vietnam War protests (Berkeley, Oakland, and San Francisco); tear-gas-shrouded protests over the formation of ethnic studies departments at San Francisco State University; Black Panther rallies, shootouts, and arrests; the Zodiac serial killings; the kidnapping of local newspaper heiress Patricia Hearst by the radical Symbianese Liberation Army; the brainwashed Patty "Tania" Hearst caught on tape, wearing a wig and a trench coat, taking part in a bank stick-up in the Sunset District; other assorted bombings, street actions, and sit-ins.

- 1975–1981: The Jonestown Massacre of 914 former Bay Area residents in Guyana; the assassinations of San Francisco mayor George Moscone and Supervisor Harvey Milk; widespread riots protesting the light sentencing of Dan White, the former San Francisco supervisor convicted of killing Moscone and Milk; the attempted assassination of President Gerald Ford at a San Francisco hotel; and even more assorted bombings, sit-ins, and street actions.

It seemed to me that journalists were important people. In the pages of the two local daily newspapers—the morning *San Francisco Chronicle* and the afternoon *San Francisco Examiner*—and on the television airwaves, I came to see journalists as smart, dedicated, fearless investigators who worked important magic: using words and images to explain and lend context to happenings that were, let's face it, quite insane.

By the time I graduated from high school in the summer of 1981, the prospect of using language to communicate with scores of readers in a handy, low-cost format such as newspapers seemed like a most excellent way to make a living. It did not occur to me that the world of journalism might not be open to people like me: a black woman from a working-class family who would not attend an Ivy League university. As a child of the post–civil rights era, a late-hour baby boomer, I believed that if I got a journalism education and worked hard at learning the trade, my opportunities for joining the ranks of working journalists were good.

Sure, I knew that black women were more likely than whites to face challenges in the media industry. I also knew at least a bit about the effects of corporate ownership on newspapers: one of the leading works of media industry analysis, *Media Monopoly* by veteran journalist and editor Ben Bagdikian, had been required reading in my college journalism department. Still, in the 1980s, after completing the magazine journalism program at San Francisco State University, I enthusiastically embarked on a reporting career, first wearing proudly the badge of "cub reporter" at the Hearst-owned *San Francisco Examiner*.

The fact that I was, for nearly two years, the only black female reporter on the Metropolitan staff at that midsize afternoon paper did not initially concern me. Yet several years later, I realized that my time working at my hometown paper marked the beginning of a long, Conradian journey through the heart of darkness of American news organizations.

The value of my byline, I learned over the years, was to editors and newsroom managers highly subjective; few managers shared my belief that my byline was more than an ephemeral presence. For many of them, the expectation was that the newspaper's reputation for quality and accuracy was to be protected, but reporters' bylines were interchangeable, the backgrounds and the insights we carried with us into the newsroom each day only marginally relevant to the work we produced.

The longer I stayed in journalism, the clearer it became that I am the only one who can safeguard the essential integrity of my journalistic identity. Much more than just safeguarding my individual reputation, though, my efforts on this front also must be focused on achieving high standards of fairness, accuracy, and ethics as part of a broader effort to defend journalism. This mission is now more crucial than ever, as the Internet expands, carrying bits and pieces of information farther and faster than we journalists could have imagined twenty years ago.

There is this, too: the Internet allows anyone to hang out a journalist's shingle—a development that is rich with promise *and* peril, especially in terms of its implications for news coverage of race and class issues in America.

First, a look at why this is proving perilous for coverage of race and class:

At a time when America is becoming ever more economically and ethnically diverse, financial challenges in the news business are diminishing the numbers of talented, experienced reporters and editors of color. Layoffs, buyouts, and a general contracting of the number of editorial workers in the nation's news organizations have been particularly devastating to the small population of black, Latino, and Asian journalists—professionals who entered news organizations in measurable numbers only in the mid-twentieth century. And, at least as of the beginning of the second decade of the 2000s, the emerging online organizations—including traditional print news outlets that have increased their online presences—have not made the recruitment, hiring, and retention of qualified journalists of color a top priority.

This in turn means that as populations grapple with the inevitable clashes (and mergings) that will occur in a multiethnic nation, news organizations will not be equipped to cover the interactions—whether positive, negative, or indifferent—even as these interactions accumulate. The 2008 presidential race—which featured our first viable African American candidate, Barack Hussein Obama, and the first electable female candidate, Hillary Rodham Clinton, vying for the Democratic nomination—exposed a national political press corps ill equipped to comprehensively and accurately inform audiences of the many complicated elements that had brought those two individuals into the forefront of presidential politics. Too often, rather than informing accurately, calmly, and with authority, news organizations—led predominantly by white males from middle-class backgrounds—deliver coverage that inflames audience's fears about a multicultural America.

At the same time, the Internet also is fertile ground for enterprising journalists of all races, ages, and class backgrounds to chart their own path and to deliver reporting and opinion that is fully contextualized. The growth of online-only journals, news websites, and socially conscious publications has been explosive, with writers, editors, and activists of color seizing the opportunity to cover and disseminate news and information that resonates with those populations. "Controlling your own narrative" has become as commonplace as it once was to order a subscription to your local daily newspaper.

There is a big drawback, however, in that the one-stop-shopping aspect of Old Media did, at least, come with a degree of professionalism baked in. The New Media landscape is more like the Wild West, with social media and independent news and opinion sites barreling along at breakneck speed while lumbering Old Media outlets chug along behind, desperate to keep up but seemingly incapable of stopping the Internet train from speeding out of sight. This would be completely exhilarating, except that there are two damsels tied to the tracks in the distance: journalists of color, and the increasingly frustrated audiences of ethnic citizens in the United States who see the train coming and suspect it will not stop for them.

Years passed between the Los Angeles riots, the episode that first sparked my interest in thinking about race and the American press, and my first sustained opportunity to explore race and media in a mass-market publication, the web journal Africana.com, in 2000. My work in corporate news organizations up to that point had been guided in part by role models and mentors, male and female reporters and editors who were black, white, and Latino. Along with their real-time examples, I had also had limited knowledge of black journalists of long ago, including Ida B. Wells-Barnett, who had written passionately about lynching in African American newspapers early in the twentieth century. It wasn't something I thought about all the time, but in a symbolic sense, I believed I could build on their legacy—or at least not destroy the chances for any other journalists of color who would come after me.

As the second decade of the twenty-first century begins, the prospect of young journalists of color finding mentors capable of relating to their particular ethnic and cultural experience has assumed new urgency. So many veteran journalists of color are leaving the business before their "natural" retirement ages that one can legitimately worry that the future of accurate, comprehensive coverage of people of color, poor communities, and other marginalized populations and issues will fall completely by the wayside of large, well-funded news organizations. This is to say (not imply) that the shrinking ranks of journalists of color employed at major news outlets does not inspire confidence that coverage of people of color—and of poor people and other historically marginalized groups—will improve in years to come. Yes, the blogosphere is rising; but how many pure journalism websites thus far have shown a willingness to hire significant numbers of trained journalists of color, or to focus on issues of particular relevance to people of color? Time's up—the answer, as of this writing, is three: TheRoot.com, TheLoop21.com, and Black AmericaWeb.com, a site founded by the popular African American disc jockey Tom Joyner. And those sites are small operations with few full-time staffers.

Black journalism academics and veteran journalists, including Alice Bonner at the University of Maryland and Pamela Newkirk at New York University, have written extensively of the soul-numbing challenges faced by the first- and second-generation black, Latino, and Asian journalists over the years: the existential loneliness from being the "first" in a big newsroom; the constant pressure to prove themselves in the eyes of white male editors; the subtle and overt signs of doubt from top editors about their skills and worthiness.

Consider Gwen Ifill, the first black woman to regularly host a national news program, *Washington Week in Review*, on PBS. Ifill came of age in journalism not long after the turmoil of the civil rights era and the urban riots of the 1960s. Throughout her successful career, which began at daily papers, she had worked relentlessly and brilliantly. Yet for all her bona fides—staff writing jobs at the *New York Times* and the *Washington Post*, a trove of big journalism awards—Ifill drew criticism in October 2008 from some media watchers who questioned her ability to objectively moderate a televised debate between vice presidential candidates Joseph Biden, a Democratic senator from Delaware, and Sarah Palin, the Republican governor of Alaska. The criticism reached a crescendo after reports emerged that Ifill had written a book about black political leadership that used the candidacy of Barack Obama as its peg. The book was scheduled for publication in 2009, and Ifill had spent the better part of 2008 researching and writing it, with the large theme of the generational evolution of black politicians since the civil rights era. In a marketing sense, the book's title, *The Breakthrough: Politics and Race in the Age of Obama*, was designed to capitalize on the rapid ascent of the soon-to-be-president. But Ifill's editorial net also captured other post-civil-rights-era black politicians, including Newark mayor Corey Booker and Adrian Fenty, mayor of the District of Columbia. The younger-generation black politicians were described in the press as "postracial," in that they were said to appeal to progressive and independent white voters while also being somewhat less "threatening" to conservatives than their predecessors—Rev. Jesse Jackson, who had made a bid for the Democratic presidential nomination in 1988, and black regional elected officials such as Harold Washington, former mayor of Chicago. Yet Ifill's attempt to examine this political evolution drew criticism from some consumers and "media critics" who questioned Ifill's "objectivity" in having worked on the final stages of the book while also hosting a high-profile vice presidential candidates' debate.

It didn't seem to matter that Ifill had begun work on the book long before Senator Obama clinched the Democratic nomination for the 2008 presidential election. An outburst of criticism erupted from some politically conservative commentators, and implicit within the question of Ifill's objectiveness was an assumption that has dogged black journalists for decades—that we can't possibly cover black people or issues of particular relevance to blacks fairly and dispassionately.

As I see it, the more pressing questions center on the ever-shrinking number of black journalists at the national level, rather than whether journalists of color can "objectively" report on the policy and activities of the nation's first black president. Despite the amazing triumph of Barack Obama, the fact remains that black journalists continue to represent an infinitesimal percentage of the high-profile journalists who can be said to wield significant influence in coverage. Along with Ifill, only a few African Americans fit that description: Eugene Robinson, an op-ed columnist at the *Washington Post*; Michele Norris, cohost of *All Things Considered* at National Public Radio; and Bob Herbert, an op-ed columnist at the *New York Times*. (At the *Miami Herald*, national columnist Leonard Pitts Jr. is a valuable and influential voice, while at the *Atlanta Constitution*, Cynthia Tucker is a columnist with a national profile; both have received Pulitzer Prizes for commentary. But I daresay that Bob Herbert and Gene Robinson wield more influence among decision makers in Washington, D.C.—though even their influence is small in comparison to that of David Broder, éminence grise of the *Post*'s op-ed page.)

As I began working at newspapers during the mid-1980s, I learned bits and pieces about a few of the black journalists who had been successful in mainstream newsrooms in the mid-twentieth century, including Robert Maynard, one of the first black reporters hired at the *Washington Post*. Maynard's big break happened during the racial tumult and street riots of the 1960s. He went on to great heights as a reporter and editor at the *Washington Post* and was even—for a short period, anyway—the only black person to own and publish a daily newspaper in a metropolitan market, the *Oakland Tribune*.

At that time, the incentive for newsroom leaders to begin hiring journalists who were black, Latino, or Asian grew out of the riots of the late 1950s and '60s. Sealing the deal for many newspaper editors was a groundbreaking federal study commissioned by Democratic president Lyndon Johnson in 1967. The National Advisory Commission on Civil Disorders, known in shorthand as the Kerner Commission, studied the causes of, and fallout from, the recent urban unrest.

The Kerner Commission's report outlined the role of mainstream news organizations in fanning the flames of urban unrest through biased, shoddy, or scant coverage of minorities—and through coverage and editorial writing that sometimes was blatantly hostile and antiblack. In one of the report's more pointed passages, the eleven-member commission wrote:

The media report and write from the standpoint of a white man's world. The ills of the ghetto, the difficulties of life there, the Negro's burning sense of grievance, are seldom conveyed. Slights and indignities are part of the Negro's daily life, and many of them come from what he now calls "the white press"—a press that repeatedly, if unconsciously, reflects the biases, the paternalism, the indifference of white America. This may be understandable, but it is not excusable in an institution that has the mission to inform and educate the whole of our society.

The Kerner Report spurred owners and publishers at several large news organizations to at least take baby steps in the direction of recruiting journalists who were black, Latino, or Asian. Was hiring journalists of color simply a cynical bulwark against political pressure, or was it a means of "getting the story" on the racial upheaval that gripped several American cities during the 1960s? Both, I say. According to biographer Alice Bonner, Robert Maynard observed many years later that the urban unrest of the mid-1960s was "the black journalist's ticket to a place in the newsroom. There is no doubt in my mind that practically all the black reporters who worked at that time for daily newspapers were hired to cover this violence."

Well before the election of Barack Obama late in 2008, the U.S. Census Bureau had released demographic data indicating that people of color are likely to constitute a majority of the nation's total population before the midpoint of this century. In some regions of the country, including the Southwest, white residents are already a minority. Yet in editorial staffs at traditional news organizations—as well as at startup, online-only, or hybrid print and online news outlets—the percentage of journalists of color lags far behind the percentage of people of color who live and work in communities. The annual newsroom demographic survey conducted by the American Society of News Editors found in 2010 that black journalists accounted for 4.88 percent of all editorial workers in the news outlets nationwide that responded to the survey. At the same time, the U.S. Census reported that blacks made up 12.9 percent of the nation's population in 2009.

Interestingly, notwithstanding two black columnists who cover media full-time (Richard Prince at the Maynard Institute and Eric Deggans at the *St. Petersburg Times*), this occupation gap is rarely covered by journalists and columnists who report on the media industry for large mainstream news organizations. It is an odd void, especially considering the growing interest—bordering on obsession, some would say—that the industry now shows in covering itself.

It wasn't always that way. In the late 1990s, as Internet use became more commonplace among consumers, the media industry was itself becoming news. By coincidence, monitoring the press's coverage of race-related stories in the United States, as well as charting the in-house battles around race and class that take place in newsrooms, had become my journalistic focus.

The LA riots—with their dramatic arc that began with the brutal beating of a black motorist, Rodney King, by a group of Los Angeles police officers and ended with the week-long violence that erupted after those white officers were acquitted of criminal charges—very literally sparked my interest in media criticism. Unlike Robert Maynard and other of my predecessors, I was already a full-fledged staff writer by the time I had my trial by urban unrest. But following that harrowing week in Southern California, after I returned to the Central Valley, I reviewed other newspapers' coverage and saw plenty that was problematic.

After covering the LA riots, I moved on to the *Miami Herald*, a newsroom in a media market that is legendary for its racial fractiousness. From there, in the itinerant spirit of many modern-day journalists, I moved to Boston; to St. Paul, Minnesota; and to Washington, D.C., along the way writing about racial issues in America and talking to, commiserating with, and learning from other journalists. This book is an outgrowth of my years working in my home state of California and in these other cities, and of my experiences and observations along the way. My trajectory is in its broadest outlines similar to that of any ambitious contemporary journalist with the stamina to keep moving forward: from staff writing at "legacy" daily newspapers to writing or editing at magazines, to the supposed Valhalla of book writing. I have done this . . . but not exactly in a straight line.

And gradually, along the way, what had seemed immediately after the Los Angeles riots an intriguing quest—finding places where I could affix my byline to coverage and analysis of the news industry's race and class struggles—eventually became my passion.

The questions I raise here aren't likely to instantly produce definitive answers. Yet I believe that in airing the confounding subject of race and the American press, in questioning the larger implication of a media culture and industry that struggles to positively inform Americans' understanding of each other at a time of immense demographic changes, there may emerge some valuable lessons for others.

Should this book reach that goal, it will be my best byline yet.

ONE

San Francisco

A Race and Media Paradox

Its motto was "Monarch of the Dailies." The masthead of the *San Francisco Examiner* had carried that grandiose tag for almost a century by the time I first walked into its newsroom in the summer of 1988.

I'd started writing for the afternoon paper while a junior at San Francisco State University, covering campus rallies, budgets, and anything else that made news. I'd been recommended by my campus journalism advisor and was brought on at the metro desk by Tim Reiterman, the *Examiner*'s city editor. It was a plum assignment, and I saw it as a foot in the door, a great opportunity that would lead to a full-time staff position. It was my hometown paper, and I felt that my skills and my knowledge of the city made me a natural: I'd already had two summer internships at dailies, the *Philadelphia Daily News* and the *Fresno Bee*. But as a native San Franciscan, my fondest wish was to land at the "Ex." I envisioned a long, successful career there.

Reiterman, a six-foot-three, soft-spoken man with thick, auburn hair, welcomed me to the staff by taking me to lunch with a couple of the paper's assistant city editors. He told me he wanted me to be successful. I looked at him with awe and respect—Reiterman was legendary in San Francisco journalism. He was also a somewhat tragic figure: a decade earlier, in November 1978, he'd been on the ill-fated trip to the tiny South American nation, Guyana, when followers of the Peoples Temple fired on a group of Congressional investigators, journalists, and a few church members who'd decided to leave the jungle encampment. Reiterman was shot, along with Congressman Leo Ryan, a Democrat from San Mateo, California; Ryan's aide,

Jackie Speier; and three other journalists. Congressman Ryan, an NBC network newsman, and two photographers were killed, while Reiterman and Speier survived. The horror they experienced was eclipsed by what happened a few hours later in that Guyanese encampment, Jonestown: the group's leader, Jim Jones, ordered 914 members of the church to commit suicide. As reports from Reiterman and other journalists later revealed, those Peoples Temple members who refused to voluntarily drink Jim Jones's lethal cocktail of cyanide-laced fruit drink were injected with poison or shot by other church members, who then killed themselves. Jones died from a gunshot wound to the head.

The majority of those who died were African American, including hundreds of elderly parishioners, babies, and children. When published reports of the massacre—some written for the *Examiner* by Reiterman—first reached San Francisco, the gruesome images of hundreds of bloated bodies laying in the dirt under the merciless equatorial sun had fascinated and terrified me, a fifteen-year-old sophomore at Abraham Lincoln High School in the Sunset District.

Those photographs—and learning that for several years Reiterman had been exposing Jones's abuse of those black parishioners—helped convince me to become a journalist. I didn't anticipate getting shot at in the pursuit of a story, mind you. But I believed that Reiterman's willingness to face potential danger to get to the bottom of the apparent exploitation of hundreds of vulnerable American citizens was an honorable way to make a living. He'd taken a bullet and nearly died to tell the stories of black folks who, it turned out, wouldn't live to tell their own stories. I'd set my heart on becoming a journalist before the terrible events of November 1978; that story cemented my determination.

In addition to Reiterman and other San Francisco print reporters, my journalistic role models included some local broadcast news people: Belva Davis, a black news anchor at a network affiliate station; Vic Lee, a Chinese American reporter at the NBC station KRON; and a deep bench of other female reporters and anchors, including Terry Lowry, Karna Small, Faith Fancher, and Wendy Tokuda. Along with their counterparts at the two daily newspapers, these workaday journalists described with flair and passion the ups and downs, ins and outs of regular citizens and city and state officials, as well as the goings-on in the many institutions and cultural outlets of the Bay Area. They were distant yet real—alluring, through-the-looking-glass figures that ignited my imagination. I had no sense of the challenges they faced in-house at their news organizations; my uninformed assessment as an outsider was that they led exciting lives by virtue of their being journalists of color in a work force that was clearly dominated by whites.

But over the years, at discrete points of contact, I learned the high personal price paid by some journalists of color working at mainstream news organizations.

Joining the news staff of the *Examiner* as a campus correspondent in 1988, and being welcomed by Tim Reiterman, was beyond exciting. In April 1989, I "graduated" from covering campus news to a full-time staff writer position, one that was funded under a new internship program that the paper's leadership had recently instituted. Before that, unlike some other big-city newspapers at that time, the owners of San Francisco's two largest newspapers hadn't bothered to institute formal internship programs, let alone internship programs designed to recruit and train young journalists of color. But under persistent pressure from some journalism educators—including the chair of the journalism department at San Francisco State at that time, Betty Medsger—and from black, Latino, and Asian journalists in the Bay Area, editorial leaders at the *Examiner* and at the *San Francisco Chronicle* set up small internship programs that began in 1988.

To those unfamiliar with the racial and ethnic peculiarities of San Francisco's civic and corporate institutions, the fact that the city's largest news organizations had lagged far behind in racially integrating their operations may come as a surprise. Some journalism educators and minority journalism trade organizations, including the Bay Area chapters of the National Association of Black Journalists and the National Association of Hispanic Journalists, had a vested interest in pushing owners and publishers of the "Chron" and the "Ex" to fund internship programs and to encourage them to bring their newsroom staffs in line (or more closely in line) with the ethnic makeup of Bay Area residents.

That interest has been heightened in the twenty-first century
by the massive downsizing and shrinking of news staffs in the Bay
Area and around the nation. The contraction of traditional new organizations' editorial staffs, along with the erosion of their business
model, has the potential to further diminish consumers' options for
obtaining well-sourced, comprehensive coverage of their own communities. The chicken-and-egg nature of this is difficult to tease out:
Did the multiethnic populations in the Bay Area abandon traditional
news organizations because the available content failed to meet their
needs and expectations, thereby contributing to declining circulation and ad revenues? Or has the drop-off in circulation caused Bay
Area newspapers like the *Chronicle* and the *San Jose Mercury News*
to make staff cuts in editorial departments, eroding their ability to
deliver content desired by the increasingly diverse readership? Either
way, as of midspring in 2008, it was clear that the Bay Area's venerable print news organizations were grappling with a cold new reality:
their print, production, and personnel costs had rendered their business models unsustainable, no matter how many newsroom positions
they eliminated.

The *San Francisco Examiner* met its financial Waterloo in 1999
when its owner, the Hearst Corporation, bought the competing *San
Francisco Chronicle*, then sold the *Examiner* to a small investment
group led by a longtime San Francisco political and business family,
Florence Fang and her son, Ted Fang. Hearst paid the Fangs' investment group several million dollars to get the reconstituted paper up
and running, then effectively left the storied *Examiner* to wither on
the vine. At the time of the sale to the Fangs, some Bay Area industry
watchers read a multicultural silver lining into the deal, hailing it as
a sign that an Asian family had at last entered the big leagues of the
region's media ownership class. But the Fangs couldn't stop the *Examiner* from losing money, any more than the Hearst Corporation or
forty years of a joint operating agreement could before them. They
gave up on it a few years later. The *Examiner* is now part of a nationwide chain of free dailies owned by Phillip Anschultz, a billionaire
whose portfolio includes media, real estate, entertainment, and energy properties, under the banner of the Clarity Media Group. The
Examiner's distinct neo-Gothic masthead now tops the front page

of tabloid-sized free daily papers in a dozen major U.S. cities. Its editorial scheme is a hybrid of small, old-fashioned news-gathering staffs producing printed and online dailies, and a growing collection of "citizen journalists," called "Examiners," who are recruited in individual cities to report news items and write blogs. And somewhere amid the recent twisting, turning fortunes of that legendary brand, its editorial brain trust ceased reporting its newsroom demographic numbers to the annual census produced by the American Society of News Editors (ASNE), the dominant news industry trade group.

While dozens of small and midsize Chinese-, Spanish-, and Vietnamese-language papers are published in the Bay Area, the loss of the big dailies will be especially devastating to those populations in the Bay Area in the future. The big papers were never perfect in terms of their ability to consistently cover all facets of a dauntingly kinetic population. Yet they provided a form of social and cultural glue that small ethnic-language papers aren't likely to replicate. Still, it is hard not to question whether years' worth of inattention to the growing communities of Cambodians, Vietnamese, Salvadorans, and other international residents by editorial staffs of the big mainstream papers did not somehow lead them to their current bleak fates.

It is a long-standing paradox of the Bay Area, one which generations of journalism educators and journalists of color have not yet been able to resolve: How can a region so rich in multiethnic, multicultural populations and institutions, and with a corporate and civic leadership class that is politically sensitive to serving the needs of diverse populations (some would say overly so), have gone on for so long allowing its largest daily newspapers to get away with ignoring the depth of experiences of ethnic populations?

In San Francisco and its surrounding cities, the newsroom diversity parity index has long been out of whack, which is to say that the gap between the ethnic makeup of journalists and the ethnic makeup of populations in circulation and audience areas is large. While mainstream news organizations in some other urban regions have for the past thirty years attempted to shrink such gaps—by establishing minority internship programs and by conducting recruiting and outreach programs in ethnic communities—the presence of virtually all-white newsrooms in San Francisco and the surrounding Bay Area has been a stubborn source of frustration for journalists of color, consumers, and some journalism educators.

I received a solid journalism education at San Francisco State, one that emphasized both the fundamentals (the nuts and bolts, shoe-leather reporting skills of verification, accuracy, ethics, and classic inverted-pyramid writing style) and approaches to covering diverse communities. But that dual emphasis was not shared by most other journalism departments. Similarly, the evolution of SF State's journalism program during the 1980s from a passive conduit of labor—from which at least a handful of fortunate, usually white graduates were hired by the *Chronicle* or the *Examiner* in most years—to a persistent nudge on ethnic diversity made it unique among Bay Area college journalism programs. (No offense to the Berkeley Graduate School of Journalism, but its coursework built around covering ethnic communities and its administrative efforts to recruit and place student journalists of color arrived almost as an afterthought, during the 1990s.)

How is it that the San Francisco Bay Area, a bastion of cultural hipness, political liberalism, and high-earning populations, continues fielding editorial staffs of mainstream news organizations that are virtually all white? And how could it be that even entreaties from journalism educators were ignored for so long by gatekeepers of the region's news organizations?

For perspective, I turned to Betty Medsger, a former *Washington Post* reporter and former chairwoman of the journalism department at San Francisco State. Medsger, who is a mentor to me, is the author of a 1996 comprehensive study of accredited university journalism programs, "Winds of Change: Whither Journalism Education?" Her broad professional experience in general and her experience at San Francisco State give Medsger great insight into several key aspects of the link between university journalism training programs (and their shortcomings) and the status of racial inclusion within the news business.

Medsger arrived at SF State in the late 1970s as a part-time lecturer and was hired as an associate professor in the early 1980s. In short order, she became the first woman to lead the department; she was also the first department chair to make the recruitment of minority journalists for faculty and lecturer positions a top priority. Along with championing efforts to increase ethnic diversity in the academy and in newsrooms, Medsger has written extensively about the ill-advised trend in university journalism departments to emphasize "media communications theories" rather than vocational-level journalism instruction.

"In university hierarchies, journalism departments and schools have long suffered from inferiority complexes. This led many to begin requiring every professor to have a PhD," Medsger said when I phoned her in mid-2009 at her home in Manhattan. "And that began to pull journalism education away from the practical."

The fallout of that trend has been far-reaching. Most notably, it has discouraged generations of college journalism professors from remaining up to date with industry developments, including the rise of digital media and the growing need for reporters and editors who excel at covering ethnic communities and issues. By the end of the 2000s, many university journalism programs had updated their curricula and facilities to accommodate students' interest in digital media, somewhat to the detriment of the fundamental aspects of reporting, writing, and editing. When I interviewed her, Medsger was undecided about how that lopsided equation might shake out in terms of producing well-rounded journalists equipped to report high-quality journalism in the twenty-first century. Will young journalists hereafter focus on mastering the technical expertise needed to deliver news and information in multiplatform formats, while ignoring or deemphasizing the valuable interpersonal skills and basic fundamental reporting skills that are required? And if college journalism programs continue to emphasize digital acumen over fundamental reporting skills and the "softer" skills required to effectively cover issues of class and ethnic communities, how accurately will news organizations of the future cover people of color and related topics?

In the 1980s, the technological aspects of those questions were less urgent, in Medsger's view, than the quest to build a teaching staff that was more reflective of the Bay Area populations. (However, Medsger did oversee the computerization of the journalism department at SF State. When I began taking classes there in the early eighties, each classroom had electric typewriters for student use;

by the end of the decade, the classrooms and the newspaper and magazine production facilities had been shifted to networked PCs.) Back then, Medsger sought to place greater emphasis on meeting the fast-changing demographics of SF State's student body and the surrounding populations.

Looking at the rich ethnic and income diversity of SF State's student population—in the 1980s nearly half the students were ethnic minorities, and most came from working-class families—and of the surrounding Bay Area population, it only made sense to attempt to build a journalism staff that was more reflective of those it sought to serve, Medsger told me. Twenty years on, in 2009, ethnic minorities represented almost three-quarters of the 29,628 students enrolled at SF State. In the journalism department in 2009, five of nine tenured or tenure-track professors were ethnic minorities.

I didn't know it when I enrolled there in 1981, but San Francisco State University's journalism department was "unusual," Medsger said. "We were an all-white faculty with a nearly all-white student body [among the journalism majors] on a very diverse campus. It didn't take a genius to see that something was wrong with that." She encountered "open hostility" from some on the faculty when, during interviews to become chair, she said that one of her goals would be to "racially diversify the faculty and students." Nevertheless, a majority of the faculty committed to the idea from the beginning, which over time made it possible for Medsger to succeed. In 1990 she launched the Center for the Integration and Improvement of Journalism (CIIJ), a nonprofit training and service organization based at SF State. Initially it was hard to raise money, but over the years, CIIJ has received funds from the Ford and the John S. and James L. Knight foundations to support its student and professional training initiatives.

While in the undergraduate program at SF State, I and other students viewed Medsger as scarily smart and fiercely dedicated to high-quality journalism and journalism education. We didn't have a clue about the behind-the-scenes battles that took place, but we certainly knew that we could count on Medsger to deal with us like adults, which is to say fairly and with candor. In hindsight, I understand that it wouldn't have been diplomatic for Medsger to have shared all the details with the students she was charged with educating and placing.

In the ensuing years, though, I've read numerous studies and papers focusing on journalism education and diversity, and I now have an even greater appreciation for Medsger's intelligence, foresight, and courage.

Medsger's goal of placing well-qualified young journalists of color in professional newsrooms is even more crucial today—and also more daunting, given the epic changes wracking the news industry. In the midst of the reordering of most news organizations' business models (from healthy budgets for news gathering to comparatively paltry budgets for reporting and producing news and information), another long-standing factor also poses a challenge to contemporary journalism educators seeking to encourage greater diversity from the point of hiring graduates: the old myth of the shallow pool of qualified minority journalists.

The position long held by some white newsroom leaders, however sotto voce, was that there simply weren't enough qualified minority journalists and journalism graduates. A Freedom Forum study by Lee B. Becker, a professor at the University of Georgia's Grady College of Journalism and Mass Communications, is one of many to highlight a supply and demand problem. (By another name, it has been a problem of willful oversight on the part of newsroom gatekeepers.) Becker and his colleagues reviewed decades' worth of college journalism program graduation rates. They found that while the nation's college and university journalism programs graduated comparatively few students of color, the rate of hire was significantly lower for minority journalism graduates than for their white fellow graduates.

In 2002 Becker published a report (also for the Freedom Forum) examining diversity in hiring at newspapers nationwide. The summary, published at the Freedom Forum's website, was headlined "Diversity in Hiring: Supply Is There. Is Demand?" Becker wrote, "It's a myth that there are not enough minority applicants to alter the face of America's newsrooms. . . . The problem is that there is not a suitable link between supply and demand." In 2001, for example, only one in five minority journalism graduates who sought work with a daily paper actually landed a job in an editorial department; three of ten took a job in a related media field, such as marketing or public relations, Becker's study found. "It's another myth that minorities have an easier time in the job market," Becker concluded. The ASNE survey for 2001 indicated that 2,292 journalists were hired in the newsrooms that responded, with minorities representing 19.5 percent of those hires.

My entrée to Bay Area professional journalism reflected the dynamic described by Becker. Despite my having studied alongside dozens of eager, talented, and qualified (if relatively inexperienced) nonwhite classmates, and even considering Medsger's persistent contact with top editors at both papers, I was the only nonwhite graduate who found a place in the main newsroom of the second-largest newspaper in San Francisco. In the Bay Area of 1989, when I landed my first "real job" at the *Examiner*, I appeared on the metro desk like a speck of pepper atop a heap of mashed potatoes. Actually, along with Gregory Lewis, who was an assistant city editor and reporter, and one other black male reporter, I was one of three pepper specks in a newsroom that contained roughly a hundred and fifty reporters, photographers, and editors.

This ratio, with some slight variation, still exists in many news organizations, and has since journalists of color first began entering mainstream newsrooms in the 1950s and '60s. But in the Bay Area, the dearth of journalists of color on staff at the major daily papers was a constant source of grinding frustration for forward-thinking educators like Medsger and for the small community of minority journalists who already worked at the established news organizations. Their frustrations were exacerbated by an awareness that the newspaper industry's official position was to increase minority representation at properties nationwide.

During the late 1970s, top editors at daily newspapers convened an ASNE study group that looked at the issue of minority journalists—how to better recruit, promote, and retain journalists who had expert technical qualifications but nevertheless faced major challenges in getting hired and advancing up the editorial ranks. In 1978, fewer than 4 percent (3.95 percent) of all journalists working in the nation's newspaper editorial departments were minority, according to ASNE's census data. By 1989, when I started at the *Examiner*, 7.4 percent of the nation's newspaper editorial employees were minority; and by 2008, the figure was 13.41 percent at the newspapers responding to the ASNE survey. In 1978, when ASNE members first pledged to bring the staffs of their news organizations in line with the demographics of their respective circulation areas by 2000, it was not inherently an unrealistic goal. Yet by 1998, minorities made up 26 percent of the total U.S. population, while the percentage of minorities in ASNE's 860 member newspapers stood at 11.6 percent. In October 1998, ASNE issued another mission statement on diversity, saying it acknowledged that its member organizations were falling "far short" of the newsroom parity goal that had been established in 1978. It revised its projected date for achieving newsroom parity from 2000 to 2025 "or sooner." In the meantime, ASNE's board members outlined a revised broad strategy to help close the gap:

- Conduct an annual census of employment of Asian Americans, blacks, Native Americans, Latinos, and women in the newsroom.
- Encourage and assist editors in recruiting, hiring, and managing diverse newsrooms.
- Expand ASNE efforts to foster newsroom diversity.
- Establish three-year benchmarks for measuring progress.

Viewed today, the well-meaning rhetoric and action planning by ASNE's leadership reads like an earnest relic of bygone aspirations, the romantic jottings in a Victorian diary. The mission statements and newsroom parity goals came without teeth, since ASNE holds no operational or financial oversight of the individual newspapers that form its membership. And as its surveys have noted over the years, there remain dozens of newspapers nationwide where no journalists of color are employed, dozens more where the sprinkling of journalists of color is so small as to make their impact on coverage negligible, and still more newsrooms where no journalists of color hold top editorial positions. The effect of the relative whiteness of newsrooms on the quality of coverage—in particular, coverage of people of color, or of issues with particular relevance to people of color—has been the topic of hundreds of professional and academic studies since the mid-twentieth century.

And in the San Francisco Bay Area, the wide gap between the ethnic makeup of the residents and the journalists at local news organizations has been especially egregious. In my view, it has contributed to the steady decline of readership and advertiser loyalty for news organizations in that region. Coupled lately with the rise of the Internet—which has stripped daily papers of millions of dollars in revenue from classified advertising—the decline has put daily papers in the Bay Area in the unfortunate and ironic position of serving a population that is among the nation's most educated, affluent, and plugged-in—and which appears to have lost faith in its venerable print news media.

The desperate cost-cutting measures undertaken by the *Chronicle* and the *San Jose Mercury News*—laying off or buying out hundreds of seasoned staff writers, editors, and photographers, including many who are ethnic minorities—has not stemmed the tide of disappearing revenues. I also believe that dumping journalists of color and closing ethnic-language publications aimed at building audiences among minority readers is precisely the wrong strategy, both in the Bay Area and nationwide. Yet some early initiatives from large mainstream news corporations that were designed to build readership among ethnic communities were smothered in the cradle amid the economic upheaval of the past several years.

For example, Knight Ridder—the former publisher of dozens of major daily papers, some located in regions with large populations of ethnic minorities, including Miami and San Jose—summarily sold *Viet Mercury*, its six-year-old Vietnamese-language newspaper, in October 2005; that same month it also closed *Nuevo Mundo*, a Spanish-language weekly that it introduced in the Santa Clara Valley in 1996. For the estimated 125,000 Vietnamese Americans living in the South Bay at that time, the sale of *Viet Mercury* (to a local group of Vietnamese investors) removed the one news source available in their native language that did not publish heavily biased reports in the tradition of most other advocacy-based ethnic-language journals available in that market. Local reports of the sale quoted some Vietnamese residents who were angered and saddened by Knight Ridder's decision, while others expressed confusion about why the *Viet Mercury*, with a small but growing circulation of thirty-five thousand, had not been given an opportunity to come into its own. A few months later, though, the corporation's motive became clearer: its chief executive officer, P. Anthony Ridder, announced that the Knight Ridder News Corporation was for sale. The closings of *Viet Mercury* and *Nuevo Mundo* had apparently served the interest of "trimming sails" before Knight Ridder went on the market. The reconstituted *Viet Mercury* struggled to find its footing without the support of the large sales and distribution team that Knight Ridder had provided. It is troubling to consider that Knight Ridder abandoned an opportunity to increase its revenue by gearing publications toward a growing ethnic market at the very moment when the Internet was beginning to offer new means of presenting news and information to "nontraditional" audiences.

It seemed to me, in 1989, that the burden was on me to obtain the skills and experience that would allow me to join a major news organization in my hometown. And in that pre-websites era, when most residents in big cities took at face value the institutional power of news organizations in their midst, most nonjournalists held a vague sense of the big gaps that existed between the ethnic makeup of news staffs and that of communities. The resulting inadequate coverage, in my experience, was accepted by minority residents as almost an existential fact of life, as in, *These newspapers don't care to get our experiences right, but we can't change it, so what're you going to do?*

More than once, while on the job for the *Examiner* in the late 1980s, I encountered black residents who expressed that sentiment or some slight variation. What I couldn't see at the time was a bigger picture of percolating African American angst.

In 1990 the number of San Francisco residents who listed their race as black on census reports was 79,039; by 2000 that number had declined to 60,515, representing 8.6 percent of the city's 776,733 residents in that year. This decline was first described not by me or any journalist at a Bay Area paper. (Indeed, I departed San Francisco in 1990 for a staff writing job at the *Fresno Bee* in the San Joaquin Valley.) A San Francisco–based reporter at the *New York Times*, Evelyn Nieves, wrote a scalding report in August 2001 outlining the disillusionment of black San Franciscans with their native or adopted city.

"For many blacks here," Nieves wrote, "San Francisco is the sweetheart who loved 'em and left 'em, who promised the moon and stars only to forget them when new blood came to town." Apart from the purple prose, I had no quibbles with Nieves's analysis. It also hit me that her chronicling of a significant migratory shift among a population of San Francisco residents that had grown steadily since the 1940s—when thousands of blacks from the South and Midwest first came to the Bay Area to work in industries supporting the United States' World War II military efforts—represented a scoop of the two largest daily papers in the city; they should have seen the story in their own backyard. Nieves's report gave substance to the complaints of many black Bay Area residents when they considered the way the daily papers covered their communities: only the "pathology" stories, those describing high crime rates, drug busts, or gang activity, drew the attention of reporters and editors at the *Chronicle* and the *Examiner*. During the two years I worked at the *Examiner*, I resisted covering those kinds of stories exclusively, believing that I would eventually bring a more balanced brand of coverage to black communities in the city and elsewhere around the Bay. It didn't turn out that way.

I was the first intern under the *Examiner*'s nascent program, but I was expected to perform just like any other staff writer on the metro team. By mid-May 1989, I had filed for graduation from SF State and took a desk in the main newsroom of the *Ex*. My schedule was Thursdays through Mondays, and in keeping with the paper's afternoon publishing schedule, I often worked the "night shift," covering general assignment news around the city from 1 to 9 p.m., or from 2 to 10 p.m.

I didn't care about the late hours—at age twenty-six, I was a bona fide reporter.

I earned almost two thousand dollars per month, big money for me at that time. And as the youngest staff writer on the metro desk— in addition to being the only black woman—I saw myself as the natural evolution of a classic, twentieth-century newspaper type: a young, talented local who gets a foot in the door at the big-city newsroom and gradually works her way up.

In San Francisco, the journalism community was small and tight-knit. It was also, as I've outlined, overwhelmingly white, especially the staff writer and editor ranks of its newspapers. Still, I was determined to fit in as best as possible, both by working hard and well at the technical aspects of reporting and by getting up to speed on the cultural peculiarities of the *Examiner* newsroom.

In my first few months on the metro desk, Tim Reiterman encouraged me to pair up as often as possible with some of the senior reporters as they worked their beats. My first stop was in the "cop shop" at the Hall of Justice. There, a veteran *Examiner* reporter named Malcolm "Scoop" Glover let me tag along for a week while he covered criminal justice. The press room in the Hall of Justice, at 850 Bryant Street, was even more of a throwback to the old *Front Page* days of big-city American journalism than the main newsrooms of the *Chronicle* and *Examiner* were. The dank smell of overflowing ashtrays, the clackety-clacking of fingers pounding computer keyboards, and the blue language from police-beat reporters gave the big, open room a clubhouse feel. I had a ball and didn't at all feel unwelcome in that cloistered space.

Along with a handful of other longtime reporters who then worked at the *Examiner*—including Larry Hatfield, Lynn Ludlow, Paul Avery, and Gerald Adams—Glover welcomed me into the fold without question. Unlike some of the younger staff writers and reporters, the old-timers didn't seem at all threatened by my presence, nor did they question my skills. It appeared that the color of my skin didn't faze them: they too had once been green reporters, and I sensed that they saw me as green rather than black. They seemed able to focus on that common link rather than on my race or gender.

Included in this group was Frank McCulloch, the *Examiner*'s managing editor. McCulloch might have been a stunt double for the World War II–era five-star U.S. general George S. Patton. Like Patton, McCulloch had a ramrod military bearing in addition to a shiny, bullet-shaped bald pate and a booming voice. He had earned his early journalistic stripes covering wars in Korea and Vietnam for *Time* magazine and other national news organizations. At the *Examiner* he was the editorial quality control chief, the arbiter of content standards. McCulloch made a nice balance to the executive editor,

Larry Kramer, who was the paper's number cruncher, and to its publisher, the affable Hearst heir, William Randolph Hearst III, whom everyone called "Will."

Will had gotten his family members at the Hearst Corporation and other board members to pump millions of dollars into the paper in the mid-1980s. The newsroom got a fancy makeover not long before I arrived, and we worked in a big, open space with spiffy black metal cabinetry. We walked around atop soft, low-pile carpeting. A giant masthead logo, with a fierce-looking eagle sprawled above the words "The San Francisco Examiner," was stenciled on the wall overlooking the metro desk. A fluttering banner draped along the eagle's outstretched wings carried the words "Monarch of the Dailies."

One hot afternoon in September 1989, McCulloch called the staff to gather around the city desk for an announcement: the *Los Angeles Herald Examiner*, our sister paper to the south, would be closing. Furthermore, we would soon face company-wide layoffs, although negotiations were underway to offer buyouts. A couple of the veterans who sat near me in the newsroom murmured as McCulloch spoke, and I made out the words "bastards" and "cheapskates."

McCulloch finished with a short pep talk about how our work would continue and said the *San Francisco Examiner* was not in danger of closing, only of having a period of "belt-tightening." After saying he was available to speak with anyone who had questions, he strode back to his office near the conference room.

A few of us gathered around Larry Hatfield's cubicle, across from the main city desk, and gossiped. Someone said they'd heard we would be "absorbing" at least a few of the soon-to-be-out-of-work reporters from the "Her-Ex." I returned to my desk and got back to work. It occurred to me that the "belt-tightening" McCulloch had mentioned might threaten my future at the *Ex*.

Over the next few months I worked hard to demonstrate my worth to the *Examiner* editors. I had developed a knack for covering large street protests and had delivered a string of front-page stories on a riot that had broken out between members of the anti-AIDS group ACT UP and city police officers in the early fall. Then on October 17, 1989, a massive earthquake struck the Bay Area. Dozens of residents were killed, and two billion dollars in damage occurred to property and highways in cities around the region, according to the U.S. Geological Survey and the California Association of Insurance Companies. I worked nonstop for the week after the quake hit, contributing reports and interviews from Chinatown and from black, low-income residents in the city's Fillmore District, a neighborhood that had been overlooked by charitable groups that flooded the city with free goods and services in the aftermath.

It was exhilarating, harrowing work, conducted amid recurring aftershocks and a shortage of basic necessities. Also, the buildings housing the staffs of the *Examiner* and *Chronicle* didn't have electrical power for the first few days after the temblor hit. Consequently, the print runs of both papers in the immediate aftermath were small (although in fairness, even if the companies had been able to produce full runs, the delivery trucks wouldn't have been able to carry them around to all circulation areas, since key bridges and highways had been severely damaged). Interestingly, although it was not far from the quake's epicenter, the Mercury News building in San Jose sustained very minor damage. It was also equipped with an auxiliary power system that allowed the paper's staff to produce high-quality daily coverage in the immediate aftermath of the devastating quake. For its efforts, the *Mercury News* received a Pulitzer Prize for general news coverage.

Back in San Francisco, most of us on the *Examiner* editorial staff weren't privy to front office details, but we speculated that the Chron and the *Ex* had lost millions of dollars in retail and classified advertising during the month after the quake. Still, as winter arrived, I felt great about my work at the *Examiner* and about my place in the metro staff pecking order.

In December, my position at the *Examiner* was eliminated.

The metro editor, Tim Porter, called me to his sleek office off the main newsroom. He was a wiry, dark-haired man, a San Francisco State alumnus a decade my senior. (Tim Reiterman, my mentor, had taken a job as investigations editor at the *Los Angeles Times* early in the fall of 1989.) When I expressed disappointment at the decision, Porter tensed up: "Look, you're young. You're a woman. You're black—you won't have any trouble finding another job. Besides, this is not the only job in the world. It won't hurt you to go out and get some more experience for a while. When you come back here, you'll really be ready. But right now, anyway, the money just isn't in the budget to keep you."

I walked out of his office and went to my desk, sharp stabs of embarrassment and anger knotting the muscles at my shoulders. I was stunned and humiliated—how could Porter have said such a thing? One of the old-timers came over and asked what had happened. I started weeping.

(In 2005, I spoke with Porter about that exchange we'd had fifteen years earlier. He said he had made a mistake in letting me go and in using the language he'd chosen during our exchange back in 1989. "It was how things were then," he said. We'd met for coffee at Peet's on West Portal Avenue in San Francisco on a drizzly morning. I was surprised and also humbled by his implicit apology; we remain friends to this day.)

The day after I found out I was losing my job, an electronic message flashed across the top of my computer screen: Frank McCulloch wanted to see me. I went to his office. He gestured to a chair next to his desk, and I sat down.

"I talked to Betty, and I know you're upset," he said, referring to my mentor at SF State, the journalism department chairwoman. I had phoned her the previous evening. Apparently, in the interim, she'd contacted Frank McCulloch.

I nodded; I felt my mouth begin to tremble, but I breathed deeply. I was still stung by Porter's pronouncement that I was young, a woman, and black. If those were such advantages, why weren't they enough to keep me at the *Examiner*? Other than me, there were only two blacks on the metro staff, and both of them were men.

I exhaled. "Yes, I am. I mean, I know I don't have a lot of experience, Mr. McCulloch, but—what, my little salary is breaking the budget? I don't think I believe that. And, well, I hope you don't take this the wrong way, but doesn't anyone notice that I'm the only black woman reporter out there? If I leave, there will only be two other blacks on the metro staff. And no black women. Out of forty or fifty reporters! That just seems . . . wrong."

McCulloch had been listening quietly; he had pale blue eyes and bright pink, healthy-looking skin. He turned his chair toward me and placed his hands on his knees.

"You're right. Of course you're right. That's the thing, isn't it? They've set up an internship program to bring on you and others who are needed here. But when the chips are down, it is all lip service, isn't it?"

I was stunned. He continued.

"So here's what is going on now: I spoke with Kramer. He says he can get you at least another eight or maybe ten weeks, if you want it. But there is no guarantee after that. What do you think of that?"

I swallowed and sat up straighter in the chair. Betty had told me that Frank was a good guy. He certainly seemed to be dealing straight with me. But I was angry and dispirited; I didn't know what to say.

"I don't know . . . I should probably think about it, right?" I said.

He nodded, his bald head reflecting the fluorescent overhead lighting.

"Sure. Absolutely. You can do that. But do you want to know what I think?" he asked.

"Yes."

He said, "I think you should tell Kramer 'No thanks.' I think you should walk out of here with your head high, get a good job at another good paper, and become the journalist you are meant to be."

He stared at me.

I smiled and shifted in the chair. This was a very strange conversation.

"Oh. Well, that's an option. Sure. But I really don't want to leave California again. This is my home," I said.

"Yes, of course. But there are other papers here. And I know most of the editors at them. Where would you like to go?"

I told him I'd interned in Fresno in '87.

His eyes lit up: "Ah, well, I go way back with Don Slinkard, the executive editor there. I will call him, if you're sure. Anywhere else? Just think about it for a couple of days and let me know. You're going to do well, Amy. Don't let this put you off your game."

I thanked him and went back to the newsroom.

Two weeks before Christmas, I cleaned out my desk and said goodbye to the metro staff.

■ ■ ■

In the second week of January 1990, my roommate and her boyfriend helped me load the few pieces of furniture I owned into a rented van. They drove the van down Highway 99 to Fresno while I followed in my Datsun, with my two cats in their plastic carriers wedged onto the backseat. After we arrived at the one-bedroom apartment I'd rented just south of downtown, we moved my things in. Then we went to a fast-food joint, loaded up on bad food, and stopped at a convenience store to buy beer and other provisions. We went back to the apartment, sat on the hardwood floor in the living room, and had dinner.

My friends slept on the small futon couch in the living room. The next morning we found the coffee maker and everyone had a cup, standing at the counters, since I didn't have a kitchen table.

After they left, I took a shower, fed the cats, and unpacked my work clothes. I was due at the *Fresno Bee* by 10 a.m.

TWO

Fresno

Race and Class Coverage,
the McClatchy Way

On January 2, 1991, a year after I started work as a staff writer at the *Fresno Bee* metro desk, a twenty-seven-year-old African American woman named Darlene Johnson appeared in a district courtroom in nearby Tulare County. Days earlier, she had pleaded guilty to two counts of child abuse. Her sentencing hearing was presided over by Superior Court judge Howard Broadman, a dark-haired ringer for the filmmaker George Lucas.

Broadman issued the following sentence:

- Darlene Johnson must attend parenting classes and counseling sessions.
- She must refrain from striking any of her four children.
- She must quit smoking cigarettes. (Johnson was pregnant with her fifth child at the time of sentencing.)
- She must agree to have a Norplant birth-control device implanted in one of her upper arms. (The slow-drip-release form of contraception had received Federal Drug Administration approval late in 1990.)

Should Johnson refuse any of the terms of probation, she would be sentenced to seven years in state prison, Broadman said.

Johnson asked a question about the birth control—what exactly was it and how did it work? Broadman helpfully explained that it was an inch-and-a-half-long plastic, pronged device that fit beneath the skin and flesh of the upper arm; its insertion did not require surgery, and it would prevent pregnancy for up to five years. He told Johnson she was to wear the device for at least the duration of her three-year probation. Johnson agreed.

Within days of their exchange and her accepting that sentence, Johnson and Broadman had become the hot center of a national debate over reproductive rights, class, criminal justice, and race.

In the *Bee* newsroom, thirty miles north of Tulare County, I volunteered to follow the story, picking it up after a court reporter first broke the news of Broadman's terms. For several months after, I had to contend with not only the usual difficulties of staying on top of a big story with layers of social and political implications, but also strong resistance from at least one *Bee* editor. "She has been convicted of beating two of her children with extension cords and a belt buckle," said Mike Reddin, the assistant city editor to whom I reported. Reddin was a Wisconsin transplant in central California, a middle-class white man in his thirties. "You will not portray her as sympathetic," he told me as I prepared to write a profile of Darlene Johnson.

I didn't argue with him. But carefully, over several months, I gathered the necessary information anyway, including hours of interviews with Johnson, her fiancé, and other family members. In early August 1991, Reddin edited my profile of Darlene Johnson, excising or shrinking paragraphs that he believed portrayed Johnson sympathetically—such as my quoting civil libertarians who had objected to Broadman's attempt to force contraception on Johnson, and comments from local NAACP officials who said they didn't believe a white woman, and certainly not a middle-class woman, would have been ordered to accept the birth control implant. He left in a quote from Darlene saying pretty much the same thing, a point that I insisted on during the long, tense edit of the profile.

I didn't feel sympathy toward Johnson, exactly, and I'd written what I considered to be a straight-ahead account of the events surrounding and leading up to that Norplant sentencing. Rather, I believed that if I didn't give readers a full, dispassionate account of her backstory, Johnson would go down in history as one-dimensional, a cardboard cutout of a bleak racial stereotype: the uneducated, poor black "welfare queen" whose irresponsible sexual behavior and lack of discipline creates an economic burden on society. In my thinking, it was not unethical to argue that Darlene Johnson did not deserve to be forced by a court of law into accepting a relatively new, invasive form of birth control. Judge Broadman's order was Orwellian, with a thick overlay of race and class bias. I would have sought to profile the defendant in such a bizarre case whatever the color of her skin.

Not long after I profiled her, Johnson was interviewed by Mike Wallace on the CBS network news program *60 Minutes*. Then, late in 1991, while her case made its way through the appeals process, Johnson was arrested, charged with cocaine use, and sent to jail. She hadn't received the Norplant device—the terms of her earlier sentence were vacated after the drug bust—but her tangled case and hard-luck life brought me to an unexpected decision: I wanted to move from reporting general assignment news and education to covering African Americans in the San Joaquin Valley.

The prospect of ongoing fights with Reddin or any other *Bee* editors were I to focus exclusively on covering blacks in the Valley seemed like a reasonable tradeoff. I just had to get the green light from someone high enough on the *Bee*'s editorial food chain to ensure that I could work such a beat.

If I didn't do it, who would?

I believed I had a good grip on race and class issues in my home state, California. But moving smack into the five-hundred-mile-long middle of the Golden State broadened my understanding of the complexities of those subjects far beyond what I thought I knew from growing up in Northern California. Working at the *Bee* also opened my eyes to the tender balance between perception, performance, and reality in newsrooms—as distinct from my time at the *San Francisco Examiner*, where most of my colleagues viewed me as a young but talented reporter who happened to be black. At the *Bee*, I was also a newcomer to the ways of the San Joaquin Valley, which led some editors on the metro staff to comb my copy extra carefully.

I appreciated close editing, especially from the editors on the copy desk, the last line of content quality control. But as I began my second year at the *Bee*, I had mastered the peculiarities and regional colloquialisms of the region, including the correct spellings of the prominent local politicians, educators, and business people with

Armenian or Latino surnames. The Darlene Johnson episode, and
a few others that evoked a similar dynamic, gradually convinced me
to give up my desire (harbored since my time in San Francisco) to
focus on covering disasters and other large-scale environmental and
manmade catastrophes. I thrived on the excitement and immediacy
of covering disasters. Race relations coverage, though, was more ur-
gently needed.

It is a familiar dynamic to most journalists of color who entered
mainstream news organizations during the last part of the twentieth century—if we don't cover ethnic communities, no one will.
Or worse, coverage of blacks or Latinos or Asians will be handled
so poorly as to further alienate groups that already look upon the
press skeptically. Pamela Newkirk, a professor of journalism at New
York University, captured the dilemma eloquently in her 1990 book
Within the Veil: Black Journalists, White Media:

> As a daily journalist at four different news organizations, I
> was, on occasion deeply satisfied with the extent to which
> I could shed light on compelling issues affecting the com-
> munities I covered. But when it came to writing about Afri-
> can-Americans, I often encountered difficulty filling out the
> puzzle that is race in this country because my editors resisted
> perspectives that were foreign to the white cultural main-
> stream. They found it easier to exclude or malign alien view-
> points than to attempt to understand ideas that did not mesh
> with their own.

I hadn't read Newkirk's book during the three years I spent at the
Bee, yet I now know that her observation jibes entirely with what I
encountered in that newsroom and others over the years. In the San
Joaquin Valley, the gap between the demographic makeup of some
mainstream news staffs, like that of the *Bee,* and the general population didn't appear to be that large—on paper. On the ground, though,
the gap is large, and the resulting inadequate coverage is inescapable.

During the three years I worked at the *Bee,* the vast majority of
my stories were edited by white men, not counting a period of a few
months in which the metro editor was Ricardo O. Pimentel, a Latino

who had come to Fresno from the *Sacramento Bee*. I also spent several months being edited by a female Enterprise Team editor, Brenda Moore, when I worked on special projects.

I hadn't gotten to know Pimentel well during his brief time leading the metro staff. Yet on one of his last days in the *Fresno Bee* main newsroom, he came over to my cubicle and perched on my desktop, next to my computer. (He had worked as the *Bee*'s metro editor for about six months, and his quick departure was something of a mystery to us "worker Bees.") He said he was sorry he wouldn't have an opportunity to work with me further, and that he wanted me to know something: "If you don't have one already, find an agenda. If it is something you believe in, trust yourself and stick with it." I didn't know how to respond. But I thanked him and wished him well. (Pimentel went on to edit the editorial pages of the *Milwaukee Journal* and become a leader of the National Association of Hispanic Journalists.)

This kind of encounter between reporters and editors who are from distinct ethnic groups is not captured by the annual ASNE demographic surveys. But the minority trade groups, like the National Association of Black Journalists and the National Association of Hispanic Journalists, have over the years conducted small-scale studies that reveal that these kinds of intraethnic dynamics do accrue benefits—to audiences receiving the coverage and to the news organizations. From the outside, were one to assess a news organization's racial inclusiveness simply by reviewing the demographic data it reported to ASNE, it would be easy to come away believing that newsroom staffs are not too far away from matching the ethnic and racial demographic of consumers. But the numbers alone, in any case, do not provide a full picture of the subtleties of how minority journalists enrich coverage.

In 1990, for example, 5 percent (33,423) of Fresno County residents were African Americans, 35.5 percent (236,634) were Latinos, and 8.6 percent (57,239) were Asian Americans (primarily ethnic Hmong and Laotians), based on U.S. Census data and a report by the Center for Comparative Studies in Race and Ethnicity at Stanford. The *Fresno Bee* newsroom, meanwhile, listed 22.9 percent of its editorial workers as ethnic minorities by the end of the 1990s, according to the annual newsroom census conducted by ASNE and released in 1999.

ASNE figures describing the ethnic breakdown of newsroom supervisors, however, are a more relevant measurement of the most important dynamic in newsrooms: who holds the power to approve, edit, and place stories.

In 1999, slightly more than 8 percent of supervisory positions in the nation's newspaper newsrooms were held by minorities; in 2009, following a three-year downward spiral in which the industry shed thousands of editorial jobs, that figure increased to 11.2 percent. This increase is an irony that the news industry has yet to unravel. Perhaps it represents a bit of good news: even as journalists of color disproportionately suffered from the historic shrinking of editorial operations during the 2000s, opportunities for advancement still exist within some of the news organizations that survive. The bad news: the rate of increase in the number of newsroom supervisors who are ethnic minorities falls far behind the increases in ethnic populations on the streets and even in some other workplace sectors, including government, according to data compiled by the economist Darrell Williams, PhD, publisher of a black-oriented website, TheLoop21.com.

More pointedly, just having a black or brown person sitting in at daily editorial meetings does not ensure that accurate, comprehensive, smart coverage of ethnic communities will consistently take place, especially if that editor is the only person of color in the meeting.

Author and journalist Jill Nelson observed, in her rueful memoir of working at *Washington Post Magazine* and other mainstream news outlets, *Volunteer Slavery: My Authentic Negro Experience*, that skin color by itself does not instantly result in racial solidarity. The person of color in a supervisory position may share key cultural values, experiences, and affiliations with her white professional peers and superiors—affiliations and a worldview that may, in essence, override any potential or perceived benefits of racial solidarity derived from shared skin color. In fact, shared cultural values and points of reference may result in a form of compliance that resembles acquiescence to the dominant group—also known as a black, Latino, Asian, or woman who is viewed by other women or ethnic minorities in the organization as a "sell-out."

This is not to say that all journalists of color who become editors deserve to be tagged "go along to get along" or as an Uncle Tom or Aunt Jemima. It does mean that those individuals likely experience more pressure than their white peers or their minority subordinates to share the perspectives of those who represent the majority in the management rank.

It is fair to say that in some instances, should a person of color in a supervisory role object when their white coworkers' biases or cultural blind spots seep into the decision-making process, they put themselves at risk of being marginalized or typecast as a "radical" or a "complainer."

Would injecting larger numbers of ethnic minorities directly into the editor ranks automatically correct imbalanced or negligent coverage? Not necessarily.

Determining the critical mass or tipping point at which increased numbers of a minority group become effective at counterbalancing the prevailing groupthink is an imprecise science. And over time, even if handled good-naturedly in the moment, the accumulation of such tense encounters can stunt career growth for those minority editors perceived as bucking conventional beliefs. Furthermore, the shifting nature of news itself—wherein financial resources have to serve many masters, including daily breaking news, enterprise reports and special series, and large-scale developments such as natural disasters—has historically given editorial managers reason to view full-time coverage of ethnic communities as a low priority.

"Every time I call it a game, they call it a business; and every time I call it a business, they say it's a game," joked an editor at a major newspaper in the Northeast when I asked him what it was like to be the only black in the "budget meetings." These meetings are twice-daily editors' gatherings in which the lineup of the next day's stories is determined. His comment was a riff on the famous line by former Dallas Cowboys football player Peter Gent, author of the 1979 classic NFL roman à clef, *North Dallas Forty*. Gent's novel was written from the perspective of a talented insider-outsider, a pro football player who had the "right stuff" technically and physically to perform in his role but who struggled with the ancillary political and corporate trappings of the pro sports world.

Typically, before the rise of the Internet upended the twenty-four-hour news cycle, editorial budget meetings took place twice in the course of each weekday: at midmorning, to determine the day's coverage, and at around 4 p.m., to assess progress on the stories reporters had been assigned or had followed up and to determine page placement for each story. My conversation with that black editor at a large northeast daily newspaper occurred in the mid-1990s, before the advent of websites and minute-by-minute news publishing rendered the big afternoon budget meeting all but obsolete. The editor chuckled when he described that frustrating dynamic—the mercurial shifting of the metrics of "success" for an editor of color in a big-city newsroom. But like Jill Nelson's recounting of her time in corporate journalism, his bemusement was tinged with bitterness and a deep sense of frustration. He had dedicated himself to working at a news organization because he believed he might help reframe the coverage of people of color and the dispossessed in the United States—only to find that the rules for scoring a touchdown could change seemingly at whim.

In the early 1990s, the McClatchy Company was among the more "progressive" of the large news corporations in terms of its hiring, promotion, and retention of journalists and business employees who were ethnic minorities. (It still is, in the second decade of the twenty-first century, although total hiring for all McClatchy news properties is down significantly from the 1990s.) The company owned the Central Valley–based *Bee* dailies, in Sacramento, Modesto, and Fresno, along with the *Anchorage Daily News* and a string of small and mid-size papers elsewhere in the West and the Southeast. The company's summer newsroom internships were highly competitive, in no small part because they often led to full-time jobs. Not only had my experience as a features department intern at the *Fresno Bee* been relatively smooth in 1987, but I'd also, before I returned for a staff position in January 1990, talked with a few minority journalists who reported having great experiences at McClatchy papers.

Journalists of color represented less than 20 percent of the corporation's total editorial workforce when I first worked there. Yet for the most part, those employed by McClatchy had ample support to succeed, including the close attention of their editorial superiors.

A decade later, in the late 1990s, minorities made up 22.9 percent of all editorial workers reported by the *Fresno Bee*, a figure that likely included staff members who weren't actually reporters or editors—clerks, receptionists, librarians, and the like. This kind of demographic trickery was common among big news organizations. But folding Mexican American clerks and African American research librarians into the total number of editorial workers identified as "newsroom staff" didn't necessarily indicate an institutional disregard for the value of hiring, promoting, and retaining journalists of color. That kind of numbers game—for that is what it amounts to—often betrays a well-meaning news organization's inability to make deep and long-term commitments to smashing the cultural barriers that so often prevent journalists of color from rising to the editorial suites. During the eighties and nineties, mainstream news organizations like McClatchy were vulnerable to criticism that they were taking a slow approach to full integration of their editorial ranks. But over the years, I came to believe they also deserved encouragement for at least taking baby steps.

Making my way through newsrooms over a decade between the late 1980s and late 1990s, I learned that the process of building editorial staffs that matched the demographics of America itself was ill-fated from its inception by ASNE in 1978. Why? The answer, as I saw it, was tough but simple: the same newsroom leaders who had grown up in a predominantly white work environment would not revise their habits, belief systems, and criteria of what constitutes a "qualified" journalist without first receiving intensive reeducation or direct, financially based incentives from their superiors, the owners and publishers of their news organizations. The culture of newspaper owners and publishers first and foremost had to change, and during my time at big newspapers, I saw little evidence of that particular evolution.

There were scattered exceptions—a few publishers who tied newsroom editorial managers' raises and bonuses to the rates of minority hiring and retention, among other benchmarks, such as staying within newsroom budgets. At least one of those publishers, Gary Pruitt, was quite emphatic about editors meeting hiring and retention goals for minority journalists. During the early 1990s, when he was our publisher at the *Fresno Bee*, Pruitt increased pressure on newsroom managers to hire more journalists of color. He radically changed the culture of management simply by insisting that it change. During the first few months after he arrived at the Bee building on E Street near downtown Fresno, he told the staff that he wanted to meet with each newsroom employee privately for a no-holds-barred, off-the-record, "temperature-taking" conversation. When my turn came, I was anxious but not intimidated: Pruitt was in his mid-thirties, Surfer Dude handsome, and displayed an easygoing personality marked by sharply tuned "people skills" and a quick intellect.

I can't describe the details of what we discussed—it was, after all, off the record—but I feel safe in disclosing that Pruitt is the rare news industry executive who genuinely understands and believes in the common-sense, bottom-line value of fully integrating a news operation. (Arthur Sulzberger Jr., chairman and publisher of the *New York Times*, also seems to "get it.")

At the same time, Pruitt had a pragmatic view of the complex collection of factors that together represented entrenched obstacles to changing the culture of newsrooms, including, most prominently, outdated beliefs held by older generations of editors and publishers. In the late 1990s, after he ascended to the chairman and chief executive officer position, overseeing all McClatchy newspapers, I watched from a distance as Pruitt built an executive team that was talented, well educated, experienced, and also ethnically diverse.

But remaking the demographics of the corporate suites at McClatchy headquarters in Sacramento was an accomplishment that was harder to replicate across a large, far-flung collection of news outlets. I believed, though, that if anyone was going to accomplish the seemingly impossible task of meeting ASNE's newsroom parity goals, it would be Pruitt: he had the power, the will, and the intellectual acumen to be successful. The economic landscape, however, and its overwhelming influence on the health of the entire news industry, was out of his control.

In 2005, a demographic report by the Knight Foundation determined that newsroom diversity had "passed its peak at most newspapers." Based on data from 1,410 U.S. newspapers, the report was commissioned to provide deeper context for the annual ASNE surveys. At the time of the Knight study, conducted by journalists Bill Dedman and Stephen K. Doig, it was clear that ASNE's 1978 goal of having its member papers' staffs match the demographics of consumers in their respective circulation areas had not been achieved.

The Knight study revealed a number of interesting aspects of the industry's diversity efforts. Seventy-three percent of the nation's large newspapers (those with daily circulations over 250,000)—including the *New York Times* and *USA Today*—employed a smaller percentage of nonwhites in comparison to the nonwhite population of their circulation base in 2005 than they'd reported employing in some years between 1994 and 2004, indicating a retreat. The slippage, according to Doig and Dedman, was mostly due to rapid increases of ethnic minorities in cities, an indication that the news organizations were unable to keep up with the pace of demographic change taking place on the ground. In sum, the gap between the ethnic makeup of editorial staffs and of their circulation areas was widening faster than most newspapers were capable of filling it in. Once the economic downturn that had been a slow-creeping reality for many newspapers and corporate media groups since the early 1980s began to rapidly accelerate with the rise of the Internet in the late 1990s, the slowdown in overall hiring quickly resulted in a decrease in total numbers of minorities hired across the industry. As Doig and Dedman wrote, "Of the newspapers who reported to ASNE, the analysis shows that every 10 point increase in community non-white percentage [of resident populations] is accompanied by only about a 4 point increase in newsroom percentage."

Also, the researchers found that by 2005, some 37 percent of the 691 newspapers participating in the Knight survey reported that their newsrooms had no minorities. (Most of those papers were small, with circulations of fifty thousand or less.) The Knight report also found that diversity initiatives worked best when they were emphasized and enforced from the top down. "Ownership [of the newspaper] is a large factor in determining a newspaper's newsroom diversity index," according to the study. But other particulars also play a big role, and some of those are nearly impossible to quantify: "desire to meet the goal, desirability of the community as a place to live, racial change in the community, the reputation of a newspaper, supply of non-white journalists in that area, and extent of the newspaper's recruiting."

In my experience, the "desirability" aspect is not just about livability but about how desirable the demographic makeup of the community is to advertisers. This too is a deterrent to change: the news organization's fate rests in large part on how many residents in its circulation or viewing area are "desirable"—meaning possessing middle-class income levels. Advertisers view "desirable" audiences as incentive to continue buying space in the news publications with the potential to "penetrate" those markets. And until roughly the mid-2000s, it was advertisers such as major retail department stores and regional automobile dealer groups that, along with money from classified ads, provided the bulk of daily newspaper's revenue.

In the late 1990s, as many middle-class and wealthy residents moved out of urban centers, McClatchy and other large newspaper chains began focusing higher percentages of their editorial fiscal resources on covering suburbs. This gradual shift in newsroom personnel and editorial focus from urban centers to more affluent—and in some instances, whiter—readership circulation areas had a domino effect on staffing in newsrooms.

My personal preference was to work in the main newsrooms of the papers that employed me, but I didn't always get my wish. In Fresno, for example, I was assigned during my first year as a metro reporter to cover a small suburb, called Clovis, twenty miles east of Fresno proper. Its residents were wealthier, its schools boasted higher student test scores, and its homes were more expensive than in the city of Fresno. I was told by my bosses that covering the city council and general news developments in Clovis was a "prime beat," since the company was in the midst of a big push to capture more readers in that locale. (There is a separate newspaper in Clovis, the *Independent*, now owned by the *Bee*. Yet the town's political leaders and some residents derided the larger, Fresno-based *Bee* for covering their town only as an afterthought.) In the early 1990s, I was in touch with other journalists of color coast to coast who expressed unease about being assigned to cover virtually all-white communities in far-flung or even "inner-ring" suburbs. Still, if we wanted to get our feet on the editorial ladder, we had to be prepared to take whatever rung presented itself.

In the aggregate, however, corporate owners' decision to decentralize news coverage in an effort to chase advertising dollars into suburbs ultimately created a larger drag on newspapers' revenues once the Internet-fueled downturn escalated in the early 2000s. During the 1980s and early '90s, many such companies, including the *Examiner* in San Francisco, built printing facilities in far-flung suburbs in order to better accommodate what they hoped would be increased circulation in those regions; but when the bottom fell out, those facilities became too expensive to maintain.

Moreover, that strategic shifting of resources, from focusing almost exclusively on covering city news to a hypersuburban focus, overlaid the traditional obstacles to achieving more ethnically diverse newsrooms: it did little to mitigate the downside of a nondiverse hiring plan. If newsroom managers don't desire a diverse newsroom, it probably won't happen.

And in the middle of those two parts of the stubborn diversity-gap equation—advertisers' needs and the need for a diverse editorial staff—was another hard-to-pin-down essential factor: the news organization's reputation among readers, wherever they resided. If consumers don't trust a news organization, they will not subscribe to its products. The diversity index gap and the shift from urban to suburban coverage didn't ensure a safe path to revenue gains, since millions of once-loyal newspaper readers—in cities, suburbs, and rural regions—have effectively decided they can simply live without a paid subscription to their local paper. The reasons for that drop-off are numerous, if intertwined; over the years, I have talked with former regular newspaper readers across the nation who said they just didn't feel their newspaper was fairly and compellingly capturing the issues that mattered to them. Most, but not all, of these former readers in my unscientific survey were people of color.

I didn't spend much time reading such data or pondering signs of larger industry trends when I worked in newsrooms. On a daily basis, at the *Bee* and other papers where I worked, I wanted more than anything for readers to trust my byline. I couldn't control the actions and thinking of newsroom managers, but I sure as hell could produce high-quality journalism as often as possible.

At McClatchy, I had a good shot at achieving that goal. It wasn't a perfect place to work, but the "lip service" dynamic that Frank McCulloch had astutely identified back in San Francisco was, at McClatchy, buffered by the generous salaries and generally laid-back nature of employee-management relations across the company properties. (Although a long-simmering standoff over a Newspaper Guild contract for newsroom employees at the *Fresno Bee* was at a stalemate before it was resolved, with Pruitt's oversight, in the early 1990s.) Working for a McClatchy paper was a "velvet coffin," said Don Coleman, the only other African American reporter on the *Bee*'s metro staff during the three years that I worked there. Don and I became friends immediately after I returned to the paper as a staff writer in January 1990. He was in his late thirties and had worked in other industries before returning to school and getting a journalism degree. Don joined the *Fresno Bee* in the late 1980s and covered county government by the time I arrived. He told me, "They'll try to assign every Black History Month story to you, but don't go for it. If we have to know how to cover government, schools, crime, and everything, then they should expect their white and Latino reporters to know how to write about black stuff too."

Don had resisted being pigeonholed as the "black affairs" reporter. But after I confided in him that I wanted to focus on covering African Americans in the Valley, he supported my low-key campaign to win that beat. Besides, a white male reporter, Alex Pulaski, covered immigration full-time, a beat that comprised writing about Mexican Americans and the growing population of Southeast Asians who lived in Fresno County and throughout the region. Don cautioned me that management's view of Pulaski, though, was very different from how they viewed me. "Alex is Bwana," he laughed, invoking a hoary stereotype of the pith-helmeted white colonialist leading "civilized savages" through the jungles in the African interior during the early nineteenth century. "They trust him to cover these poor brown people, but don't think you will get the same kind of freedom," Don said.

Not long after I covered the LA riots, I was reassigned to writing about African Americans, though not quite full-time; I had to pitch in on big breaking stories and large-scale projects. This change was made possible by three things: my performance covering the LA riots, Pruitt's arrival as the *Bee*'s publisher, and the arrival of a new metro editor, Terry Jackson. Like Pruitt, Terry came from Sacramento in 1991, along with his wife, Marji Lambert, a veteran enterprise reporter. Terry became my editor, and that was fine with me: he was sharp as a tack, had a blue sense of humor, and carried himself like the Big Man on Campus, notwithstanding the twisted landscape of his body. Terry had been born with a severely curved spine; he used a cane and stood barely five feet tall. He sat down at my desk, not long after arriving at the *Bee*, and told me that he intended to be my advocate as long as I was willing to work hard and focus on growing as a reporter and writer.

In late April 1992, on the night the verdict was announced in the trial of the white police officers charged with assaulting a black motorist, Rodney King, Terry sent me, Marji, and photojournalist Russell Yip into Los Angeles. The next week, after I learned that Mike Reddin had been the editor back in Fresno who'd sprinkled offensive language into my riot stories, Terry assured me that it wouldn't happen again. But he also cautioned me against getting hung up on it, since our work had largely been successful. Besides, he said, there was no guarantee that readers even noticed the loaded language that Reddin had inserted. And by that time the newspaper was well into a new, systemic plan designed to help close the gap between the ethnic makeup of its news staff and the region we covered.

In 1990 McClatchy developed a new initiative to address the challenge of covering a region that was growing more ethnic than its news staffs: it dove into the mini-trend that had taken hold in the industry at that time and began publishing a separate daily paper, *Vida en el Valle*, aimed at Spanish-speaking readers.

Some of us in the main newsroom snorted when we learned of the plan: how typically *safe* of them, we said. Rather than doing the arduous and psychologically challenging job of devising mechanisms to force white newsroom managers to change their beliefs and ways of thinking about race (something that is especially difficult when individuals believe they already "get it"), you just put up a new, separate-but-equal newspaper and hope for the best.

Vida en el Valle, McClatchy's Spanish-language paper, has survived fairly well since its inception in 1990. By 2008 its daily circulation was 58,000—clearly not big numbers, but undoubtedly McClatchy appreciated even that modest amount, since the *Fresno Bee*'s circulation had been stagnant. According to the Audit Bureau of Circulation, the daily *Bee* in 2008 had a circulation of 166,000; when I worked there in the early 1990s, its circulation was in the mid-150s, which means that the region's steady population growth during the 1990s did not bring comparable increases in readership. Still, *Vida en el Valle* represents a corporate effort to appeal directly to the growing Spanish-speaking population in the San Joaquin Valley. Our knee-jerk, cynical response to the advent of *Vida* in the early 1990s was naive and, in hindsight, unhelpful.

Vida's editorial staff at that time was not housed in the main *Bee* newsroom on E Street in Fresno. Our staffs did not mingle, and truth be told, many of us who worked in the main newsroom in downtown Fresno didn't know the staff of *Vida en el Valle* at all. This detached dynamic was repeated in other cities, including Miami, where *El Nuevo Herald* had been launched by Knight Ridder. However well-intentioned the owners might have been with these efforts, it stigmatized those Spanish-language publications right out of the gate, effectively relegating them to stepchild status in their respective markets. I suppose that was unavoidable, in the main, but at the least the newly launched publications might have experienced a greater appearance of legitimacy had their staffs worked alongside the staffs of the larger, English-language sister publications. McClatchy and Knight Ridder were not alone in fumbling this kind of effort. The *Los Angeles Times* partnered with *La Opinión*, the region's largest Spanish-language daily, in 1990, a relationship that continued after the Tribune Company bought the Times Mirror Company, publisher of the *LA Times*.

But as the decline of the big mainstream newspaper companies like the *LA Times* and other Tribune Company properties accelerated through the early 2000s, some publishers of Spanish-language dailies began to chafe at those ties. In 2004, José Ignacio Lozano, the former publisher of *La Opinión* and vice chairman of the newly formed ImpreMedia, brought in a private investment firm—CPK Media, owner of New York's largest Spanish-language daily paper, *El Diario/La Prensa*—to help buy back *La Opinión*'s stake from the Tribune Company.

Lozano said he thought a new company, with a coast-to-coast reach, had a better chance under his leadership of not only surviving into the future but of thriving and beating mainstream papers at gaining readers among the nation's growing Latino population. By the late 1990s, the circulation figures of *La Opinión*, *El Diario*, and other Spanish-language papers nationwide were exploding, while circulation at most large corporate-owned English-language papers were declining dramatically. Obviously we couldn't have known it at the time, but the relatively stable environment of the *Fresno Bee* newsroom in the early 1990s—with its mini–rainbow coalition of reporters, photographers, editors, and designers—mirrored other midsize to large newspapers on a couple of crucial fronts: its staff at that time was at the peak of its ethnic diversity, and its long period of continual revenue growth was coming to an end.

In June 1992, two months after the LA riots, I drove from Fresno to San Jose and attended the annual awards ceremony of the California Newspaper Publishers Association. The *Bee* received the Spot News Award for our coverage of the epic civil unrest that had roiled LA in the last week of April.

When I returned to the newsroom in the Central Valley the following Monday, I sat at my desk and looked around at the stacks of used notebooks. There were piles of folders stuffed with budget reports from the Fresno County Unified School District—I had spent much of the previous year covering the education beat. Another mound of police reports—whenever I worked a weekend shift, I covered the cops beat. I had environmental reports from Pacific Gas and Electric, the big utility company that had been battling neighborhood and teachers' groups in Fresno after reports that its massive power lines above a district elementary school had caused rare forms of cancer in teachers and pupils; the stories I had written about that controversy resulted in a reporter from the *New Yorker*, Paul Brodeur, profiling the topic and my work at the *Bee* in a six-thousand-word story.

Every few months, I culled through those piles and threw out documents and used notepads. But I kept papers and notepads that I felt held potential for more stories down the road. I placed the dozen notepads I'd filled during the LA riots into a bottom drawer of my metal desk.

The week we'd spent in LA had been exhilarating. Interviewing "real people" and public officials under insanely stressful circumstances had recharged my batteries and reaffirmed the earliest beliefs that had led me into journalism: clearly and adeptly telling the stories of complex, inexplicable developments to wide audiences so that they can better understand their communities. Now the question was, Could I recreate the same level of grace under pressure on a bigger stage?

THREE

Miami

The *Herald* Tightrope

One Herald Plaza is the Floridian version of an American architectural gem: the big-city newspaper building. Built in the early 1960s—long after the skylines of Chicago, New York, and Los Angeles first sprouted their neo-Gothic newspaper temples—the *Miami Herald* building is squat, finished in a tastefully muted shade of yellow. It replaced a 1920s-era building a few blocks away and occupies a stretch of prime waterfront real estate along Biscayne Bay.

Inside, the lobby of One Herald Plaza is two stories high. A discreet bank of elevators is tucked to one side, and two narrow escalators—one ascending, one descending—dominate its midsection. It is hushed, airy, and grand. Postmodern columns and terrazzo floors give the wide space a stateliness that seems out of place in kitschy South Florida.

Just before 6 p.m. on July 27, 2005, a fifty-nine-year-old black Miami politician walked into the lobby and asked the security guard whether he might use the in-house telephone.

Arthur Teele Jr. dialed the extension of a *Miami Herald* columnist, Jim DeFede, who was at work in the building's newsroom. After speaking with DeFede, Arthur Teele hung up. Next he spoke briefly with the security guard on duty and asked him to give a sheaf of documents to DeFede.

Then he took a Sig Sauer handgun out of the green canvas case he carried and placed it at his temple. The security guard called city police.

Moments later, as patrol cars roared up to the glass double doors of the lobby, Arthur Teele shot himself in the head. He died two hours later at a Miami hospital.

■ ■ ■

That night, from my computer in suburban Washington, D.C., I clicked into a journalism industry website.

Chills rippled through me when I read of Teele's suicide.

I had first walked into the same lobby in late May 1992, several weeks after covering the Los Angeles riots for the *Fresno Bee*, and I had returned in 1993 to begin work as a staff writer at the *Miami Herald*. The suicide of Art Teele twelve years later in that lobby struck me as a tragic symbolic encapsulation of the declining fortunes of the *Miami Herald* in South Florida. Like other once-powerful regional newspapers in the United States, the *Miami Herald* by 2005 was under economic siege from shrinking classified and display advertising revenues. The precipitous drop in *Herald* ad revenues coincides with a defection of readers over the years, a development that I attribute to the paper's outsize (if questionable) reputation as an oppressor of ethnic communities and as an apologist for the status quo political leadership in the region, which is dominated by whites and Cuban Americans.

At the same time, the *Herald*, perhaps more than any other big-city newspaper, occupies a no-win position in terms of its ability to meet the needs of its readership. As the largest news organization in South Florida, it represents a big, splashy target for thousands of South Florida residents who don't agree on much, but who can usually agree on their dislike of the region's biggest newspaper.

Charged with providing accurate, fair, and ethical coverage of a quicksilver ethnic landscape, the *Herald* operated for decades like an all-seeing, if sometimes imperfect, referee. And the high level of emotions that the *Herald* evoked among readers was like nothing I'd ever seen. In the four years that I worked there, I witnessed a steady stream of protestors from across the spectrum of ethnic groups turn up in front of One Herald Plaza to wave placards and shout their disapproval of the newspaper through bullhorns—the late-twentieth-century version of the viral advocacy campaigns that now are organized through online social networking websites. Before the rise of the Internet threw the very survival of daily papers into question, such raucous protests were exciting and invigorating to those of

us who worked at the *Miami Herald*. Editors and reporters sometimes
had to walk through lines of protestors to get to work at One Herald
Plaza, and they did so resolutely, believing that the protesters' anger
simply proved that they were doing their jobs honorably, with favor
to none.

I was cast back to that contentious place in 2005 by news of Teele's
suicide. His final, fatal act struck me as especially sad and shocking,
in part because I knew firsthand the pain his family members likely
experienced when they learned of his death. My oldest brother killed
himself in 1979, and I am familiar with the emotional fallout that
ripples far beyond an individual suicide.

But more than anything, Art Teele's death reminded me that ethnic minorities in South Florida have long had intense, occasionally
volatile dealings with the *Miami Herald*, owned by McClatchy, and
with its sister paper, the Spanish-language *El Nuevo Herald*. In 2009,
the combined circulation for both papers stood at 273,440, with *El
Nuevo*'s average daily circulation representing 71,318 of the total
number. *El Nuevo* had been launched in 1976 by the *Herald*'s previous
publisher, Knight Ridder, and was designed to appeal to the large,
educated, and politically active community of Cuban Americans and
other well-educated Latin Americans who live in South Florida. By
1995, *El Nuevo*'s daily circulation reached a high of 126,000 copies
sold of its Sunday editions; but by 2010, readership and circulation
for *El Nuevo* and the *Miami Herald* had declined significantly.

Despite having editorial staffs that are among the most ethnically
diverse in the industry, the *Herald* and *El Nuevo* suffered from a perception among many South Florida residents that they were biased
in their coverage. (In 2008, 42 percent of editorial workers at the
Miami Herald were ethnic minorities, with Latinos accounting for 29
percent and blacks 10.2 percent; at *El Nuevo*, 98 percent of editorial
workers were Latino, according to ASNE.)

The disconnect between the *Herald*'s solid track record of employing journalists of color and the public's perception that it doesn't
do a good job of covering minority communities highlights the complexities facing big, full-service news organizations nationwide. And
it also demonstrates a need for news staffs that not only are ethnically diverse, but also encompass diverse economic backgrounds.

Often, ethnic minorities who hold midlevel or top editing positions attended elite universities or come from families that are assimilated—creating, sometimes, a cultural gap between their experiences and those of recently arrived Latinos or other ethnic minorities in circulation areas.

When I worked at the *Herald*, I gradually came to see why blacks and some Latinos in South Florida—including some who worked at the *Herald*—had a love-hate relationship with the newspaper. The *Miami Herald* played a powerful role in setting the political and social agenda and driving cultural debate in the region. When it covered topics involving Haitians, Cubans, Jews, or African Americans, it inevitably angered someone. Haitian Americans and other Caribbean-born blacks living in South Florida viewed the paper as favoring the politically and economically powerful Cuban exile community in Dade and Broward Counties. Thousands of Cuban Americans—in particular, those who coalesced around Jorge Mas Canosa, an influential businessman in the large community of Cubans who had fled the island in 1959—viewed the *Herald* as favoring Cuban president Fidel Castro and promoting a pro-Castro agenda. To Jewish Americans in South Florida, the *Herald* was too sympathetic to Palestine whenever it covered U.S. diplomatic efforts in the Middle East.

Many African Americans, meanwhile, suspected the *Herald* of focusing on Latino issues and Haitian affairs at their expense. Caribbean blacks, including the Bahamians from which Art Teele descended, tended to believe that the *Herald* ignored their concerns about fair employment laws, educational opportunity, and economic development in the neighborhoods where they lived.

At the time of his suicide, Teele had been under investigation by state prosecutors for allegedly taking bribes from residents in predominantly black Caribbean communities in his role as a Miami-Dade County commissioner. The *Herald* had covered the case for months, along with other local news organizations. On the day that Teele shot himself at One Herald Plaza, an alternative weekly, the *Miami New Times*, had published a lengthy story detailing alleged episodes of Teele using cocaine, hiring prostitutes, and shaking down business owners for suitcases filled with money. The journalists at both papers felt they were just doing their jobs in covering Teele's legal troubles. To them, the Teele investigation represented another in a long, rich history of corruption by elected officials in Miami-Dade and Broward Counties. The color of Teele's skin and the striver narrative of his Bahamian background were beside the point.

I didn't believe that the *Herald* as an institution, or its staff members, had directly caused Teele to take his own life. But it was likely that Teele had come to see the *Herald* as a powerful symbol of a larger system that was crushing him. Teele wasn't the first public figure in South Florida for whom the looming presence of the *Herald* represented an intractable, possibly destructive force. A trophy case in the hallway outside the main newsroom held two dozen awards for *Herald* stories that over the years had exposed corrupt dealings of a multiethnic rogues' gallery of elected officials in the region. Few blacks had ever worked on investigative teams at the *Herald*, but those of us who occupied other beats at the paper had no reason to believe that editors unfairly singled out black elected officials. (By contrast, in 2001 hundreds of black San Franciscans staged a protest on the streets outside the offices of the *San Francisco Chronicle* after it published stories outlining accusations that the city's first black mayor, Willie Brown, had larded his administration with cronies and loyalists. I followed that flap from a distance, and I had more doubt about the *Chronicle's* motivations for covering what amounted to circumstantial evidence about Brown's leadership than I did about *Herald* investigations of elected officials who had clearly engaged in unethical behavior. I also knew from experience that the editorial leadership at the *Chronicle*, unlike that of the *Herald*, had not ever seriously attempted to fairly and comprehensively cover ethnic communities or minority elected officials in its circulation area.)

Moreover, what *Herald* critics didn't immediately get is that journalists of color on staff, too, sometimes found themselves in the uncomfortable position of failing to successfully reconcile their personal allegiances or beliefs with their professional identities as *Herald* employees.

Liz Balmaseda, for example, a Pulitzer Prize–winning metro columnist at the *Herald*, was called on the carpet by her editors in 2000 after she joined a sidewalk prayer-circle-cum-public-protest by Cuban Americans who were incensed by the U.S. government's handling of a case involving a Cuban-born schoolboy named Elián González. In that moment, Balmaseda chose her personal identity and beliefs over the strictures of her profession. It is a dilemma that is not unusual for journalists of color working in a corporate news organization anywhere in the United States, but one that is especially fraught in the racial hothouse of South Florida.

Barely two months after Teele's suicide, the *Herald* again made unhappy national news in the incendiary place where race, media, and identity politics collide. At *El Nuevo Herald*, three writers were found to have taken money from a U.S. government–funded organization in exchange for producing anti-Castro news; they were summarily fired. The fallout from that September 2006 imbroglio included the rehiring of the writers—staff members Pablo Alfonso and Wilfredo Cancio and a freelancer, Olga Conner—and the resignation of *El Nuevo*'s publisher, Jesus Diaz.

The *Herald*'s parent company—the McClatchy Company, which had bought Knight Ridder a few months earlier—conducted an investigation and learned that Diaz and the paper's executive editor had known that the administration of president George W. Bush, through its Office of Cuba Broadcasting, had been paying journalists since at least 2001. The fired journalists were indeed "on the take," but once it investigated and learned that Diaz had effectively signed off on the arrangement, McClatchy made the brave decision to rehire the journalists after reprimanding them. That ethics scandal mirrored disclosures that in 2004, African American radio talk show host Armstrong Williams had been paid $240,000 to promote the federal government's No Child Left Behind Act on his program. Both situations, rich with irony, showed that the ethical lines that should be hard and bright for journalists can become blurred when a government entity is the one seeking to circumvent the rules.

The case of the *El Nuevo Herald* publisher striking a deal with a government agency also represented an intriguing clash of Old versus New in terms of journalistic practices in America. The presence of partisan coverage—or questionable ethics, by our American journalistic standard—is part of the history of ethnic media in the United States, when newspapers such as the Jewish *Forward* and the *Amsterdam News*, both based in New York, were compelled to

take strong advocacy roles on behalf of their politically and economically marginalized constituents. By the late twentieth century,
though, the struggles of large corporate media groups attempting
to capture readers in emerging ethnic markets in the United States
included, among the usual logistical challenges, the trick of balanc-
ing competing expectations: readers' preference for strong partisan
coverage of issues that concerned their lives and traditions, and the
media organization's adherence to strict ethical standards of objectivity. Given the *Herald*'s historically tense relationship with Cuban
exiles in its circulation area, news that editorial workers had been
taking money from the Bush administration to write anti-Castro
news seemed to confirm the conspiracy theories of many non-
Latino South Floridians that the *Herald*, and *El Nuevo Herald* in particular, engaged in government propaganda favoring the Cuban exile
community.

Historically, some immigrants, in particular those who arrive in
the United States after fleeing war-torn countries with oppressive
governments, have gravitated to news outlets where coverage reflects
strong political advocacy. A few exceptions have emerged in recent
years across the nation, including *Viet Mercury*, which Knight Ridder
published for six years in Northern California, and the independent
Haitian Times, a small Brooklyn-based weekly published by a former
New York Times reporter, Garry Pierre-Pierre. The *Haitian Times*,
under Pierre-Pierre's leadership, is making a go of it with relatively
small circulation numbers and a modest budget. When I interviewed
Pierre-Pierre, he told me he felt it was more important to provide
high-quality, nonpartisan news and information for Haitian Americans than to make a financial killing. And I found it laudable that
Pierre-Pierre had bailed out of a financially secure staff writing job
at the *New York Times* to found the *Haitian Times* in the early 2000s.

Still, Pierre-Pierre, like his corporate newspaper publisher counterparts, has not solved the puzzle of reconciling reader preferences
with high journalistic standards of objective news coverage. And in
fairness, the urge to seek out news and information that confirms
your own beliefs and values is not unique to immigrants in the United
States—just look at the recent growth of highly partisan political
blogs and websites directed at specific constituencies, including *Talk-*

ing Points Memo on the political left and Townhall.com, a politically conservative site. These online sites, fashioned as news and information portals, offer loads of opinion writing, along with the occasional "investigative report," and make no pretense at being "fair and balanced." The lines between online news publications and those that are purely partisan are becoming increasingly murky, representing a throwback to the earliest days of mass media in the United States, when hundreds of "penny papers" espoused strong political ideologies and had robust circulations.

But the seemingly unstoppable impulse among consumers to favor publications that reinforce their existing beliefs over those that offer "straight news" presents a tightrope act for contemporary American news organizations, companies that strove for most of the past two hundred years to offer unbiased, objective reporting in their news columns. Now, editorial leaders at traditional news organizations constantly ask, "Is it possible to win and keep readers' loyalties while also adhering to high ethical standards? Can we compete with websites that primarily offer opinion writing and that appeal to audiences' preconceived ideas about current events?"

These questions have become more urgent in the twenty-first century, and their philosophical, navel-gazing quality is made more confounding when combined with the kinetic demographic landscape of multiethnic America.

I don't like to think I am a cynic, but the "pay-for-play" scandal that emerged at the *Herald*'s sister paper, *El Nuevo Herald*, was less of a surprise to me than the suicide of Art Teele. As a former *Herald* staff writer, I had witnessed the high emotions that grip many Cuban Americans in that region when it comes to the *Herald* and Fidel Castro; I didn't feel I had a dog in that fight, although I was a bit embarrassed for the leadership at the *Herald*, which at first responded clumsily to the *El Nuevo Herald* scandal. Art Steele's suicide, by contrast, struck a deep chord of recognition and sadness within me.

Both of those developments reminded me that I have mixed emotions about the *Miami Herald*'s performance on covering minorities and issues of relevance to ethnic communities.

In a pragmatic sense, I know that the *Herald*'s big footprint in

South Florida and its effort to stand as an aggressive, elegantly written paper devoted to covering events and communities fairly are somewhat naturally in conflict with its earnest attempts to juggle competing interests within a circulation area that is among the most ethnically diverse in the United States. In modern history, its journalistic successes—whether exposing local government corruption, championing fair immigration laws, or detailing the vast tapestry of cultural and religious rituals practiced by ethnic residents—have historically doomed it to occupying a contentious place in South Florida's political and cultural scene.

By the end of the 2000s, the double-whammy scandals of Art Teele's suicide in the *Herald* lobby and the *El Nuevo Herald* journalists' "pay-for-play" episode seemed like foggy memories from a distant era. In the wake of the swift unraveling of the American economy that began in late 2007, the accusations of racial and ethnic bias that once regularly flared at the *Miami Herald* have receded. It is almost as if the paper's traditional antagonists—Cuban Americans, Haitian activists, and assorted elected officials who loathed the *Herald*'s scrutiny—are now waiting and watching to see what will become of the paper itself.

In December 2008 the McClatchy Company put the *Miami Herald* up for sale. Its building and property at One Herald Plaza at the foot of Biscayne Bay, worth millions more than the newspaper itself, was viewed by McClatchy as a viable lure to potential buyers. Guessing games about the *Miami Herald* center on whether it will survive, not on what or whom it decides to cover. Moreover, staff layoffs and buyouts, once anathema to the owners, have sapped the collective spirit of the remaining editorial personnel (and have diminished the total number of writers, editors, and photographers across all departments and bureaus). It is interesting to consider that the decline of the *Herald*'s fortunes is as closely tied to the roiling ethnic makeup of South Florida as it is to the emerging power of the Internet. (At this writing, in 2010, no buyer had emerged for the *Herald* or for its property at Biscayne Bay.)

I can't imagine South Florida without the *Miami Herald*, imperfections and all.

■ ■ ■

In the spring of 1992, during my maiden visit to Dade and Broward
Counties, I was seeking relaxation. I also wanted badly to work at the
legendary *Miami Herald*.

I had recently covered the Los Angeles riots, and by taking in the
lush landscape and peppery ethnic mix of greater Miami, I hoped to
soothe my jangled nerves. For the first time in my life, I found myself
in dire need of decompression and a change of scenery: it occurred
to me, in the days after I returned to Fresno from Los Angeles, that
I suffered from the journalist's version of posttraumatic stress syn-
drome. I had become twitchy and short-tempered and was drinking
too much. My editors at the *Bee* were in full agreement that I needed
a break.

And then again, unofficially, there were two other reasons why I
chose South Florida as my decompression preserve: I had been dating a *Miami Herald* reporter I'd met in 1990 at a journalism convention, and things between us were heating up. I also wanted to catch
some "face time" with editors at the *Herald*.

I'd first met the journalist—let's call him Romantic Prospect—
and a few *Herald* editors, separately, at a big gathering: the annual
convention of the National Association of Black Journalists (NABJ).
The professional group had met in Los Angeles in July 1990, and
although I'd been on staff at the *Fresno Bee* only since January of that
year, I decided to go.

Why not? The group's convention hotel, the Century Plaza in
Los Angeles, was a few hours south of the San Joaquin Valley, within
driving distance of Fresno. I'd never attended an NABJ gathering,
but from colleagues and mentors, I knew that the convention was the
best place for networking and professional development.

Founded in 1975 by a group of black journalists who had broken
in at mainstream news organizations, the NABJ is based in Maryland.
Its founding principle is similar to that of other large professional
and educational associations in America—to provide a protective
structure and training designed to bolster the effectiveness of its individual members within their profession. Unlike most other such
groups, however, it does not actively lobby elected officials or federal

agencies. That would present a major conflict, since aside from the narrow confines of the Federal Communications Commission's regulatory oversight of broadcast airwaves, the First Amendment makes clear that government shall not seek to interfere with or prohibit a free press. And for all the influence of the Kerner Commission's landmark report in the 1960s about the press's role in contributing to the urban unrest of that era, the NABJ took no official action to correct the problems the Kerner Report identified in news organizations regarding their lack of ethnic diversity. In turn, while the NABJ has issued many official statements over the years about developments that involve government actions—and in 2009 urged the nation's first black president, Barack Obama, to be aware of the need for a diverse national press corps—it stops short of directly lobbying federal officials.

Over the years, NABJ members have included college students, greenhorn journalists, and midcareer writers, photographers, designers, and editors, as well as top veteran editors and reporters at major print and broadcast news organizations. The group's annual conventions have sometimes made news, including the 1996 gathering, when Nation of Islam minister Louis Farrakhan told attendees they were carrying water for oppressive white corporate and political leaders in the United States. At the 1992 NABJ convention in Detroit, Democratic presidential candidate Bill Clinton stunned attendees by engaging in a heated exchange with Clarence Page, a *Chicago Tribune* columnist, over affirmative action.

As an advocate for fair hiring and retention practices in the news business, the NABJ has sometimes found itself torn between fulfilling its mission to support journalists of color in a notoriously insulated business and holding to the bright line of high standards and ethics for its members. Since 1981, when a black journalist named Janet Cooke was exposed as a fabricator at the *Washington Post*, the NABJ has sometimes had to remind industry leaders that should a lone African American journalist commit a journalistic sin, like plagiarism or fabrication, it should not reflect badly on the larger number of hardworking, qualified, and law-abiding black journalists. The NABJ's activist and educational functions, too, have gained sharper focus in the group's fourth decade.

By the beginning of 2009, the group's membership had shrunk to four thousand members, from a high in the late 1980s of close to eight thousand. Although the drop reflected the downsizing taking place across the entire news industry, NABJ president Barbara Ciara, a veteran broadcast journalist, was concerned that blacks and other journalists of color were losing their jobs at a faster clip than other journalists and that the negative implications for a news industry effectively shorn of journalists of color would be significant.

On January 5, 2009, Ciara released an open letter to president-elect Barack Obama that read in part: "We are writing you to express our urgent concern about the current crisis in the news media industry and the impact it is having on diversity in our nation's media system. We are also writing to offer a few recommendations that we urge your administration to support to increase media diversity." Among the recommendations Ciara outlined was for the president to prevent further consolidation of media organizations, since few minorities historically have been in a position to buy into large conglomerate media structures, and to support a "robust" public-interest media. Ciara didn't have specific recommendations for how the president might show support for increasing diversity in print media. Her letter did, however, ask President Obama to "provide greater access to journalists of color" assigned to the White House beat, an entreaty that picked up steam as the new administration got underway and the president began holding regular press briefings to outline his economic recovery plans.

Although the president had earlier appeared to be at least open to the concerns of NABJ members—he attended their 2007 convention in Las Vegas, as well as the Unity: Journalists of Color convention in Chicago in 2008 (a quadrennial gathering of the four leading organizations for journalists of color, including NABJ)—Obama initially kept silent about the big drop in numbers of working journalists of color as the massive downturn continued to reshape the industry throughout 2009. By the second year of his term, however, Obama's press office quietly began making outreach efforts to black bloggers, and the lineup of White House correspondents (historically a virtually all-white corps) held nearly a dozen black, Latino, and Asian journalists. That increase, while not directly attributable to presidential intervention, was nevertheless a signal that assignment editors had recognized potential value in assigning journalists of color to cover the nation's first African American president.

Still, the withering of ranks in large newsrooms has had a devastating impact on the NABJ and other trade groups for journalists of color. Even during better economic climates, the NABJ, like the professional trade organizations of Latino and Asian journalists of color, had little more than a symbolic effect on the corporate news industry and the U.S. government's influence on, and oversight of, media companies. These organizations are in effect toothless, relying on advocacy and letter-writing campaigns to encourage elected officials and corporate overseers to pay attention to diversity at news outlets. It is "lobbying lite," and to date, no one in government has raised objections to such outreach efforts.

The NABJ continues providing high-quality training workshops and professional support for its members, including free or low-cost courses in digital technology. It is in survival mode these days, and as in the past, I am bolstered by its dedication to helping its members remain relevant in an increasingly volatile business. As the number of black journalists continues to decline in mainstream news organizations, the NABJ has begun offering its members free sessions with industrial psychologists and other clinical professionals specializing in workplace issues. In a sign of the times, the NABJ has added a new item to its portfolio of support services for its members: grief counseling.

In the early 1990s, though, I mostly saw the NABJ as a vehicle for networking with editors at other newspapers and as a place to meet other black journalists. At the time of the NABJ convention in Los Angeles, I had been at the *Fresno Bee* less than a year, but I was feeling lonely, in a cultural and professional sense. Other than Don Coleman, my colleague at the *Bee* who was also African American, and a couple of African American broadcast journalists at local television stations in the San Joaquin Valley (including an energetic reporter named Steve Pickett, who, as of late 2010, was a top reporter at the CBS affiliate in Dallas, Texas), I didn't have any peers who looked like me or came from similar backgrounds. I'd loosely planned to remain at the *Bee* for at least two years, but I'd also made a silent promise to

myself: that by my thirtieth birthday, in May 1993, I would be working at a larger daily newspaper. My plan for accomplishing this was
simple, if not wholly formed: report and write my way out of Fresno.

Since the NABJ conventions at that time drew hundreds of recruiters from newspapers and broadcast organizations across the
country, it couldn't hurt to scout around, drop some clips, and chat
up some editors. Best of all: NABJ conventions drew thousands of
black journalists to one location for a week's worth of milling at
sumptuous receptions and banquets by night, and soldiering through
a smorgasbord of workshops and panels by day. Sounded like a good
time to me.

I couldn't afford more than one night at the Century Plaza Hotel,
so my first convention experience was brief but eventful: I hit one
cocktail party after another, schmoozing with dozens of well-known,
novice, and midcareer journalists with carefree bonhomie. By the
time I drove back to Fresno, I had thoroughly enjoyed myself, having managed to speak with a handful of recruiting editors—including
two from the *Miami Herald*—and engage in restorative socializing
with other black journalists, among them Romantic Prospect.

And by the spring of 1992, I was (to my surprise) eagerly engaged
in chaste, long-distance dating with Romantic Prospect, a former police reporter from a Mid-Atlantic newspaper. He'd left there for the
Miami Herald not long after we'd first met in Los Angeles.

In terms of the professional prospects, I had also kept in touch
with those two *Miami Herald* editors since meeting them in LA. For
months after, I would periodically send them copies of some of the
stories I published in the *Bee*—carefully mounted "clips" that I put
together with the help of a *Bee* news aide. (How quaint, right? These
days, any editor interested in scouting a talented prospect at another
news organization simply logs on to the Internet, while ambitious job
seekers can just e-mail their work to a prospective editor.)

I'm not sure where I got such bravado, but I sent clips to the
Herald's recruiting team members every few months, accompanied
by short notes that I hoped sounded smart and pithy, not desperate:
"We often have to parachute into forest fires, but this one was a real
challenge," I wrote, adopting what I hoped was a cheerily intrepid
tone, in a note accompanying a *Bee* story about a big fire in Yosem-

ite National Park. (The parachute was metaphorical—I was intrepid, but had never actually jumped out of an airplane for a story!) This "constant contact" method, bold and possibly presumptuous, carried some risk—foremost, the current boss learning of the contacts—but was recommended by my closest mentors in journalism. It didn't always work, and over the years I've known many reporters at midsize newspapers who never managed to turn that particular trick. Timing, resources, skill, and a mysterious alchemy of personality and compatibility all have a lot to do with determining who gets lifted out of the middle of the pack of midmarket papers and invited onto the A-Team—a big regional or national news organization.

In my case, the stars aligned just so during the spring of 1992. I later learned that my coverage of the LA riots for the McClatchy papers helped accelerate my hiring at the *Herald* and that my earlier clips had been only moderately successful at priming the pump, so to speak, since the slush pile of prospective hires at the *Herald* was tall and deep.

The main point is that we all had kept in touch after the 1990 NABJ conference in LA—an odd, parallel flirtation that conflated my personal life with my professional one. And by the time The Call finally did come in late 1992, when I was offered a staff writer position at the *Miami Herald*, things had progressed from theoretical to physical with the Romantic Prospect, lending the entire enterprise an air of kismet.

But before that moment, during that warm spring of 1992, I hedged my bets on both fronts: combining a much-needed vacation with an opportunity to scope out the Romantic Prospect and the professional one.

FOUR

On the South Florida Rainbow Beat

On the midmorning in May 1992 when I first walked through that lobby at One Herald Plaza, I felt exhilarated and nervous. Like many young newspaper journalists at that time, I was enthralled by the *Miami Herald* and its reporters and editors. To call it a "great newspaper" at that time was to severely understate the *Herald*'s standing in the industry and in South Florida: a few months after my first visit, the *Herald* capped a twenty-five-year period of exceptionally hard-nosed, creative, and brave journalism by winning the Pulitzer Prize for public service, the big daddy of the annual awards, for its coverage of Hurricane Andrew.

Its parent company at that time, the Knight Ridder News Corporation, was for me the epitome of a smoothly run, world-class newspaper company, one that nurtured and encouraged precisely the kinds of journalists who lived to take risks in service of getting the story. It was most definitely my kind of outfit, and the *Miami Herald* was its flagship paper.

As I crossed that vast lobby for the first time, I fretted: *Do I have the stuff to make it here? The reporting and writing skills? A hide that is thick enough?*

In the late 1980s a former *Herald* reporter, Edna Buchanan, had written a funny, scary book about her time on the police beat at the height of the "cocaine wars" in South Florida. With its terse, vivid descriptions of the insane goings-on in Miami during much of the 1970s and '80s—drug-crazed killers, corrupt cops, and murder victims both deserving and undeserving—*The Corpse Had a Familiar Face*, first published in 1987, was required reading for print journal-

ism students at my college. After I'd inhaled it, I had instantly fallen
in love with the newspaper and its editorial energy. Miami seemed
like a foreign land within our national borders, while Buchanan herself struck me as a logical, organic evolution of the archetypical "intrepid girl reporters" I had also read about in college—Nellie Bly and
Ida Tarbell.

Buchanan, who had won a Pulitzer Prize in 1986, no longer
worked at the *Herald* full-time by the early 1990s. But plenty of other
world-class reporters, columnists, and photographers did, including
Dave Barry, Carl Juste, Martin Merzer, Carl Hiaasen, Patrick Farrell,
Leonard Pitts Jr., Liz Balmaseda, and many more, all contributing to
the *Herald's* reputation as a big, fast, smart newspaper with a boatload
of Pulitzer Prizes to its credit.

The intimidation I felt, though, ebbed soon after I reached
the main newsroom, where I was greeted warmly by the recruiter,
a middle-aged Latina editor who had perfected the mix of humor,
casual seriousness, and sharp intuition that is a hallmark of great
journalists. We sat in her office for nearly half an hour, chatting ami-
ably about my trip to South Florida, my adventures in Los Angeles,
and the like. Since my visit was "unofficial," she said, I would not
meet the full complement of top editors, but she did think it prudent
for me to take "the test" and to meet at least one editor that she was
sure I'd "hit it off with." My eyes widened at the words "the test." She
laughed. "Everyone reacts that way. But really, it is nothing—kind of
a personality test, mixed with a reporting test . . . designed primarily
to try to gauge how people react under pressure. It only takes about
thirty minutes, okay?"

I looked away and swallowed: I hated tests.

I took a deep breath and smiled at the recruiting editor. "Oh.
Sure, no problem," I lied. "Will I meet the editor you mentioned
first, or do the test first?" I asked, hoping I sounded enthusiastic and
confident.

"He's in a meeting right now," she replied, "so I'll set you up with
the test, and when that's done, we'll go check on him." Her coworker
brought me to a desk just outside their small suite of offices. I sat
down and tried not to look nervous while I waited.

How do they get any work done with that view from their windows?

I mused. One side of the *Herald*'s newsroom had a wall of windows overlooking Biscayne Bay. Seen from the recruiting editor's small office and the other, larger offices of higher-ranking editors, the shimmering, turquoise-teal expanse must be one of the most spectacular views in America. The bay glinted just beyond the windowpanes, seemingly at my fingertips, stretching to the horizon, a dreamy vista dotted every few miles by a string of luxuriantly green artificial islands.

I simply wanted to not fall on my face. By lunchtime I had completed a psychological assessment as well as a Knight Ridder "reporting exercise" without completely falling apart. I had even survived a brief, friendly meeting with a top newsroom editor—Joe Oglesby, a middle-aged, soft-spoken assistant managing editor. He was African American, with a bemused glint in his eye. I knew that Oglesby had won a Pulitzer Prize for editorial writing several years earlier. He struck me as sublimely, calmly confident as he questioned me about some of the clips I'd sent to the *Herald*. He laughed in odd places as I recounted some of my reporting escapades in Fresno and San Francisco, and he seemed to watch me closely for signs of exaggeration or self-aggrandizement. His questions were sharp: How had I worked a particular beat for news outside of "official" channels? And how many hours did it take me to get to the top of Half Dome in Yosemite to write about a paraplegic national park ranger?

Later that evening, I talked with the Romantic Prospect about my meetings. He had put me up at his apartment in Hollywood, in Broward County, just north of Miami. He confided that he still sometimes doubted that he had "the goods" to really be successful at the *Miami Herald*. But he encouraged me to think optimistically about my chances of being hired: Oglesby was "good people," Romantic Prospect assured me.

"He's smart, fair, and has a good sense about people," he said. "It's a good sign if he said they'll be in touch."

The only question I had left was *When?*

In March 1993, two months shy of my thirtieth birthday, I left California for South Florida. I had been hired at the *Miami Herald* to cover minority affairs in Broward County, directly north of Dade County (which has since been renamed Miami-Dade County).

Saying goodbye to the *Bee* was more emotionally difficult than I anticipated: I'd made a dozen lovely friends among the reporters, editors, and photographers at the paper and my neighbors in Fresno. Romantic Prospect and I drove my VW across country, while Knight Ridder hired a truck and moved my household goods. I'd never driven coast to coast before, and our trip was a week-long adventure enlivened by deep rust-colored Southwest landscapes, midpriced hotel rooms, and parched, pastel horizons of Texas that suddenly morphed into lush, Louisiana bayou country. Every time we crossed a new state line, I couldn't stop myself from tearing up.

When I reported for work at the *Herald* newsroom in Fort Lauderdale, everyone there seemed confident that I had the makings of a successful *Miami Herald* staff writer. I had butterflies, but I was confident that, at the least, I had the intellect and reporting skill to meet the *Herald*'s standards.

At that time, from Edna Buchanan's book and from stories that I had read both in the *Herald* and in Fort Lauderdale's newspaper, the *Sun Sentinel*, I knew more about the roiling ethnic mix of residents in South Florida than I did about the demographics of this newsroom. Jewish retirees from northeastern states, including New York, New Jersey, and Pennsylvania, had over many decades given a decidedly Borscht Belt flavor to the cities of Miami and Miami Beach and to the neighboring northern counties, Broward and Palm Beach. Both counties were home to the popular "snowbird" cities of Hollywood, Fort Lauderdale, Palm Beach, and Boca Raton. Cuban Americans, of course, also represented a large portion of Miami's residents and a growing number of Broward's. (Though I have to admit that at that point, I was fairly ignorant about the strong dislike of the *Herald* that many Cubans had: their frequent protests outside One Herald Plaza had sometimes resulted in news stories that had reached even my arid swath of central California, but I did not grasp the full implications of what ignited them.)

When I began working in the Fort Lauderdale bureau, my editors provided me with a thick binder and several folders filled with reports from local agencies and their own marketing research, material that would background me on the demographic particulars of the region. Most interesting to me were the research files stamped with the newspaper's corporate logo: culled from state and federal census data, the studies were produced by the *Miami Herald* parent company to aid its advertising sales force. My editors had obtained copies for me, believing that the documents would also help ground my understanding of the region's two largest ethnic groups, Latinos and blacks. The reports showed that slightly more than one million Latinos lived in Dade and Broward Counties, compared with 591,440 blacks; that 22 percent of Latinos and 19 percent of blacks in Dade County were college graduates; and that 16.4 percent of Latinos and 18 percent of blacks in Dade County had annual incomes of $50,000 or higher.

Missing from the data, though, was research on the points of interethnic contact that caused tension among blacks, Latinos, and whites in Dade and Broward Counties. Over time, I would learn that many blacks in the region—including Caribbean immigrants and native-born Floridians—held simmering resentments toward some Cuban Americans in South Florida, primarily due to perceived advantages that they believed Cubans received in politics, education, and corporate arenas.

Since 1959, when they began arriving in significant numbers following Fidel Castro's revolutionary coup against the Batista regime, Cubans had become a powerful economic and political force in local governments and businesses. Prior to my first visit to Miami, I had never actually met a Cuban. But having grown up in Northern California, where Mexican Americans and Central Americans had been my classmates since preschool, I believed I had the cultural IQ needed to quickly absorb and adapt to this variation of Latinos. How different could Cubans be from the Latinos I'd been friends with for decades?

My editor, Patricia Andrews, was beloved by the reporters in that office. She was highly skilled at the interpersonal aspects of reporting: how to "read" a source or situation, how to quickly locate relevant information amid official structures and organizations, how to cultivate sources, and the fine art of knowing when to push a source or contact and when to back away.

As the senior of two full-time assistant city editors in the Fort

Lauderdale office, Pat presided over a dozen reporters who covered everything from Broward County businesses to cops, schools, and city and county government. I had been hired to cover a relatively new beat at the *Herald*, minority affairs. I was told upon being hired that the company considered the beat essential.

The reporter who had initiated the beat at the *Herald*, a laid-back, whip-smart journalist named Tony Pugh, had recently been reassigned to covering news in the main office in Miami. This was the trajectory for most of the reporters who began their *Herald* duties in the Broward bureau or other bureaus around the state: work hard, break great stories, write the hell out of them and you might win a coveted spot in the main newsroom, known as Downtown. It was encouraging to know that Tony, who is African American, had successfully followed that path. Pat Andrews, who also is African American, had been Tony's editor too.

Romantic Prospect said the Fort Lauderdale office was a great place to work: the bureau, located in a former bank building on Sunrise Boulevard, was less than one mile from the storied beachfront district immortalized in the all-time greatest spring break movie ever, *Where the Boys Are*, from 1960. It was a mid-twentieth-century, two-story, unremarkable building, with one exception: a teal-blue neon *Miami Herald* sign marked its main entrance.

Pat instantly brought me under her wing. I took to her easy sense of humor, down-home advice, and historic knowledge of Fort Lauderdale and Broward County. Pat had been at the *Herald* for nearly a decade, having arrived there from a small paper in her home state of Wisconsin. She seemed to "get" me immediately, and the fact that Pat is an African American woman implicitly helped ease my early job-performance anxieties.

I had taken a one-bedroom garden apartment in a small complex not far from downtown Fort Lauderdale. I learned quickly that this section of town, located less than a mile from beaches and not far from the high-end shopping district along fancy Las Olas Boulevard, was in the throes of gentrification when I arrived. I briefly considered, but then rejected, the idea of living in the historically black part of Fort Lauderdale, a midsize neighborhood, delineated by Sixth Street and Sistrunk Boulevard, that was part of the business district.

For one thing, the city's black neighborhood, known as informally as Sistrunk, had only a tattered commercial area made up of bar-bershops, seafood shacks, and liquor stores; for another, its housing stock was limited to single-family houses and large apartment com-plexes—nothing that appealed to my budding sense of sheltering. Did my choice of a "nonblack" neighborhood mean that I was out of touch with the black residents, businesspeople, and community leaders that I had come to South Florida to cover? Maybe. But dur-ing my entire time in South Florida, none of my African American sources expressed any opinions at all about the fact that I didn't live in a "black" neighborhood, and I didn't feel out of touch with the black communities I covered.

South Florida summers are beyond hot.

My mother had warned me that living in a subtropical region full-time would present challenges that I probably hadn't noticed in my previous visit.

She also reminded me, in the weeks before I left Fresno, that Florida is "still the Deep South." Like me, she had never actually *lived* in the Deep South, but my mother—a native of Rock Springs, Wyoming—carried with her the searing images of all the horrible in-cidents of racist terrorism that black Americans had endured in that region for so many years.

I had read about the civil-rights-era racial turmoil that had taken place in Miami and Fort Lauderdale as Jim Crow discrimination dis-sipated at local hotels, businesses, and other public institutions. It was ancient history in my view, although I thought it prudent to keep an eye out for lingering signs of old pressure points as I familiar-ized myself with the city and the beat. I had also read in almanacs and official regional histories that summer temperatures in South Florida were "hot"—but until I experienced it, I didn't really under-stand how South Florida's summer heat differed from that of Fresno, where temperatures routinely topped one hundred degrees in July and August. The biggest difference: San Joaquin Valley summer tem-peratures can be blast-furnace hot, but there is little or no humidity; in South Florida, "hot" also means "damp," since the humidity can climb to 90 percent in the high summer months, leaving you feeling wrung out and sluggish by early evening. For the first time in my adult life, I took to sprinkling talcum powder under my arms and between my breasts after showering.

Another lesson learned quickly during my first year in Broward County: the care and feeding of African American hair can be a big challenge. When I worked at the *Herald*, I permed my hair to a fare-thee-well and, even in the deathly hot, soggy South Florida summers, wore it in heavy, shoulder-length waves, the better to fit in among the glamorous ladies who fill newsrooms in that part of the country. (After I quit the *Herald* and moved to Boston in the winter of 1997, I cut my hair to a length above my ears and wore it that way until 2008.) A paradox, but there it was: my journalist's identity matured and gained in confidence even as my sartorial sense of self caved in to high-school-era peer pressure.

Still, I dug in, and during my first few months as a *Miami Herald* staff writer I produced a regular stream of stories that explored inter-ethnic relations in South Florida. One that stands out was a fun story looking at the concept of "political correctness." I found a group of blue-collar workers at the maintenance shop of Fort Lauderdale–Hollywood International Airport who engaged in workplace banter that might have struck white-collar workers as decidedly politically *in*correct. By highlighting their practical take on the subject—which had been in the news frequently during the early 1990s, after public figures like Rush Limbaugh drew criticism for rhetoric that some viewed as insulting to gays and ethnic minorities—I demonstrated the absurdity that characterized much of the debate around what constituted "safe speech."

In recent years, a few high-profile skirmishes rooted in speech have renewed that debate. In 2006, U.S. senator George Allen, a Republican from Virginia who was running for reelection, was excoriated for calling a brown-skinned worker from a rival's campaign a "macaca." In 2007, national radio talk-show host Don Imus lost his job after he referred to a group of black female college basketball players as "nappy-headed hos." The letters of protest from civil rights groups, consumers, and ethnic advocacy groups in both those instances whipped up a frenzy of acrimony that elevated both episodes to the national stage. I'm not convinced, though, that hounding unreconstructed racists out of jobs will persuade regular Americans who hold racist beliefs to change their behavior. But the coordinated protests of the mid and late 2000s—in the form of thousands of letters being sent to corporate sponsors of Imus's radio and television programs, which convinced MSNBC to drop their simulcast of his radio program—demonstrated that citizens now have highly effective forms of organizing: digital media and online social networking tools have created a revolution in rapid-response capability for Regular People.

And the swiftness with which Americans can now respond to outrageous comments or behavior by public figures—or to news coverage that is perceived to be biased—has thrown many old-school journalists for a loop. When I wrote about the blue-collar airport workers who regularly, jokingly used words like "spic" to refer to each other, I presented a hidden-in-plain-sight aspect of the larger debate around politically correct speech: that the intent of the speaker usually has a big impact on how such language is received. And those articles, published in the summer of 1993, drew not a single letter of protest from *Herald* readers.

By midsummer I was becoming familiar with the culture of the *Herald*. Along with attending the weekend parties thrown by *Herald* editorial employees and volunteering to write for the annual year-end fundraising publication, the Wish Book, I also had begun participating in an in-service training program designed to increase multicultural awareness among *Herald* staffers. These infrequent, hour-long sessions were called "diversity training," and they could be comically touchy-feely: reporters and editors were taken to offices of a local consultant and led through a series of team-building exercises designed to help us recognize our respective gender, age, and racial biases.

Some reporters and editors found the training sessions dopey and condescending, but I enjoyed them—at the very least, they revealed things about ourselves that we didn't often have time or inclination to consider, the sometimes subtle expressions of opinions and beliefs that crept into our dealings with each other and into our work. Knight Ridder was one of the few big newspaper companies to insist on this kind of training for its employees. Its former editorial leader, James Batten, had a progressive take on diversity in the news business, and the *Miami Herald*, the *Philadelphia Inquirer*, and other Knight Ridder news outlets were viewed as leaders in building staffs that at least attempted to reflect the demographic compositions of circulation areas.

Inside newsrooms, though, these initiatives were sometimes met with eye-rolling by editorial workers of all ethnic stripes, who suspected the Knight Ridder leadership of using the training as a cynical brand of corporate apple polishing, a way of one-upping other big media companies. It may sound twisted to outsiders, but even while we journalists of color experienced frustration at our relatively low numbers in big newsrooms, some of us bridled at what we viewed as the superficial quality of the diversity initiatives. Apart from the few minority recruiting and internship programs that focused on the intensive training and placement of young journalists of color —like Knight Ridder's formalized summer internship programs and METPRO (Minority Editorial Training Program), an initiative funded by Times Mirror, the former publisher of the *Los Angeles Times*—corporate-sponsored initiatives somehow didn't manage to translate into significant numbers of minority journalists ascending to top jobs in newsrooms. And now, of course, with big newspaper companies fighting total obsolescence, many of these initiatives have vanished.

During my first year at the *Herald*, I caught a race-related story that was unaccountably tragic: a six-year-old African American girl had stood on a set of train tracks near Hollywood, just south of Fort Lauderdale, and allowed herself to be mowed down by an onrushing engine. It was an unfunny version of what we called an "Only in Florida" story, a shocking development or event that *Herald* columnist Carl Hiaasen usually captured with rapier wit and irony. Most of those stories involved comically corrupt politicians, drugged-out socialites, or wildlife run amok. The story of Jackie Johnson, though, fit another "Only in Florida" archetype: the unfortunate fates that often befell poor, undereducated residents.

In this case, Carla Johnson, Jackie's twenty-nine-year-old mother, had been diagnosed with HIV, the virus that causes AIDS. Carla had

five children, including Jackie, all under age twelve. At Easter, Carla
had been stricken with a fever that required hospitalization for treatment. Jackie had overheard some older relatives discussing her mother's illness and speculating whether Carla might be dying. But when
Jackie and an older sibling asked an aunt to explain, the aunt denied
that their mother's health was in jeopardy. And when the Johnson
children visited their mother in her bed at Broward Memorial Hospital in Hollywood, Carla had assured the children that she was fine.
"Mommy is not going to die," she told them. By early June, Carla
had been released from the hospital and was recovering at her aunt's
home in Dania, a suburb that bordered Hollywood, where she lived
with her children.

A few weeks after Carla returned from the hospital, three of her
five children were walking to school. Their route to the elementary
school included a stretch of train tracks that ran through town. As
Jackie's older brother later described it, he, Jackie, and another sibling had been walking to school around 8:30 a.m. on that hot morning
when they began talking about their mother's illness. Jackie had been
upset ever since they'd overheard the relatives discussing Carla's illness, and as they walked to school, the six-year-old girl began crying.
She told her two siblings that if Mama was going to die, she wanted
to be in heaven when she arrived, waiting there with the angels.

At that moment a train approached, and Jackie ran to the tracks
and stood with her back to the oncoming locomotive. Her brother
and sister dragged her off, but she wrestled free and ran away from
them, further along the tracks. Her brother and sister tried to catch
her, but she leapt back onto the tracks, where she was struck by the
train. The conductor had seen the whole thing but was unable to stop
the multicar train in time. The six-year-old girl was thrown away
from the train, her skull horribly broken by the impact. She died at
the scene.

I was in the Fort Lauderdale newsroom when the police beat reporter, listening to the scanner at her desk, heard public safety workers responding to the incident. (Police reporters at that time usually
had shortwave radios that picked up public safety agency frequen-
cies.) She went out immediately, and Pat asked me and a few other
reporters to begin making calls. We also turned on the television in

the newsroom: in South Florida, the hyperkinetic, aggressive local television news teams are relentlessly on top of breaking news, and we knew there would be immediate reports. The news teams from local television outlets, while ethnically diverse, were more notable for their willingness to run fast and loud with any sliver of information on a hot story than for displaying sensitivity to racial matters or just about anything else that required a deft touch. *Herald* reporters regularly griped about the shabbiness of the local television journalists' reporting, even as we sometimes used it to our advantage with sources, as when appealing to citizens who unexpectedly found themselves the subject of news stories by telling them that *Herald* journalists were ethical and thorough—unlike those sensationalistic local television reporters.

I decided to take the social services angle, since the early reports from law enforcement indicated that the child's mother might be a patient at a Broward hospital; Pat and I guessed (correctly) that the child's mother might be receiving public assistance, which meant there probably was a social worker involved. By lunchtime, the television news programs had the basic outline of the story: a six-year-old Broward girl commits suicide by jumping in front of a train.

Late on the afternoon of Jackie's death, I talked with Carla Johnson's aunt, Laura Scott, a heavyset woman in her late fifties. She had taken in Carla and her children after Carla lost her job. (The children's father, an ex-inmate, was not involved in their lives.) Aunt Laura was in shock when I visited her. She told me she had a hard time believing the story that the two older siblings described. Laura and Carla had been at home that morning; a neighbor ran up to the front door and told Carla there had been an accident involving her children. Carla and Laura jumped into Laura's car and rushed to the scene, then followed the ambulance to the hospital as it carried Jackie in. The news that her daughter had died, and in such a manner, sent Carla into seizures of despair and grief; she was readmitted to the same hospital she had checked out of only weeks earlier. When I asked if I might visit Carla at the hospital, Laura said she doubted that Carla would want to speak with me, but that it was okay with her if I tried.

I talked it over with Pat Andrews, and we decided that I should seek an interview with Carla Johnson. The local television news reports had been typically overwrought and insensitive. By the evening of Jackie's death, all three major television news outlets reported that the child's mother was suffering from AIDS; apparently an emergency worker who had talked with Jackie's two siblings at the scene had relayed that information to a reporter, and the television journalists seemed to believe that by attributing the medical diagnosis to "officials," they were not breaching any ethical boundaries. No one, however, had actually interviewed Carla Johnson. Trish Power, my *Herald* colleague who covered cops in our bureau, agreed that I should attempt to meet Carla as soon as possible. All three of us—Trish, Pat, and me—decided that our breaking story of the girl's suicide should sidestep the exact nature of Carla's medical condition until formal confirmation was obtained (if in fact it was—we were aware that medical personnel and social service workers rarely provided diagnoses of patients and clients on the record.)

So on day two of the story, I drove to Memorial Hospital in Hollywood and parked. Before leaving my car, I hung my *Miami Herald* press badge inside the front of my shirt, carefully tucking the lanyard beneath my collar. There were several TV news crew vans stationed near the hospital entrance, confirming my suspicion that other reporters would also be trying to interview Carla Johnson. I had asked Pat how I should proceed: contact the hospital spokesperson or just turn up at Broward Memorial? Pat had answered, "Amy, do what you think is necessary, but please don't get into any trouble."

Earlier that day, I had talked with Carla Johnson's social worker, Marie Brown. She was an African American woman in her late twenties, and she had been sad but straightforward during our conversation. Jackie Johnson's death might have been avoided, Marie told me, if the chain of events leading up to that moment had been broken at any point along the way. Carla Johnson, Aunt Laura, and the other older relatives lacked the education to understand that lying about Carla's illness only created more anxiety for the children. Marie had been gently urging Carla for months to sit down with her older children—the youngest two were under age three—and tell them in clear but nonscary language that she did indeed have a serious illness. The social worker had even drafted a script for Carla to use.

But Carla apparently experienced the same degree of confusion, shame, and denial experienced by many other young black women after learning they are HIV positive. And not talking about the reality of the disease with close friends and family members often led to a tangled knot of related problems that further compromised their chances of successfully coping with the illness, Marie explained.

I had written about AIDS over the years, in San Francisco and in New York, but had not reported a story that involved blacks' experiences with the illness. I had been reading more and more stories, though, about how black Americans faced unique challenges in regard to the virus—and how the shame, fear, confusion, and denial experienced by most HIV patients could be especially acute among blacks. I also knew, from Centers for Disease Control and Prevention data and from the Broward County Health Department, that increasing numbers of blacks nationwide and in Florida were being diagnosed with HIV.

The basic outline of the Carla and Jackie Johnson story deserved further exploration, I decided. My own family's experience with suicide had taught me that blacks, much more than whites, were vulnerable to trauma from mental illness, terminal diseases, drug and alcohol addiction, and severe emotional or psychological-related illnesses, in part because of our history in America. We were conditioned to be "stronger than the average bear," owing to the generations of us who had endured physical oppression and thick Jim Crow segregation and discrimination. Internalizing negative messages around being black and holding on to some coping skills that provided immediate comfort (like overeating or drinking too much) had begun to work against our long-term health. So had a high degree of emotional stoicism, sometimes called "John Henryism," after the legend of the "steel-drivin' man" who had worked himself to death rather than give up and rest at signs of physical exhaustion.

My older brother, Carl, committed suicide in 1979 at the age of twenty-five. I knew that the drug addiction and erratic behavior he had shown in the last two years of his life had been part of his attempt to self-medicate; he had been diagnosed with a form of schizophrenia in his early twenties. But we had never talked about his illness in my family, and his suicide threw my siblings, my mother, and our extended family into a deep well of despair that affected us for years after. It was not until the late 1990s, when I began researching Carl's story for a book on African Americans and mental health, that we finally talked openly about what my oldest brother had experienced—and what he meant to us.

I walked through the double doors of Memorial Hospital, sailed past the clutch of reporters milling around the front desk and visitors' area, and went directly to the elevator bank. Aunt Laura had told me Carla Johnson's room number, and I had decided during the short drive from Fort Lauderdale that I wouldn't bother the public relations person at the hospital. One of the television reporters seemed to recognize me as I waited for the elevator to arrive, but I turned away from her. The doors opened, and I stepped in and punched the floor number. I took my narrow reporter's notebook out of my handbag and slid it into the back pocket of my skirt. I also took out a business card and palmed it in my right hand.

Once on the floor, I walked quickly down the hall, avoiding the nurses' station near the elevator bank. To an observer, I was either a hospital administrator or a family member, so confident were my footsteps. I turned a corner into a new hall, walked another ten feet, and found Carla's room. When I reached the door I stopped, took a deep breath, and exhaled slowly. The door was ajar; I knocked gently and slowly pushed it open. I stepped into the room and pulled the door back to its previous position behind me. Carla Johnson was half-reclined in the bed. When she saw me, her eyes widened and she pulled the sheet up sharply to rest beneath her nose.

I said, "Hi, Mrs. Johnson. I'm Amy Alexander, from the *Miami Herald*. I'm so sorry to bother you without calling first, but I hope you don't mind . . ."

She made a "hmmp" sound and nodded slowly.

I took a short step toward the bed and stopped. I told Carla that I was very sorry about her daughter's death. I offered her my business card. She reached up from the bed, her long, dark-brown fingers gripping the card tentatively. Without looking at it, she slid the card beneath her pillow and returned to holding the sheet tightly over the lower half of her face. I stepped back.

"I hope you feel better soon . . . and I also hope you haven't been upset by what the TV people have been reporting. I mean, we really think it's awful that they're airing stories about your family when no one has even bothered to talk to you," I said. "I won't write stories unless I have all the information. It just isn't responsible, do you know what I mean?"

She nodded. I heard movements beyond the door, and Carla did too. She sat up and arranged the bedclothes around herself hurriedly. Her body was stick thin beneath the floral-print hospital gown; her dark brown hair stuck out in all directions; her mouth was partly opened, a symptom of the thrush that had caused her tongue to swell painfully within her mouth. I learned later that stress from the news of her daughter's death had caused her health to decline severely.

"I won't take up more of your time," I said. "I'm guessing you really need to rest. But Mrs. Johnson, when you are ready, I hope you will speak with me. We won't write anything that isn't true, or anything that makes your family feel badly. I just want you to know that."

The door pushed open, and a nurse—middle-aged, with auburn hair and a stern expression—appeared.

"Are you a family member?" she asked me.

"Thank you, Mrs. Johnson," I said, sidestepping the nurse. "Just let me know," I said, backing out of the room, "whenever you are up for it."

Carla's eyes were smiling as I brushed past the woman in the doorway. I double-timed toward the elevator. A few seconds later, the nurse left Carla's room. She stopped briefly at the charge station, where she was met by another woman, who wore a business suit: that would be the hospital flak, I thought.

The two women spotted me waiting in the elevator bank and began run-walking toward me. "Excuse me! What were you doing in her room?" the woman in the suit called out. "If you're a reporter, you are *not* authorized to be up here! You can't just . . ."

The elevator arrived, I stepped inside, and the sound of her voice fell away as the doors closed.

Three weeks later, the phone at my desk in the Fort Lauderdale newsroom rang. It was Carla Johnson.

I had cowritten the breaking story but had taken over the story thereafter. I had gone to the Baptist church in the tiny city of Dania for Jackie's funeral, where hundreds of people gathered. The ceremony ran nearly two hours and was marked with wails and cries of despair from Carla and other family members; they filled the front pews of the stately chapel. I wrote about the ceremony, including extensive quotes from the minister and some Johnson family members who had eulogized little Jackie. I folded in comments from health department officials and suicide specialists and made note of the debate that had been sparked nationwide in response to Jackie Johnson's shocking death. (Most of the national stories and op-ed pieces focused on the question of how a child as young as Jackie Johnson could possibly make the decision to end her own life. To me, that question was not as important as this: What were the dynamics that had created such distress in the little girl?) Again, my story did not refer to Carla Johnson's HIV diagnosis. After the ceremony, I had greeted Laura Scott and once again expressed my condolences; when Carla left the sanctuary, supported by relatives on either side, I nodded politely as she moved past me.

Two weeks after her daughter's funeral, she phoned me at my desk. Carla said she was ready to talk about her little girl. It never came up, but I sensed that along with my expressing the sincere desire to let Carla tell her own story, it also helped that I was black and a woman.

On July 6, 1993, my interview with Carla was stripped across the front page of the *Miami Herald*. It carried the headline "A Child's Suicide, a Mother's Anguish" and was laid out just beneath the masthead. It jumped inside, where it filled an entire page. A sidebar that I'd written, detailing the state and national data on the growing numbers of blacks with HIV and AIDS, accompanied the interview.

It was my finest journalism to that date, and it remains the newspaper story I am most proud of.

It also nearly undid my reputation at the *Herald*: during the editing, Pat and I fought miserably.

My first draft of the story carried a lead that (in hindsight, I now admit) was much too long. My original lead had described a photograph that Carla Johnson had showed me of Jackie's body in the coffin at her funeral. Pat had shortened that lead considerably, saying its length—about four paragraphs—increased the prospect of losing the reader before the meat of the interview presented itself. I disagreed, and not in a calm, diplomatic manner.

When I pulled my chair next to Pat Andrews's computer to go over the draft I'd filed the evening before, I was a wreck: Carla Johnson's life story had really resonated with me. Not only were we the same age—she was twenty-nine, and I had recently turned thirty—but during my interview with her it was obvious that in other circumstances we might have become good friends, or at least acquaintances.

Her story—of poor choices, bad men, and low-self esteem, all contributing to her being diagnosed with HIV—had aroused in me a degree of sorrow and anger that I didn't know I was capable of. I was, in other words, quite invested in the story.

In my own life I had made dumb decisions, and I considered it pure luck that I had a network of family members, friends, and teachers who had managed to save me from myself at various crucial points. *There, but for the grace of God* . . . I thought as I mapped out the structure of the Carla Johnson profile. For two weeks I worked virtually around the clock on the profile; it was all I thought about.

By the time Pat showed me the draft she had edited, I was sleep-deprived and anxious. The state of our working relationship—typically jovial and mutually respectful—was threatened in this edit. I broke a cardinal rule of newsroom protocol by saying out loud, right there in the middle of the entire Broward staff, that I felt she was "ruining" the story. I protested just about every phrase and sentence she sought to trim, questioned every word she said we should consider changing. After a half hour or so, I rolled my chair away from her desk and stalked out of the newsroom. When I returned, during lunchtime, Pat was out of the office.

Soon after, Pat returned and asked me to come into her office.

I was mortified—and furious, at myself and, paradoxically, at Pat. I hung my head and stared at my hands in my lap. "But Pat, this story *needs* to open with that picture of Jackie in the coffin—it's just . . . it's the best way to show how awful this whole situation is," I said.

Pat agreed, but added that the description I'd written in the draft simply went on too long.

She was right, and Pat's shortened lead is the version that was published. I had delivered the kind of story that I'd always dreamed of: an exclusive, a competitive story that captured a tough, monumentally difficult topic with sensitivity and clarity, a story that caused government officials and policy makers to reexamine their programs and systems.

Yet several months later, Joe Oglesby—who by then had been promoted from an assistant managing editor to managing editor of the *Herald*'s Broward edition—took me to lunch and told me he was reassigning me. Instead of the minority affairs beat, I would now cover general assignment news from the Hollywood bureau of the *Miami Herald*.

By late 1994, having been reassigned, I was unhappy at the *Miami Herald*; the sunny optimism and high energy that had characterized my first year at the paper had given way to wariness—and weariness. I learned the hard way that the *Herald*'s top editors—charged with extracting consistently top-quality journalism out of hundreds of high-strung, high-performing reporters, photographers, and low-level editors—didn't suffer divas gladly. I didn't think of myself as a diva, but somehow my reputation had entered that territory. My closest reporter friends cautioned me against becoming a grumbler. Worse than getting typed as a diva or a prima donna was the prospect of being typed as a complainer, they said.

I moved my belongings to the Hollywood office with a heavy heart but resolved to work my way out of the hole as quickly as possible. My new editor was a cheery white woman who was freshly minted as a manager. We had a good relationship, even if I found her alternately crisp and chipper style somewhat superficial. I suspected that Oglesby had decided that I had grown too comfortable with Pat Andrews—and that a level of informality had begun to erode Pat's authority in terms of her ability to effectively manage me. The Hollywood office was the largest bureau in Broward, and it was where Oglesby and the two Broward assistant managing editors were located. I felt like I was being put under a microscope and that I had foolishly screwed myself out of the beat I loved.

Along the way, I realized there was one segment of *Herald* staffers from which I could probably learn valuable political skills.

The legend of the all-powerful "Cuban Mafia"—those Latino

journalists said to exert immense influence over internal politics at the *Miami Herald*—turned out to be mostly mythical. I learned this the same way that all of us, if we are fortunate, discover that our preconceived ideas (and prejudices) require revision: by firsthand interaction.

Marilyn Garateix was an education reporter on the Broward staff. Marilyn was a couple of years younger than me but carried herself with such quiet confidence and good humor that she seemed to be older. Her parents were Cuban exiles, she had grown up in Miami's Little Havana, and I was fascinated by her and her family's history.

In off-hours, over meals at restaurants in South Beach or Fort Lauderdale, we learned about each other's families. Along with Trish Power and two other women who were Broward reporters, we began meeting for dinner nearly every Friday night, no men allowed.

Over time I felt comfortable enough to ask Marilyn whether what I'd heard about the "Cuban Mafia" at the *Herald* was true: that the Cuban American editors and reporters there enjoyed a uniquely protected status. "Oh, please," Marilyn said. "What does that mean? Amy—the publisher, David Lawrence, is white. Last time I checked, the EE [executive editor], Doug Clifton, was white. Saundra Keyes [the *Miami Herald* managing editor] is white, Oglesby is black, the editorial page editor [Tom Fiedler] is white, the I-team [investigations] editor, Jim Savage, is white, and in case you haven't noticed, there's only one Cuban columnist, Liz Balmaseda."

Yes, I countered. But coverage of Cuba and the Cuban American community in the region always seemed to get the best and largest play in the *Herald*. Even a package of stories that Marilyn and I had worked on together—describing the ongoing immigration crisis, in which hundreds of Cubans and Haitians were attempting to enter the United States aboard rickety boats from their respective island nations—was published in such a way as to give the Cuban refugee story more prominence. "That sounds really paranoid, Amy," Marilyn said, adding that it had likely been a pure oversight that resulted in some copy editor placing the Cuban refugee story above the fold, whereas my story describing a group of recent Haitian refugees had been published below the fold on the front of that same day's local section. While readers may have debated the *Herald*'s use of "legal alien" versus "illegal immigrant," we staff writers referred to our in-house stylebook and did our best to give input whenever top editors announced revisions to it. Our own debates over race, favoritism, and the perceptions of both usually centered on who got hired, who got raises, and who got promoted rather than on language within news stories.

These informal conversations I had with Marilyn Garateix and the other women in our clique were carried out with good humor and directness—aided, I'm sure, by the large amounts of delicious food and strong alcohol we consumed during our gatherings. What Marilyn said was true: the top editorial leadership at the *Miami Herald*, at that time, did not include a single Cuban American. But it was also true that Marilyn and the handful of other Cuban American staff writers and photographers I was friendly with had mastered the fine art of "managing upward." Marilyn, in particular, always knew how to suss out impending personnel moves long before I did; she was plugged in with senior reporters and editors in the main newsroom (some but not all of them Cuban), who shared with her inside information about upcoming initiatives and resource allocation decisions that would affect all staffers. But that kind of skill was rooted more in an elusive, effective sense of pride, confidence, and interpersonal savvy more than in any particular ethnic code of *omertà*.

And by the time I took an extended leave from the *Herald*—in the summer of 1995, after Romantic Prospect and I had married and I decided to accompany him on a year-long journalism fellowship he'd been awarded at Harvard University—I realized a profound but simple truth: some people have those "soft skills," and some people don't.

I resumed work at the Broward office of the *Herald* in July 1996 to find that much had changed within a year. The word "Miami" had been dropped from the edition of the paper that covered Broward County, and it was odd to see the daily paper with a masthead that simply read "The Herald" in its neo-Gothic typeface. While we had been in New England, the Hollywood bureau had relocated from a large office building to a small former bank building several blocks away. Circulation and readership was declining for all editions, and for the first time in many staffers' memories, there was talk of "belt-tightening" coming from the executive suites on the sixth floor of One Herald Plaza.

A new managing editor had been placed at the main paper, an African American journalist named Larry Olmstead. In Broward, too, a new managing editor was in charge, Paul Anger. Joe Oglesby had taken a job as the executive editor at the *State*, a Knight Ridder newspaper in Columbia, South Carolina. The move didn't sit well with Oglesby, according to the prevailing scuttlebutt. A general sense of unease prevailed in Miami too, but interestingly, I returned with a bold new outlook: I had written freelance pieces for the *Boston Globe* during my time in Cambridge, Massachusetts, and I'd also signed a contract to edit a nonfiction book.

Not long after I returned to Broward, where my new official beat was transportation, I had lunch with Lynn Medford, an assignment editor on the features desk at One Herald Plaza. I had sent her copies of some of the op-ed pieces, feature stories, and book reviews I had published in the *Boston Globe*, and she said she wanted me to write for the lifestyle section of the *Herald* too. I had begun to write with genuine authority, meaning I'd attained a level of self-confidence that made my reporting and writing sing. I can't pinpoint the exact turning point, but by the time I returned to South Florida, I had clarity about the topics that interested me, about how to conceptualize stories and ideas with alacrity and skill, and about my ability to translate sophisticated ideas, themes, and concepts into evocative narratives. I was more at ease in my own skin, which translated into my work.

Pat Andrews was also now based in the Hollywood office. Though she wasn't my editor, I regularly sought her advice and insight. We had become friends and peers, and I was relieved to have gotten through our past difficulties. Romantic Prospect—by now, Hubby—had been reassigned to editing full-time at the *Herald*.

We settled into a rented house near downtown Fort Lauderdale. But we also knew a not-so-secret new piece of information: we had fallen in love with New England. In October 1996, after editors at the *Boston Globe* called and offered work, we couldn't turn down the chance to return to Boston.

There is a black-and-white photograph of me on my last day at the *Miami Herald*, taken by a photographer friend, Candace West. It shows me carrying a cardboard box out through the open glass doors of the *Herald* newsroom in Hollywood, Florida. I'm wearing a light jacket over a pale yellow silk shirt. My hairstyle is a short, curly Afro, quite different from the long, glamorous do I'd sported for most of my time as a *Miami Herald* staff writer. I am moving, and I am smiling.

FIVE

Boston

Brahmins, Fabricators, and Changing Populations

On a brisk day in February 1997, I walked into a stationery store near Porter Square on Massachusetts Avenue in Cambridge. After lingering awhile in the shop's warm, papery aroma, I ordered business cards. A week later, I returned to pick up a rectangular white box. Inside: two hundred cream-white cards imprinted with boldface, Times New Roman lettering.

They read, in part:

Amy Alexander
Writer + Editor

Below those words, my address, phone and fax numbers, and e-mail address were listed. For the first time, my business cards did not bear the logo of a major news organization.

I was officially in business as an independent journalist.

The cards looked and felt portentous as I took them out and placed a few in my wallet: so much freedom and uncertainty printed on a single small piece of paper.

Over the next few years, in fits and starts, I got used to the life of an independent journalist. (I can't explain why I never cottoned to the title "freelancer.") Taking the leap from staff writer to independent contractor was a scary proposition, yet I felt the time was right.

My search for a path from staff writing at daily newspapers to working on longer-form, literary journalism is what led us to Cambridge in the first place. In 1994, a few months before Romantic Prospect proposed marriage, I had decided I wanted to write a book.

While covering minority affairs at the *Miami Herald*, I'd connected with a literary agent in New York and began casting around for story ideas that could become a nonfiction book. I also let Romantic Prospect know that I didn't envision my long-term future in South Florida. He decided then to apply for a midcareer fellowship at three big universities that hosted them for journalists: the University of Michigan, Stanford, and Harvard. On parallel tracks, we worked on our respective plans, occasionally updating each other with progress reports and trading drafts—in my case of book proposals; in his, of personal essays required by the fellowship programs as part of the application process.

We married in July 1995 and left South Florida a month later. In early September, Hubby became a Nieman Fellow at Harvard University. The Nieman Foundation is based at Walter Lippmann House, a large, remodeled Greek Revival steps from the campus at Harvard.

Inside, the second-floor hallways of Lippmann House are covered with framed photographs of members in each "graduating class" of the journalism fellowship program. Visitors who scan these photos, beginning with the grainy, black-and-white photographs of the first few groups, may notice the evolution of the race and gender demographics—and clothing styles—of succeeding classes of fellows. The earliest images show row after row of smiling white men in dark suits, overcoats, and natty fedoras. Gradually, as you move along the rows, clothing and hairstyles worn by the fellows morph from buttoned-down and Brylcreemed to the swinging, mod bell-bottoms and muttonchop sideburns of the 1970s to the pegged-jeans-and-skinny-necktie punk-casual of the 1980s. By the 1970s the photos begin to depict sprinklings of light and dark brown faces. Most all the fellows are smiling, and why not? Each class is posed in stiff formations of rows in these photographs, but their faces, whatever the skin color, radiate the good fortune, amazement, and feast of intellectual bounty they have experienced as Nieman Fellows. But the fact that ethnic minorities make up a tiny fraction of the domestic and international fellows that have been fielded since the foundation's inception is made obvious by these photographs.

By the foundation's seventieth anniversary in 2009, some thirteen hundred journalists from around the globe had participated as fellows. But although the program has welcomed international journalists for half of the seventy years—including hundreds from war-torn nations in Africa, Latin America, China, Southeast Asia, and elsewhere—women and men of color from the United States have historically been underrepresented in each fielded class. The first women were selected in the class of 1946 (Charlotte FitzHenry Robling and Mary Ellen Leary Sherry), almost a decade after the fellowships began. The first African American fellow, Fletcher P. Martin, followed in the class of 1947. The elite nature of the program—it receives hundreds of applications for the dozen spots available to domestic journalists—inevitably means that each year several dozen writers, editors, producers, and photographers who apply will not be selected. But its competitiveness doesn't necessarily indicate the journalistic unworthiness of applicants who fail to win a fellowship.

The criteria for selection are a mix of quantifiable factors—time in service, quality of work, and the subjects that candidates propose to study should they win the fellowship—and a somewhat mysterious alchemy of personality and professional potential known only to the Nieman selection board members who interview each year's candidates.

It is the second part of that equation—the "unknowns" baked into the subjectivity within the selection process—that has discouraged some journalists of color who might otherwise have applied for the Nieman over the years. In recent years, the Nieman Foundation has included at least one or two academics or journalists who are ethnic minorities on their selection committee, undoubtedly with an eye toward neutralizing cultural biases that might adversely affect the interviewing process whenever minority candidates are brought in. Over the years, African American journalists who received Nieman Fellowships have included several who went on to hold top editing positions at major news organizations and to collect a raft of Pulitzers and other big journalism awards. Among them are Robert Maynard (a reporter turned owner and publisher of the *Oakland Tribune*), Gerald Boyd (a reporter and editor who became the first black managing editor of the *New York Times*), Alice Bonner (a reporter, editor, and journalism professor), Cynthia Tucker, and Joe Oglesby (both re-

porters and columnists who received Pulitzer Prizes). Oglesby, managing editor of the Broward edition of the *Miami Herald* in the early
1990s, had coached Hubby through the application process leading
to his being selected for the Nieman class of 1996.

In the same way that generations of white male journalists have
passed the secrets of their training and professional connections down
to novice reporters who reminded them of themselves, Oglesby had
seen something in my husband that made him believe that he too
might have the "right stuff" to earn a Nieman Fellowship.

During the nine-month residency in Massachusetts, I had introduced
myself to the *Boston Globe* by phoning its managing editor, Gregory L. Moore. Before leaving Fort Lauderdale in the summer of
1995, a *Miami Herald* colleague who had worked at the *Globe* helped
me make the connection.

I had talked with Greg Moore's assistant; she said that he would
see me for thirty minutes. "Why can't we meet for an hour?" I'd
asked her, impulsively. She'd phoned back the next day and said yes,
you and Greg will meet for an hour. Then I mailed a few sample
clips of my work to him. My husband's salary was to be subsidized by
the Nieman Foundation and by the *Miami Herald* during the fellowship, but accompanying him for that academic year required me to
take an unpaid leave of absence from the *Herald*. Saundra Keyes, the
Herald's managing editor, had been enthusiastic about my going to
Cambridge. But she'd also made it clear that the *Herald* would only
hold a "comparable" staff writing position open for me during my
absence—and that all my pay and health benefits would cease during
the nine months I'd be away.

No way in hell was I going to miss the chance to take free
classes at Harvard, an option available to the spouses and partners
of Nieman Fellows since the 1970s. And I also planned to use the
time to concentrate more fully on writing book proposals. But I'd
need to generate at least a small amount of income during the nine-
month period. The *Globe* was the obvious place to start.

So on a sunny morning in October 1995, while my husband was
at a class, I walked to the Harvard Square subway station.

On the train, I rehearsed my pitch to the paper's managing editor: I wanted to write op-ed pieces on African American issues, as well as book reviews and possibly feature articles. My *Miami Herald* colleague who had recommended I tap the *Globe* for freelance work also told me, as an aside, that Greg Moore was African American. That detail gave me small relief: I knew it would be foolish to assume that Moore's being black would automatically mean that I'd get freelance work, but on the other hand, I hoped that at least it would mean I'd have a fair shot.

In the mid-1990s the *Boston Globe* was the big dog on New England's media scene: a strong, smart newspaper, liberal on its editorial pages, rigorous in its news coverage. Among blacks in the region, I subsequently learned, the *Globe* was viewed with caution. It had been on the side of integration during the busing upheaval of the 1970s, a wrenching period for many Boston residents. In the mid-1960s, when Thomas Winship succeeded his father, Laurence, as editor of the *Globe*, the editorial page supported efforts to racially integrate civic institutions in the city and around New England. But its news coverage didn't always deliver accurate, comprehensive coverage of minority communities or of the issues. Its editorial leadership, predominantly white, Irish, or Anglo-Saxon "Brahmin," was viewed by black New Englanders as patrician and distant, its coverage of their community leaders and important topics arriving as over-sentimentalized vignettes that belied the editors' sense of noblesse oblige.

While the *Globe*'s editorials during the busing tension of the 1970s infuriated those white residents who resisted the integration of Boston's public schools, drawing angry protests in front of the newspaper's offices and death threats to some of its writers and editors, the paper had no better luck winning over black Bostonians, especially after it published a series of stories examining irregularities in the campaign finances of the first black senator from Massachusetts, Republican Edward W. Brooke.

Yet by the mid-1990s, among the growing population of ethnic minorities in Boston, the lines of demarcation between perceived class bias on the part of the *Globe* and perceived racial bias were blurred. The *Boston Herald*, offspring of the Hearst-owned *Boston Herald-American*, is the *Globe*'s only competing daily, a tabloid in tone

and physical format: scrappy, loud, and populist in its news coverage, conservative in its editorial positions. Yet you are more likely to
see copies of the *Herald* being read in the black-owned barbershops
and clothing stores along Blue Hill Avenue or in the predominantly
African American neighborhood of Roxbury than you are the *Globe*.
This paradox is similar to one that exists in New York, where rid-
ers on subway cars heading to neighborhoods in Bedford Stuyvesant
or Washington Heights—predominantly black and Latino neighborhoods—carry copies of the *New York Post* or the *New York Daily
News*, not the *New York Times*. And in both of those increasingly multiethnic Northeast cities, the two leading ethnic newspapers, the *Bay
State Banner* of Boston and the *Amsterdam News* of New York, both
have modest circulations: thirty thousand per week for the *Bay State
Banner*, for example.

There were factors besides low circulation figures that led journalists of color of my generation to seek work at mainstream or
"white" publications such as the *Boston Globe* or the *Miami Herald*: we
wanted living wages that weren't available from small, black-owned
daily and weekly newspapers, as well as a large platform for reporting
stories that might spur changes in policy and government legislation.
It was an unsentimental position, but in my case, I don't see it as being disloyal to minority interests. And in New England, journalists
who were Latino, Asian, black, and white all viewed the *Globe* as the
place to work if you wanted to deliver high-impact journalism, notwithstanding its location in "Irish" Boston.

The city's reputation among blacks as "racist" has still not completely been eliminated in the forty years since racial turmoil erupted
during the 1970s, after a court ruling on the desegregation of public
schools led to ugly scenes of white, predominantly Irish American
residents in some neighborhoods hurling rocks, bottles, and epi-
thets at buses filled with black students. But although some corners
of Boston—like most large cities in the United States—certainly
hold pockets of residents who hang on to outmoded ideas about
race and ethnicity, by the mid-1990s it was among the more ethnically and economically diverse cities in the United States.

In 2000, the city's total population of nearly 600,000 residents included 149,202 blacks, 85,089 Latinos, and 320,944 whites, accord-

ing to U.S. Census figures from that year. By 2007, 25.8 percent of its residents were foreign born, a demographic that closely tracks with increasing immigrant populations in other large northeastern cities between 1980 and the end of the century.

In the mid-1990s, ethnic minorities accounted for nearly 18 percent of the *Globe*'s editorial staff, a figure below the percentage of minorities living in greater Boston at that time, but slightly above minority representation at many other large dailies. As I prepared to seek freelance work at the *Globe*, I didn't worry that I might run into racial discrimination. To the contrary, I knew that the *Globe* had a veritable rainbow of enormously talented journalists, including news features writer Wil Haygood and Derrick Jackson, an editorial columnist. I admired those writers, as well as Renee Graham, a features writer; Richard Chacon, a national correspondent; Patricia Smith, a metro columnist; and a dozen or so other journalists of color who consistently delivered high-quality coverage at the paper. But their presence also meant that I'd have to raise the level of my work—including sharpening my reporting antenna and my ability to think and write creatively—if I wanted to pick up work at the *Globe*.

The *Globe* had been purchased by the New York Times Company in 1993, a corporate and editorial match made in heaven—at least until the economic downturn that began in late 2007 seriously challenged the *Globe*'s financial outlook. Beginning in 2001, in fact, the *Globe* began offering buyouts of newsroom personnel in an attempt to shrink its operating budget. Those buyouts—at least five rounds between 2001 and 2009—shrank the newsroom staff from a high of about four hundred to fewer than three hundred by the end of the decade. In 2008, according to ASNE's annual newsroom census report, minorities accounted for slightly more than 20 percent of the *Globe*'s editorial workers. That census report was released in mid-April 2009, a few days after the news broke that the New York Times Company had threatened to close the *Globe*. A year later, though, the company announced that it had shelved its plan to sell the *Globe*, thanks in large part to huge cuts in the salaries and health benefits of union workers—including drivers and press operators—and to cuts in the editorial budget, primarily in the form of buyouts. Among the accomplished journalists of color who left the paper during that period were Wil Haygood, Renee Graham, and Richard Chacon.

But in 1995 I had no inkling of the *Globe*'s financial health; I just wanted badly to write for it. In key aspects, the *Globe* mirrored the *Miami Herald*: both had respectable, healthy circulation and readership numbers; large staffs of talented, aggressive reporters, columnists, and photographers; and benches that were several rows deep with smart editors and reporters. The *Globe*, like the *Miami Herald*, had earned a slew of Pulitzer Prizes since the 1970s, and the *New York Times* and the *Washington Post* regularly wooed away *Globe* staffers and editors.

I discovered quickly, though, that the *Globe* newsroom culture was more buttoned up than that of the *Herald*. At the *Globe*, reporters and editors affected the eggheady, Brahmin mien of the political and business leadership class in Boston. Even the *Globe* building itself seemed to discourage any freewheeling impulses among its inhabitants: the paper's original home had been a traditional, neo-Gothic, late nineteenth-century edifice in downtown Boston, but since 1958 the *Globe*'s editorial operation had been housed in a sleek, glass-encased structure on the city's southern tip. Its architecture was so unlike a classic newspaper building that it might have belonged to an insurance company.

Set back from busy Morrissey Boulevard at the edge of Boston's gritty Dorchester neighborhood, the *Globe* building was imposing, if uninspiring. Inside, the *Globe*'s editorial space was a warren of quiet, whitewashed hallways opening to modest-sized offices for graphic artists, columnists, and department chiefs. The main newsroom was not a wide, football-field-sized space of the kind that distinguished so many other big-city papers. Rather, it was laid out in a twisty maze of waist-high partitions and carpeted aisles. Surrounding this cubicle farm were the "glass boxes," fishbowl-like offices situated along the perimeters, where editors worked. It was whisper quiet.

I was not sure my plan to focus on African American issues would fly, given the *Globe*'s relatively decent number of journalists of color. When I walked into the lobby at 135 Morrissey Boulevard on a fall morning in 1995, I was perspiring slightly. The level of insecurity-inspired anxiety that hit me wasn't quite as strong as when I'd first walked into the *Miami Herald* building in 1992. But it was a warm day, the *Globe*'s lobby had a wall of windows that welcomed the sunlight, and the two-block walk from the subway stop to the newspaper had me running hot.

I dabbed my brow with a Kleenex, gave my name to the desk attendant, and told him who I was there to see before sitting on one of the low-slung, slick black leather chairs in the lobby. Tapping my feet slowly, I looked around the quiet lobby. I might have been waiting in a doctor's office, the furnishings were so unremarkable. Then I noticed a wall opposite the windows: it was hung with an immense map of New England carved from granite. The twenty-foot-tall carving looked as if it weighed at least a ton, its polished surface giving off a dull sheen. I got up, walked across the lobby, and stood beneath the huge granite map, craning my neck back to take it all in. It was lovely, with tiny pieces of brass and seashells set into the stone to mark cities and towns up and down the New England coast. Its sturdy beauty gave the lobby an elegant sense of history, regional pride, and gravitas. I instantly fell in love with its understated grandeur.

Finally, Greg Moore's assistant came for me. We walked through a set of glass double doors near the granite wall sculpture and, to my surprise, stepped right onto an escalator. (This conveyance is not visible from the lobby, which struck me as especially discreet, after the prominence of those long escalators in the *Miami Herald*'s lobby.)

Upstairs, Moore's assistant asked me to wait in a small alcove. I peeked around the message center—a desk on a raised, circular platform where a receptionist sat—and saw part of the main newsroom. The male reporters wore crisp dress shirts, while the women looked smart in dresses or expensive-looking pant-and-shirt ensembles. No Hawaiian prints or guayaberas—like those sported by some *Miami Herald* photographers and reporters—in sight. In the swirl of all the people I saw on that first day, I noted several blacks, Asians, and Latinos in the main newsroom and in the small offices along the hallways we traversed.

The morning budget meeting had just wrapped up, so I guessed that the metro staff members were just beginning their heavy lifting for the day.

"Amy, you can go in now," the assistant to Greg Moore said.

I hustled over to the open door of the managing editor's office. I was shown in, and the door closed behind me.

I felt myself shrink: Greg Moore had been seated at a midsize conference table on the far side of the large office, but when I entered, he got up and walked toward me, his hand extended. At six feet three inches tall, with dark coffee-colored skin and deep brown eyes, he was movie-star handsome. Looking up at him, it occurred to me that I probably should have worn a dress instead of the slacks and dress shirt I'd chosen. Maybe even a formal gown. My premeeting reconnaissance of the *Globe* and of Moore had consisted of reading the paper closely and querying Oglesby and other *Miami Herald* staffers who had knowledge of the *Globe* staff. But at that time there was no such thing as Google Images, and getting a visual peek at a potential employer wasn't easy; my research had not included digging through copies of trade journals, so I had no way of knowing how striking Greg Moore was.

I swallowed hard and tried not to show what I was thinking: *Why didn't I know I'd be meeting the Denzel Washington of the newspaper business?*

On Sunday, January 7, 1996, my first byline appeared in the *Boston Globe*. It was above an op-ed piece tied to the inauguration, that same week, of Willie Brown as San Francisco's mayor. Headlined "The Reach of the Rainbow," the twelve-hundred-word article carried this subhead: "As Willie Brown becomes San Francisco's first black mayor, ponder this: Could it happen in Boston?" Impetus for the reported essay had been simple. First, Boston in many ways resembled San Francisco, so I drew parallels between both cities' mid to late twentieth-century histories of race and electoral politics. Second, I needed money, and the Sunday op-ed page at that time paid five hundred dollars for a cover piece (an amount that seems rich indeed by current standards of low or no freelance rates at most daily newspapers). A decade later, of course, Massachusetts did achieve a big first on the race and politics front—its citizens elected Deval Patrick, a former appointee in the Clinton administration, as their first black governor.

"The Reach of the Rainbow" would not have been published

without my first meeting with Greg Moore in the fall of 1995. During our talk, Moore had flipped through the clips I'd mailed to him. It was clear that he'd already read the samples of my *Miami Herald* work, and he pointed to specific stories as we talked. Much as Joe Oglesby had during my first visit to the *Miami Herald*, Moore quizzed me closely about how I'd approached specific reporting challenges, why I'd settled on particular subject matter, and my thoughts on covering race relations in South Florida. He talked in general terms about opportunities for freelancing at the *Globe*, but did not say unequivocally that he'd open that gate for me. He wasn't rude or abrupt, just inscrutable. He praised my treatment of stories and said he thought I was a good writer.

Then, midway through our meeting, he surprised me: "Let me ask you something—if you're so good, why are you still in a bureau?"

The question was a minefield: the internal hierarchy of editorial staffs at big, competitive daily newspapers was known to all editorial employees. Bureaus, in particular those located in suburbs surrounding the paper's urban headquarters, were the place where greenhorn reporters, editors, and photographers earned their stripes before moving into the main newsroom. Suburban bureaus, however much they appealed to advertisers, could also be languishing points or dumping grounds for staffers who were viewed as not quite having the starch to succeed on the main stage. Moore knew that I had arrived at the Fort Lauderdale bureau of the *Miami Herald* in the spring of 1993—two years before. And while it was not unheard of for a new reporter to spend two years in a suburban bureau before being called into the main newsroom, he obviously wanted to know whether my work itself, or the way that I worked, might be stalling my arrival at the Big Show.

The way I chose to answer Moore's question might make the difference between ending the meeting on a polite but ultimately unproductive note or my walking out with his blessing for regular contract work at the *Globe*. I straightened my posture and smiled. "Wow, I didn't see that coming," I said, praying silently for composure. Moore's dark brown eyes were fixed on me.

"To be honest, I think it's because I'm not very good at internal politics," I said, stumbling. "I mean, I'm good at this, my editors know I'm a good reporter and writer—but at the *Herald*, there's a lot more that goes on that I just didn't quite get. I mean, I'm not downplaying my responsibility, I'm just saying that—I didn't realize how important the in-house stuff is. I'm sure I'm not always as diplomatic as I should be. But, I'm learning . . ." My voice sputtered out.

"Okay. I hear you," Moore said. "That's fine."

As our hour drew to a close, I breathed easier: Moore, while physically imposing, was also a consummate gentleman, and I could tell that he sensed I was nervous. His questions had been pointed, smart, and designed to gauge my philosophy of journalism as much as my strategic approach to the job. The "why are you still in a bureau" question had been a curveball, but I understood why he'd zapped it at me. His subdued response to my explanation did not immediately betray whether I'd passed that test or not.

We stood after his assistant reappeared in the doorway of Moore's office, signaling the end of our meeting. Moore told me he'd contact the appropriate editors and let them know that I'd be calling. After a bit more small talk about my adjusting to living in New England, we shook hands.

"Keep in touch," Moore said. "Let me know if you need anything else, okay?"

A few days after my first op-ed appeared in the *Boston Globe*'s Sunday opinion section, Moore sent a handwritten note to our Cambridge apartment: "Amy, thanks for the excellent, insightful piece in Sunday Focus. Looking forward to reading more."

It is among my most treasured mementos from my years in Boston.

In April 1996 I signed a contract with Grove Press to edit a nonfiction book on Nation of Islam minister Louis Farrakhan and black leadership. A year earlier I had signed on with a literary agent after being referred to her by a colleague from central California, writer and academic wunderkind Ruben Navarrette Jr. For a year, the agent and I frequently traded ideas for nonfiction books, with her assuming the role of an editor. By the end of 1995 we'd arrived at a great topic: the Million Man March had taken place in October 1995, and the timing was excellent for a book related to that event and to the larger topic of black leadership in America.

For months leading up to and following the Million Man March, an immense political and cultural rally in Washington, D.C., Americans had been riveted by the prospect of thousands of black males gathering for a "Day of Atonement" in the nation's capital. Farrakhan, long a contentious national figure, had staged the gathering, and the ensuing welter of controversies had preoccupied journalists, black studies academics, politicians, and nearly everyone for much of 1995 and well into the next year. Questions surrounding black political leadership were bound up in much of the public debating that occurred—including whether Farrakhan represented a "true" political leader or a mere "symbolic" leader. Journalists, in particular, had been apoplectic in the months leading up to the march.

After watching the coverage of the Million Man March, it occurred to me that a high level of hysteria had infused many of the stories, especially in some corners of the mainstream East Coast media. It seemed to me that white writers, politicians, and cultural commentators had somehow managed to hijack the conversation about not just the Million Man March but black leadership in general. What would it look like, I wondered, to have thoughtful black Americans weigh in at length on Farrakhan and black American leadership at this point in time? The sticky wicket of race, identity, politics, and media represented by the Million Man March gave a glimpse of the frenzy that would surround the candidacy of Senator Barack Obama a dozen years later. Louis Farrakhan, who had led the quasi-religious Nation of Islam since the 1970s, had fascinated and repulsed Americans for decades, mostly with inflammatory speeches and statements condemning white racism and accusing some Jews of exploiting African Americans. Interestingly, the widespread racial anxiety and ensuing discussions spurred by Farrakhan's Million Man March helped pave the way for Obama's success, I believe.

After my agent relayed my idea to an editor at Grove—a small, respected literary publisher—we reached an agreement: rather than dissect the Million Man March itself, I would edit a collection of essays from black writers, historians, academics, and activists that would place Farrakhan in much-needed historical context. I drafted a ten-page proposal, including a sample introduction and outlines of other chapters covering history, economics, education, women and black leadership, and black nationalism, and sent it to Grove.

During the few months we lived in South Florida before returning to New England (editors at the *Globe* had offered Hubby a job editing on the city desk), I firmed up the list of contributors and began receiving first drafts of their essays. My earlier proximity to Harvard, with its rich array of high-profile black academics, most certainly made it possible for me to put together that volume. We'd returned to the *Herald* in July 1996, but we left again in January 1997. That time, our trip to Boston was "for good."

So it was that on that bright, frosty February day in 1997 when I picked up my first independent journalist business cards, I felt more excitement than trepidation at the path I had chosen. It also helped that I could count on at least a sliver of institutional support in the form of regular assignments from the *Boston Globe* and that my husband earned a respectable income as an assistant city editor at the paper. Marriage also provided another crucial benefit, one that is not available to some other independent journalists—affordable health insurance.

I knew just a few journalists of color who were freelancers. In the late 1990s, after I'd spent a decade in big newsrooms, the majority of the journalists in my network were attached to established news organizations. The only models I had who looked like me were black writers at a handful of alternative papers that I had encountered over the years, including Stanley Crouch, who came and went at the *Village Voice*. In Boston, the largest alternative newspaper, the *Phoenix*, published the occasional contribution by arts writers who were minorities. And when I looked into the trade associations of freelance journalists, the Society of Professional Journalists and PEN New England (the local chapter of the international literary and human rights organization), it was with an eye toward finding a community of freelancers who probably faced the same challenge that I anticipated—finding work by establishing contacts with editors. (I am not a big joiner and had allowed my membership in the NABJ to lapse, although I did attend the group's annual convention twice during the late 1990s. Ultimately, I didn't join PEN or the SPJ, either.)

It felt strange to suddenly find myself adrift from the community of black and Latino journalists I'd fallen in with while working at newspapers, although I found kinship among plenty of journalists of every ethnicity in Boston and around New England. I didn't view my newly chosen professional designation, an independent journalist, in any kind of political context: I hadn't abandoned daily newspapers; I'd simply decided to explore other options. And the journalists I encountered around New England didn't appear to hold me in lower esteem than they did their colleagues who had staff jobs.

In January 1998, *The Farrakhan Factor: African-American Writers on Leadership, Nationhood, and Minister Louis Farrakhan* was published by Grove Press. Its contributors covered a wide range of perspectives and opinions on the history of black leadership and on contemporary blacks' concerns for the future of leadership in the wake of Farrakhan's large footprint. I learned valuable lessons about managing other writers—and about managing my own expectations.

Galleys of the Farrakhan book—the early test run of a few dozen copies—had been circulated to media outlets and to booksellers. Call me naive, but despite the warnings of Grove Press's publicist, Miwa Messer, I believed that journalists would "get" the book and be enthusiastic about covering it. Yet the stubborn insularity of the news business—in particular the race and class homogeneity that had troubled me since I entered the business in the 1980s—soon came to bear. The *Globe*, the *Chicago Tribune*, and *Newsday* were the only big daily papers to review or write stories about *The Farrakhan Factor*.

At that time, authors of all ethnicities were not yet hip to the marketing potential of the Internet, though in fairness, comparatively few journalists, authors, and publishers then had evidence that vast audiences existed online. I did, however, engage in one bit of online promotion: Grove arranged for me to participate in an online interview and chat with readers on the Barnes & Noble website. It was a strange, disconnected experience to walk around my apartment in Cambridge holding the telephone receiver to my ear while a go-between at the bookseller's office in New York read me "live" questions coming from readers through the website. I answered the questions, the go-between typed them in, and my responses magically appeared on the B&N site in real time.

Beyond that, I had no contact with blog writers who focused on books or with any other online marketing projects. In hindsight, I now understand that this wasn't a sign that Grove or other publishers were inclined to skimp on marketing resources or innovations for black authors—it was a sign that the publishing industry, like other big mainstream print industries, didn't at that time see the Internet as integral to improving their bottom lines.

What a difference a decade makes, both in the Internet's influence on the marketing of books and in the emergence of blacks and other ethnic minorities as bankable authors. It is difficult to quantify, in dollars, the role played by the Internet in the growing sales figures for books by ethnic minorities. But Target Market News, a Chicago market research firm focusing on minority audiences, charted an explosive growth in the sales of black-oriented books beginning in the mid-1990s, growth that tracks with the rise of the Internet over the ensuing decade. In 1997, African Americans nationwide spent 285 million dollars on books; in 1998, that amount had increased to 320 million. I wasn't aware, back then, of such specific sales figures for books, and I didn't really expect to sell millions of copies—I just wanted my first title to be read and appreciated by anyone with an interest in the subject matter.

Working alone required adjustments in my professional identity and in my day-to-day work habits. I missed being in the middle of a lively newsroom, even as I relished the independence of being a contractor. My workdays slid into a routine of mornings at the computer, an hour-long break for lunch, and early afternoons spent reviewing the morning's work or talking by phone with colleagues and friends in Florida or California or with my husband. At times I was lonely, and before I knew it, the four o'clock hour became a time I eagerly anticipated: with no shame at all, I had become an avid follower of *The Oprah Winfrey Show*. Oprah was at that time well on her way to becoming the Queen of All Media (to steal Howard Stern's tagline); her daily hour-long program aired in more than a hundred markets worldwide, reaching billions of viewers. *The Oprah Winfrey Show* regularly topped the Nielsen ratings for daytime national broadcasts, and the former television news journalist, as part owner of her program, had an income of more than two billion dollars by the end of the 1990s, according to *Forbes* magazine.

For a hot minute, I wrestled with my new, surprising affinity for the Big O, but in no time at all my resistance dissipated. Much of what aired on Oprah's daily talk program had a New Age patina that I avoided in my personal life, and yet Oprah's overriding message to her viewers was one of self-improvement and self-confidence. At that point in my life, I needed big doses of both, and Oprah was there to deliver them. Her outsize profile in the media universe made her a role model, although I didn't aspire to climb the mountain of worldwide fame that she had achieved.

When Oprah got sued by a national association of beef producers (she had aired a show in which viewers were cautioned against eating too much red meat, a program that had apparently led to a drop in sales of beef products), I wrote an op-ed in the *Boston Globe* questioning the beef producers' motivation for bringing the suit: Could they prove that their businesses had been significantly harmed by Oprah's comments on that program? Or was it more a matter of their egos and sense of entitlement being injured because an African American woman seemed to have the power and influence to move consumer loyalties?

The lawsuit was thrown out by a Texas judge, and even Oprah's biggest detractors admitted the obvious: she had become a cultural force of nature. I found the opportunities to share my opinions on these timely cultural and political topics liberating. It also helped that editors at the *Globe* let me know that they appreciated my contributions.

On weekends, we socialized with other *Globe* writers and editors and learned our way around the region. Most of the *Globe* staff members who worked with my husband welcomed me into the newsroom's social doings, which went some way toward filling the void left by the friendships I'd left behind in South Florida. Some of the women who were metro reporters invited me to attend their monthly "girls only" nights out, when I'd join them at a restaurant downtown for dinner or drinks, laughs, and gossip. But there was one female *Globe* staffer I particularly wanted to know more about who did not attend these gatherings.

Patricia Smith, a *Globe* metro columnist, had originally agreed to contribute an essay to *The Farrakhan Factor*. She had planned an "atmospheric" piece about Louis Farrakhan that would center on his childhood in Boston. But as the deadline for her first draft neared, Pat phoned me and said she simply didn't have time to contribute after all. I reluctantly agreed to take her off the list and found another writer to contribute a similar piece. Now that I was living in Cambridge, I wanted to catch up with Pat Smith again, but it didn't happen. And before I knew it, she had become the focus of the biggest journalism scandal to hit the *Globe*—and the newspaper industry—since the Janet Cooke scandal of 1981.

In the early afternoon of June 18, 1998, I was standing over the printer in my home office when the phone rang. Since late spring, I had been working on my next nonfiction book—a collection of short biographies of notable black women in American history, for Birch Lane Press (which has since been acquired by Kensington Publishing)—and I was in the process of printing the text I'd written that morning.

I stopped the printing job. The voice on the phone line was hushed, whispering. "Do you have a sec?" It was my husband. It sounded like his hand was cupped around the receiver as he spoke.

"Yeah, sure . . . What's up?" I glanced at my watch—it was too early for his usual afternoon phone call letting me know what time he would be home. "Why are you whispering?" I asked, sitting in the chair at my desk.

"They just sent a message out a few minutes ago telling everyone to show up at the city desk. Storin and Greg and Helen have been in and out of meetings all morning," he said, referring to Matt Storin, the *Globe*'s executive editor; Helen Donovan, its editor; and Greg Moore, the managing editor. "We knew it was something serious . . ." I could just make out the muffled sounds of other voices around him. In my mind's eye, I saw the editorial staff bunching around the *Globe*'s main news desk. I envisioned the crowd of reporters, photographers, artists, and editors from across the news divisions perching on desks or partitions or jockeying on tiptoe to see the front of the room, where the top editors probably stood.

"Why? What is it?" I couldn't figure out why he was calling me in the midst of a newsroom-wide meeting. "Is the *Globe* being bought? Is it closing? Did someone die?"

"No, no . . . It's about Pat," he said, his voice so faint that I could barely make out his words. "Storin is saying they've found problems with her work and that she's resigning." He spoke in present tense, which meant the meeting was underway—and there he was, on the phone! I knew the layout of the main newsroom, and my husband's desk was in the thick of it. As much as I wanted all the details—like, why would someone's resignation require a big staff meeting?— I knew he'd have to hang up immediately.

"Wait, why is it a big deal that someone's resigning? And who is it, Pat *who*?" I asked. He was silent, but I heard voices in the room around him. Then I caught on: "Not Pat *Smith*?!—Pat SMITH?" I asked again, my voice rising slightly.

"Yes," he hissed. "Wait—he's saying that basically she'd been making up information in her columns—or inventing sources—I think she's already resigned."

"Holy shit," I said. Then I started whispering too. Pat Smith, the high priestess of compassion, the wizardly wordsmith of the metro page? I needed more information.

"What the . . . ," I stuttered. "Is she there? How'd they—I mean, how do they know that's what happened? And she resigned over— what, a one-time mistake—or had she been . . . " My questions flooded out.

"Okay—wait. I'll call you back—I think they're gonna take questions now," he whispered. "I'll call you back." He hung up.

I let my full body weight drop against the chair's back support. In 1998 there were no websites or blogs devoted to every uptick and downturn of in-house developments at news organizations—no *Romenesko* blog, no *Gawker* or mediabistro.com where I could turn for this fast-breaking industry story. I hung up the receiver, left my office, and turned on the television in our living room, clicking to New England Cable News. I went to the stereo and tuned in WBUR, the local public radio station. Nothing. Even the *Globe*'s own website was nothing more than a big, static snapshot of that morning's front page. It was too early in the afternoon for the local news broadcasts, but wouldn't New England Cable News, the CNN of the region, have some information?

It seems hard to believe now, but I had to wait more than two hours, until my husband called back, to learn of the awful end to Patricia Smith's journalism career—and it would take several weeks more to understand what a big hole it had torn in the *Boston Globe*'s reputation.

Smith was found to have made up quotes and characters in her metro columns over a period of several years. After Walter Robinson, a veteran writer and editor at the *Globe*, raised questions about one of Smith's columns, an investigation was undertaken. The effort to locate some of the individuals Smith had been quoting—including a supposed "cancer patient" named "Claire"—produced strong evidence that Smith was inventing sources and quotes from whole cloth. When Greg Moore met with Smith and presented her with some of the findings of the research on her sources, she had no explanation. Several days later she resigned, setting off a firestorm that ultimately swept Mike Barnicle—a longtime *Globe* metro columnist, also found to have fabricated quotes and sources—from the newsroom too.

By the end of the summer of 1998, the name Patricia Smith had become synonymous with two major failings of modern journalism: poor ethical standards, oversight, and enforcement, and the poisonous fallout of political correctness and affirmative action in corporate journalism. Make that three major failings, if you also count the institutional arrogance that some accused the *Globe* of in the aftermath. Pat's ignominious departure from the *Globe* was the first small pebble in an avalanche of upheaval that spread from Morrissey Boulevard out across the media landscape nationwide. As I lived it at the time, up close, it was a stress-filled period marked by paradox upon paradox, double standards, hypocrisies, and a weirdly exhilarating sense than an old, insidious, powerful order was finally being challenged. This last response was the result of the other unexpected twist in the story of Pat Smith's fall: within days of the *Globe*'s official announcement of Pat's resignation, Barnicle, a white columnist, also came under intense criticism for allegedly committing similar journalistic crimes over the years. By summer's end, he too had left the *Globe*.

Barnicle was a major media star in Boston, commanding six figures annually from the *Globe* and a hefty supplemental income from side gigs at local television and radio stations and from speaking fees. Barnicle's shtick as the tough-talking champion of underdogs, Southie fishwives, and small-time hoods had made him a one-man franchise at the *Globe* and a beloved New England demicelebrity. His high profile and brash personality, though, had also earned enemies over the years, including one who charged, in the days after Pat Smith was fired, that Barnicle had lifted passages from a recent humor book by comedian George Carlin and plopped them into one of his metro columns without credit.

Quite unlike Smith, however—who had confessed her professional sins in a remarkable mea culpa as her final column on June 19, the same day that stories about the scandal appeared on the front pages of the *Globe* and the *New York Times*—Barnicle had initially refused to resign. For more than a month, aided by a cadre of powerful white male journalists in Boston, New York, and Washington, D.C.— including Tim Russert of NBC News and radio talk show host Don Imus—Barnicle had mounted a fierce public relations campaign to keep his *Globe* job. By mid-August, Howell Raines, who was editing the *New York Times* editorial page, wrote a scathing, signed column accusing the *Globe* editors, as well as the white male establishment of outside journalists who had been supporting Barnicle, of practicing situational ethics and perpetuating a blatant double standard.

In the midst of the first wave of public fallout, I felt for Pat Smith. And initially I felt a small bit of sympathy for Barnicle too—at least until a veritable army of journalists, former interview subjects, and others began to produce evidence that the former Kennedy speechwriter had indeed gone for years blithely making up quotes and "characters" in his columns. When Harvard Law School professor and media gadfly Alan Dershowitz turned up on local news broadcasts and in print reports saying that he had been misquoted by Barnicle a decade earlier and that the *Globe* had paid him a settlement but had not publicly admitted wrongdoing, my feelings soured.

In the weeks between Pat Smith's June resignation and late

August, the rhetoric escalated as Barnicle refused to resign, and the public's awareness of the implications quickly moved from curiosity to anger and polarization. At bars, cafés, and newsstands in Boston and Cambridge, I overheard conversations among the townsfolk that were vehement and pointed. Some civilians felt that Barnicle was being victimized by political correctness, while others felt the *Globe* alone was to blame for allowing both writers to carry on undetected—making up information and passing it off as news—for as long as they had. Still others asked, "What's the big deal, since everybody knows most of what you read in metro columns is made up, anyway?" (I found this sentiment, which I heard expressed more than once by callers to local radio talk programs, most distressing: did readers honestly not know that what appeared in a daily paper's news pages was supposed to be 100 percent factually accurate *nonfiction?*)

It was confusing and enervating, and I had the unique perspective of being in close proximity to the tumultuous fishbowl that the *Globe* newsroom had become. In short order, Barnicle's refusal to admit to having breached ethical standards wiped away the small dribble of sympathy I had felt for him, a turn that was cemented by his scurrilous claim that he was the "victim" of political correctness because the *Globe* managers felt they had to fire him to balance the firing of Pat Smith.

As a journalist, I was angry at both of them for their poor judgment and laziness, but my feelings about Pat were more personal. Nearly twenty years after the *Washington Post* had unmasked a black female journalist named Janet Cooke as a fabricator, Pat Smith had once again created the image of a black female journalist as a thief, poseur, and liar.

Cooke had humiliated herself and the *Post* by admitting she'd made up, from whole cloth, a feature story published in 1981 about a black D.C. boy who was a heroin addict. She'd received a Pulitzer Prize for feature writing, becoming the first black woman to win the award. She'd had to return it—and was fired—after someone noticed discrepancies in her official biography, a tiny thread that led to the entire unraveling of her award-winning story of the boy addict. Since that bombshell, Cooke's professional ghost hung over me and hundreds of other black female journalists working in mainstream media. We felt an extra burden to overcome the bleak legacy she'd left behind.

Now Pat Smith had again endangered the tenuous position of the small cadre of black women in the media, potentially undermining our work and reputations by association. Even though I had worked in enough newsrooms and had repeatedly demonstrated my expertise, I knew that women in general, and black women in particular, had to constantly outperform male journalists. More frustrating than that, we also had to keep our "spider senses" attuned for ephemeral, intangible factors such as the unspoken doubts of some white male editors. One black female reporter I know likened it to "trying to shadowbox a ghost—you know it is there, you see, hear, and feel its presence, but you can't lay a glove on it."

I was relieved not to have to go to the *Globe* newsroom every day in the weeks after Smith was let go and as the battle over Barnicle's job raged on. The in-house turmoil sparked by Pat's firing—for that is what happened, despite the formality of her submitting her resignation—flared up instantly following that first staff meeting on June 18, and it continued until late in the summer, when a member of the family that owned the *Globe* finally got fed up, called Barnicle in, and fired him.

During those eight weeks, the *New York Times*, which owned the *Globe*, delivered sober front-page stories about the scandal, in addition to Howell Raines's column, while national and local television news programs regularly aired reports about the "showdown" between Barnicle and the *Globe* managers. Throughout, black journalists in Boston and around the nation publicly complained about the *Globe*'s double-standard treatment of the two columnists.

And in a turn that heightened my anxiety, my even-keeled, supremely professional husband—known within the newsroom as a calm and skilled juggler of reporters' needs with those of the top editors—had become the de facto leader and spokesman of an impromptu "minority coalition" of *Globe* staffers who went public with their concerns. (The group of fifty or so *Globe* writers, editors, and other staffers who signed a "letter of protest" actually included white staffers too. But the majority of the group were journalists of color.) My husband was interviewed frequently on New England Cable

News and was quoted in the *Times*. His language was diplomatic but clear: the *Globe* had made a mistake by not firing both columnists immediately.

It was an extremely delicate dance, the business of criticizing the institution that employed you. But as journalists, we were required to "speak truth to power," right? I felt a mix of pride and anxiousness about this. I knew that my husband felt strongly, as I did, that the *Globe*'s dithering over Barnicle's fate, even as they had swiftly kicked Pat Smith to the curb, stunk to high heaven. In the end, it was clear to me—and probably to the vast majority of minorities nationwide— that contrary to the belief held by some whites that affirmative action had conferred an unfair advantage on people of color, the oppo- site had been true for Pat Smith. Her ethical breaches were firing offenses, and the *Globe* leadership—Greg Moore included—had not wasted a moment in effecting her departure. But for Barnicle—a white male columnist—the *Globe* editorial leadership seemed quite unaccountably deferential in the face of his equally egregious lapses.

Journalists of color at the *Globe* and elsewhere were not alone in calling out the double standard, as shown by the number of white *Globe* staffers who signed the petition of protest and by Howell Raines's scathing column in the *New York Times*. But still, I worried that my husband's taking the lead in expressing the anger and disap- pointment of the *Globe* staffers at such a volatile time, and on a matter that was highly contentious within the industry at large, might bring trouble for him down the road.

In a purely pragmatic sense, we couldn't afford for him to lose his job: I was pregnant.

Several weeks after I'd cleared the first trimester, I began phoning friends and family members with the news. My mom said, "That's great, Amy! How do you feel?"

Then I phoned my agent in New York, who said, "Welcome to the club!" She also advised me on how to broach the topic with the editors at the publishing house where my next book was on tap— Beacon Press, in Boston. I had written a proposal for a third nonfic- tion book, this one on African Americans and suicide, and in February 1998 Beacon had bought it. For many years I had wanted to write a book about my older brother's suicide and the larger subject of blacks and mental health. In researching the issues involved, including the history of blacks and the medical and mental health establishments in the United States, I kept encountering the name of a Harvard psychiatrist who was a leader in the field: Alvin F. Poussaint, MD.

My agent had suggested I write to him, and I did. And during a meeting with Dr. Poussaint in his office near Children's Hospital in Boston, early in 1998, not only had he agreed with the premise of my book—that black Americans face bigger challenges in dealing with mental health and emotional distress than the general population—but he'd also agreed to be my coauthor. After I learned I was pregnant and Beacon and I worked out a new delivery date for the manuscript, Dr. Poussaint agreed to keep the project moving forward by writing the final chapter—the solutions portion—on his own.

He was proving to be a Good Doctor on many important fronts.

My daughter was born in early spring 1999 at Mount Auburn Hospital in Cambridge, by cesarean section. The birth took less than two hours. Afterward, looking down at her tiny peach-colored face and pink mouth, I joked with Hubby. "I figure she's bound to have a great sense of humor," I told him.

It was April Fools' Day in the last year of the century. Privately, I wasn't sure how I would ever return to journalism full-time.

Little by little I wrote the mental health book, having completed the interviews and travel during the second trimester of my pregnancy. Being a new mother focused my concentration in a way that I found surprising but which Dr. Poussaint assured me was common. I had developed an easy rapport with him and came to relish our talks and working relationship. My time for writing articles and reviews had all but vanished, but I occasionally checked in with editors at the *Globe* to let them know of ideas that sometimes popped up.

In the summer of 2000, we bought a house in a small, out-of-the-way Boston neighborhood called Hyde Park. Greg Moore, the *Globe*'s managing editor, lived nearby in Milton. All of a sudden, I was a suburban stay-at-home mom.

In October 2000, Beacon published *Lay My Burden Down: Suicide and the Mental Health Crisis among African-Americans*. A *Globe* features writer, Bella English, interviewed me and Dr. Poussaint in early October, and I was startled days later to see our story played across the entire front of the paper's Living/Arts section. It felt odd to see myself and my latest book become the subject of a story in the *Globe*—the newspaper where my byline so often appeared. Bella English accurately captured the theme of our book and also told our respective family members' stories with compassion and an appropriate amount of drama. And over the next few weeks, our book received favorable reviews in a handful of publications, including the *New England Journal of Medicine* and the online magazine *Salon*.

As if the excitement of buying a house, moving, and publishing a book were not enough, I had also begun writing a column for a new publication: Africana.com. The web-only journal focused on blacks in the United States and abroad, the latter known as the "black diaspora." It was cofounded by Henry Louis Gates Jr., a Harvard black studies scholar, with funding from Microsoft. Originally launched as an online promotional vehicle for *Encarta Africana*, a massive encyclopedia coedited by Gates and Harvard philosophy professor K. Anthony Appiah, the website provided a range of opinions and writing styles. During a short meeting with the site's top editors at their cramped offices in Harvard Square in late May 2000, I had pitched an idea for a column on race and media. They responded enthusiastically, and we settled on the second week in July as the column's launch date. Over the next few days, in e-mails and phone calls, we also settled on its title—"Reading Between the Lines"—and agreed it would appear twice each month.

I had sold the editors on the idea based in large part on the metro columnists' scandal at the *Globe* in 1998. That ethical and racial maelstrom over Smith and Barnicle's departures proved a theory that had been bubbling in my mind for a few years: the public was growing more interested in the "stories behind the stories" at major news organizations, and the highly contentious subject of in-house race and gender politics at major news organizations was an area ripe for coverage. A few weeks later, with Gates's approval, we arrived at a payment amount: five hundred dollars per column. I would receive no health benefits, profit sharing, or stocks. My official title would be "media columnist," though I was a contractor.

A few weeks before we moved our household from Cambridge to

Hyde Park, I wrote the inaugural column, which posted on the site on July 11, 2000. Its thesis statement—the column's mission—read in part:

> I hope to raise the kinds of questions about race, class, and gender in relation to American journalism that often go unasked, such as: Who decides what is "news" and how do they decide? What kinds of personal experiences do newsroom managers bring into the daily budget meeting? Do their personal views on race and gender influence the professional decision-making process? Does the sex and race of the information gatekeeper matter more than his professional ethics? In short, I want to be there when someone decides to drop a monstrously loaded phrase like "playing the race card" into a news story. In my quest to expose the behind-the-scenes discussions on race that take place within newsrooms and publishing suites (or that don't), I will take names, name names, and bring them to you along with my opinions of the goings-on.

Africana.com was the first large-scale, ideas-oriented, black-centric news, opinion, and cultural magazine published exclusively on the web. While the idea that my work would appear only on the web seemed risky and a bit creepy, I was more excited than ambivalent about joining the editorial team so soon after its launch.

By the late 1990s, freestanding news-oriented websites—including *Slate* and *Salon*—had begun to take off with readers, although not so much that readers paid for access. I had written a profile of Stanley Crouch for *Salon*, and on the day that it posted, I was startled but ultimately gratified to get calls and e-mails from people across the country who had read it. How amazing, this Internet! Suddenly, journalists anywhere could have a national readership. I didn't know any black journalists who wrote exclusively for online publications, and oddly, I didn't think of myself as either an "online journalist" or a "print journalist." I simply viewed *Africana* as a new place where I could publish—and a new source of income.

More than a decade after I joined *Africana*, the slowness of racial integration at online publications is becoming a growing point of frustration for journalists of color. For one thing, few of these online sites pay living wages to journalists; fewer still employ journalists of color in full-time positions.

In 2006, a black female lawyer in Texas, Gina McCauley, launched an independent blog, *What About Our Daughters*, which created a minor splash in the widening universe of online-only publications. McCauley—who is an attorney, not a journalist—began writing blog entries about race-related injustices taking place in the Southwest and Southeast. Within two years she was drawing thousands of visitors to her site each day. The mixing of activism with the basic journalistic formula of reporting and verification was a revelation to those of us who had been struggling to reconcile those two things in the new world of online news and information publications. And unlike *Africana*, which had corporate funding and had been conceived and launched as a traditional magazine that happened to exist on the web, McCauley's publication had the look and sensibility of a seat-of-the-pants operation. It worked, and there was but one employee behind it.

At *Slate* and *Salon*, meanwhile, journalists from mainstream news organizations regularly contributed essays and investigative journalism that sometimes sparked coverage by "old media" stalwarts, such as the *New York Times* or the network news teams on ABC or NBC. The two sites were becoming "thought leaders," at least in media and academic circles—despite their apparent inability to find black or Latino writers. (Interestingly, *Slate* and *Salon* have long published the work of East Asian and Indian journalists and authors with much greater frequency than the work of blacks or Latinos.)

An online hierarchy was developing, though, and it had the tinge of racial apartheid to it. Neither *Slate* nor *Salon* had ever employed more than one or two black or Latino writers on their respective editorial staffs during their decade of operation. And by the time of Barack Obama's historic run for the Democratic presidential nomination, in 2008, the Washington Post Company had launched an online publication that, oddly, served the purpose of both highlighting the online racial apartheid of web magazines and lessening its effect. TheRoot.com debuted in late January 2008, providing readers with smart, sometimes raw commentary and analysis on black topics. Its co-owner is Henry Louis Gates Jr., former publisher of *Africana*. The Harvard professor said the same thing in interviews about *The Root* in 2008 as he had about *Africana* in the late 1990s: that he had conceived it as a thoroughly modern online vehicle for readers seeking well-written journalism that was sophisticated, sharp, and well-funded.

Gates had obviously learned a lot from the earlier experience with *Africana*. In 2001 he had sold his stake in *Africana* to Time Warner, saying he did so in order to save it from closure. (Microsoft's funding had been short-term, and *Africana* had struggled to bring in advertising revenue sufficient to support its full-time staff of a dozen editors and programmers; most of the writers were contractors.) Not long after the sale to Time Warner, that media company merged with America Online (AOL)—an Internet service provider that had seen its stock price leap during the height of the dot-com bubble in the late 1990s. Yet over the next few years, as the overpriced stock of AOL and other big Internet businesses corrected downward, *Africana* received fewer resources within the AOL Time Warner empire. It was folded into an AOL site, Black Voices, in 2003 and shuttered completely in 2005.

Yet in 2008, Gates formed a partnership with *Washington Post* publisher Donald Graham to launch *The Root*. The online magazine was envisioned not only as a place for sharp, well-reported, and well-written news and information about blacks around the world, but also as a place where African Americans (or anyone, for that matter) could access a DNA search company—of which Gates was an investor. In news stories about the launch of *The Root*, Gates batted away questions about potential conflict of interest by saying no such conflict existed, since he had disclosed his partial ownership of the genealogy search company.

Gates, a feverishly productive scholar and public intellectual, had been hosting historical documentaries on PBS focused on scientific developments in DNA research that were providing new tools to blacks and other Americans interested in finding their family origins. I didn't know quite what to make of Gates's stake in the DNA company, but having been a columnist at *Africana* for five years before its demise, I wanted to at least contribute to *The Root*.

Imagine my surprise, then, when I had my first conversation with an editor at TheRoot.com: freelance writers received only two hundred dollars per essay. That was less than half of what I'd been paid when I had signed on to be a columnist at *Africana* eight years earlier. In their earliest days, online publications may have offered journalists of all ethnicities more creative freedom and at least an approximation of the pay scale that existed at traditional news organizations. But as the 2000s marched on, with few exceptions, most of the marquee online news organizations offered contractors deplorably bad pay—and significantly fewer full-time staff positions than their counterparts had a decade earlier.

Between October 2000 and January of the next year, the promotional tour for the mental health book took me from Boston to New York to Atlanta to California. After the thick of the promotional duties for Beacon had passed, I settled into a routine of reporting, researching, and writing my columns and freelance articles for various publications. My column at *Africana* had become popular among journalists of color. By 2003 I could count on receiving dozens of e-mail responses to my columns, and other websites had begun linking to them. I had grown accustomed to a style of writing that was more "webby" than what I had done at newspapers and in magazines—breezier and more comfortably in line with my day-to-day conversational tone of speaking. My domestic life was getting busier: in 2002 I had been startled to find out I was pregnant again, at age thirty-nine, but overwhelmingly I was glad.

The *Globe* too had undergone some big changes since the start of the decade. Its executive editor, Matt Storin, resigned and was replaced by an editor from outside the company, Martin Baron, who is white. Greg Moore, the managing editor, should have gotten the top spot. But according to the "*Globe* family" rumor mill, he had been passed over in part because he had failed to recognize the ticking time bomb of Patricia Smith in 1998. In their public announcement of Baron's hire, company officials mentioned Baron's long track record of accomplishments. He had worked in middle management at the *New York Times* for several years, then taken the editor job at the *Miami Herald*, where he had presided over a slate of stories on lo-

cal government corruption that had won the paper a Pulitzer Prize.
He had also overseen the *Herald*'s coverage of the Elián González
saga—the strange 2000 case of a Cuban schoolboy who got caught in
a custody battle between his mom in Miami and his father in Havana,
Cuba—which garnered a Pulitzer for spot news photography (and
which had spurred the community "prayer circle" that had gotten
Herald columnist Liz Balmaseda, a Pulitzer Prize winner, into hot
water).

Moore never said it publicly, but among black journalists in New
England and around the nation, his being passed over for the editor's chair in favor of an "outsider"—something that hadn't happened
before in the *Globe*'s recent history—was seen as evidence of latent
racism. Why is it, I asked in an *Africana* column, that the minute a
black editor is in line to take the Big Chair at the *Globe*, the company
suddenly decides that it wants to go "in another direction," suppos-
edly in the name of bringing "fresh perspective" to the paper? The
company's official line never mentioned the Pat Smith debacle, but
it is possible that the deep embarrassment over the situation made it
easier for top management to pass him by for the position. Moore's
ethnicity, in the eyes of many journalists of color, short-circuited any
aspect of loyalty that might otherwise have led the *Globe*'s leadership
to show confidence in Moore by promoting him in the years immediately after the Smith/Barnicle disaster. It was not a provable theory,
but it prevailed all the same.

There were predictions that Greg Moore would not long stick
around after Baron was hired—and ultimately, he did not. By late
2002 Moore had agreed to become editor at the *Denver Post*. His
departure made me sad, but I didn't blame him for taking that step.
Moore was, and is, an exceptionally accomplished editor, both in
technical terms and in his ability to successfully manage and moti-
vate workers. The term "leadership skills" gets tossed around so frequently as to lose meaning in corporate nomenclature, but I know its
true value in the context of newsrooms.

I was due to give birth in early May 2003, and as that date ap-
proached, Hubby told me he had been in talks with editors at the *Star
Tribune* in Minneapolis. He asked for my opinion of that newspaper.
I didn't know much about it, but I told him that its parent company,

McClatchy, was a great outfit. The professional training and conference trips that Hubby attended in different cities often brought him in contact with top editors at other newspapers, and it wasn't unusual for him to get "hit on" by other team leaders. This dynamic represented another irony, if not paradox, where the subject of race and the big daily newspapers is concerned: Greg Moore, a black man, was tacitly suspected of having been too sympathetic to Patricia Smith, a black fabricator on his staff, which possibly led to his being passed over for the top newsroom job at the *Globe*. But for Hubby, his standing as an accomplished up-and-coming editor who also happened to be black made him something of a hot commodity on the hiring circuit. Of course, this dynamic was never discussed openly in mixed company—that is, between black and white newsroom managers.

But the fact remained that Hubby was African American, relatively young, and well educated, and he had a great reputation at his home paper, which was itself a leader within the industry. He had come through the Smith-Barnicle scandal relatively unscathed and with a more prominent profile in the close world of newspaper management recruiters.

I was proud that he drew so much interest from other newspapers, but I also knew I had to tread lightly. I didn't want to be in a position of squelching any opportunities for advancement that might come to him, but neither was I eager to uproot my household at the drop of a hat—and certainly not to live in a part of the country that I didn't think I would like. The Twin Cities, though, had a reputation as a politically progressive and economically affordable area. For that reason, and because I had firsthand knowledge of the McClatchy Company, I didn't dismiss Hubby's interest in the *Star Tribune* out of hand.

A couple of days before my scheduled C-section, I read an item on a journalism blog, *Romenesko*, about a possible "problem" with a young black reporter at the *New York Times*. The item was worded vaguely, but it seemed to indicate that *Times* editors were concerned about the accuracy of the reporter's work. On May 2, the day before I checked into Brigham and Women's Hospital in Boston, the *Times* published a short story inside its A section describing their editors' decision to remove the young reporter from his beat covering national affairs. They cited "improper conduct" and hinted that there was more to come.

I showed the story to Hubby and asked him what he thought. He said, "Uh-oh. That kid was an intern at the *Globe* a few years ago, and I always thought there was something . . . off about him." His name was Jayson Blair.

I turned forty years old on May 4, 2003, two days after the birth of my son. On that clear Sunday morning, the last day of my stay at Brigham and Women's, I turned on the television in my room. On CNN, Howard Kurtz, host of the network's media affairs program *Reliable Sources*, was in a frenzy. He was reporting that the *New York Times* had fired Jayson Blair for "plagiarism, and possibly for fabrications too." Lots of them. Kurtz then turned to an "analyst" who was on the set, and they began to discuss the situation. Jayson Blair, once an up-and-coming metro reporter, had apparently been caught not just making up quotes in his news stories, but also lifting entire passages and quotes from stories published elsewhere. Then—out of nowhere, it seemed to me—Kurtz and his guest began talking about affirmative action. As in, "Was Jayson Blair allowed to perform below the *Times'* standards because he was an affirmative action hire?"

I leaned back in the hospital bed and turned off the television set. My newborn son was sleeping in the tiny bassinet beside my bed, and Hubby had gone to breakfast with our daughter. I looked out of the windows, up at the sky. I knew that the minute I returned home to my office in Hyde Park, I would be on the phone with my *Africana* editors in Cambridge, planning our coverage of the Jayson Blair scandal.

Three months later, on a steamy morning in mid-August, I wheeled my son out of the front door at our house and down the block toward the local playground.

A massive tractor-trailer had just arrived out front of our home on Brush Hill Terrace, and I didn't want to be there as the workers loaded our household goods inside. Hubby had decided to take an editing job at the *Star Tribune*. I was sad and confused. Even though I had initially told him I thought it would be okay, by moving day I was experiencing buyer's remorse.

Not long after my son was born, talks between Hubby and editors at that Minnesota newspaper had intensified, and by June the *Star Tribune* editors had invited him to become him the assistant managing editor of the metro staff.

I had been torn between wanting to support his career needs and my desire to stay in Hyde Park and Boston. I loved our house and had developed a solid network of support in my personal and professional lives. But I also struggled with feelings of guilt, since the birth of my son meant that I would not be returning to full-time work for at least another year. And when Hubby had traveled to the Twin Cities in late May and returned with stories of how livable the region was and how friendly everyone he'd met had been, I swallowed and told him, "Well, okay. As long as you're sure that it's the right move for your career."

Preparation for our departure from Boston was hurried, with virtually no time to calmly sell our home in Hyde Park or, more important, comfortably find a new one. By the time the moving van pulled up in front of our Boston home, I was resentful and exhausted to the point of tears. I doubted I would find work at the *Star Tribune* or that I would want to work there; the newspaper I had been reading online was earnest, well-reported, with serviceable writing—and boring.

I could continue writing my column, "Reading Between the Lines," from St. Paul. The editors at *Africana* had assured me that they didn't mind that I would no longer live in Boston. "You're moving for your family," my editor, Kate Tuttle, told me. "There is no way we'd have a problem that."

But I had a problem with it. I just didn't know where or how to express it.

SIX

Minnesota

Is "Well-Meaning" Good Enough?

Fifteen minutes from St. Paul, the Mall of America unfurls its 2.5 million square feet of shops, restaurants, movie theaters, and amusements in Bloomington, Minnesota.

During our first two months in Ramsey County, while our house on Highland Parkway in St. Paul got a new kitchen, we lived in an apartment complex in Bloomington, a few miles from the mall. In short order, as Hubby settled into his new job at the *Star Tribune*—known as the *Strib*—I began to feel isolated. I worried that I had reached the end of my journalism work and that a future of driving children around and attending PTA meetings was what awaited me.

I tried not to dwell on it, choosing instead to dive into getting our household set up in St. Paul and finding a support community, if possible.

Fortunately, in that regard there was Duschesne Drew, a reporter covering business at the *Star Tribune*, and his wife, Angela Davis, a reporter and morning anchor then working at KTSP, the local ABC television affiliate. My husband had met them during a solo trip to Minneapolis; after our family relocated there, I was relieved to learn that Duschesne and Angela were our enthusiastic goodwill ambassadors. They are African American and had been in the Twin Cities for nearly a decade when we arrived.

Angela, Duschesne, and their family members were my lifesavers in the weeks right after we arrived. They provided tips on practical matters, like the best places to buy groceries and day-care programs we might consider. They also eased my transition into the media community of the Twin Cities.

Over our first year in the Twin Cities, I came to admire the Drews greatly, in no small part because their relationship to their work was very different from my own and from the way many other journalists I'd known on the East Coast approached their work. For Duschesne and Angela, their career choice enriched their lives but didn't define who they were. Similarly, most of the other journalists I met in the Twin Cities had side interests that seemed to help them keep their journalism work in a healthy perspective. During the two years that I lived there, I met journalists of different ethnicities who spent their off-hours engaging in "real world" interests ranging from playing music to gardening to teaching, and I marveled at their abilities to not eat, breathe, think, and live journalism 24/7.

All the same, the economic and technology-driven changes that had roiled corporate news organizations elsewhere in the country were also being felt in the Twin Cities during the early 2000s. And in 2006, after the McClatchy Company bought the larger Knight Ridder chain, the Sacramento-based corporation announced its plan to sell the *Star Tribune* and the *St. Paul Pioneer Press*, which it had acquired in the Knight Ridder purchase.

That initial report sent a shock wave through the *Pioneer Press* newsroom, where a colleague I had worked with years earlier in Fresno, Rhoda Fukushima, was covering health and fitness. "I'd say that first announcement created the most anxiety. You could see people just walking around the newsroom looking stunned," Rhoda said when I phoned her several years later to interview her for this book. But in short order the anxiety ebbed. Rhoda attributes its relatively short life span to a combination of factors: the *Pioneer Press* had been on the ropes in the past and had always managed to survive, and with a few exceptions, many on the editorial staff maintained a practical outlook on their work and their ability to readjust. When I asked whether she or other journalists of color had felt any special pressure at the thought of the *Pioneer Press* closing, Rhoda said, "I can only speak for myself, and honestly, it wasn't something that kept me awake at nights."

Yet Rhoda observed, in the early spring of 2009 when I phoned her, that those who remained at the *Pioneer Press* were determined to make the transition to whatever the future held for their paper and

for the news industry. She transitioned from covering health and fitness on the print version of the *Pioneer Press* to writing and posting
the early morning breaking local news stories on the TwinCities.com
website, a newfangled job that she said she enjoys immensely.

She is in her mid-forties now, like me, and said that learning the
digital version of daily newspaper mostly requires patience and an
open mind. "I'm glad to still be working, and I'm excited for the
future. . . . I know this is a tough time for a lot of journalists all over,
and given what's happened here in the Twin Cities, I can't even imagine what it is like to be in Denver or Seattle, where papers have actually closed," she said, referring to the demise of the *Rocky Mountain
News* and the *Seattle Post-Intelligencer*, both in 2009.

But some other journalists of color in the Twin Cities didn't
weather the changes as smoothly.

Delma Francis, a veteran black journalist who took a buyout from
the *Star Tribune* in 2007, reported on her own money struggles two
years later. Writing at MinnPost.com—a new online site focused on
local news in Minnesota—Delma described the rabbit hole of job-
lessness she fell down barely two years after she'd left the *Strib*.

"Until twenty-three months ago, I'd never been unemployed.
When I took a buyout at the *Star Tribune* on June 15, 2007, I was sure
I'd find another job quickly, although my entire career has been in
newspapers—which, as you may know, are not doing a lot of hiring
these days. Still, writing and editing are valuable assets to many businesses. What I hadn't counted on was the total tanking of the economy," Francis wrote. Her account, clear-eyed and honest, went on to
describe the tangles of bureaucracy she encountered once she began
applying for unemployment benefits and other forms of aid. Unlike
Duschesne and Angela—who held on at their respective news organizations during several periods of uncertainty—Delma had believed
that taking the buyout would give her an opportunity to explore
other work. But in a scenario that is being repeated across the nation,
as scores of black journalists with upwards of two decades' worth of
experience are laid off or "strongly encouraged" to take buyout pack-
ages, Delma discovered that being a middle-aged African American
job seeker during a deep recession is exceptionally tough.

She writes regularly for MinnPost.com, but that web publication

—founded by a former top editor at the *Star Tribune* and funded by grants from foundations and by micropayments from local readers— has only a skeleton staff. Delma doesn't receive health benefits of any kind, a frightening state of affairs. But she continues writing at *MinnPost*, grateful for the platform to share her views on local and national cultural affairs—and she keeps pounding the pavement in search of another Real Job.

When we arrived in Minnesota, despite finding this supportive community, we discovered that the newsrooms of both papers had only small numbers of minority journalists. At the *Pioneer Press*, or *PiPress*, where Rhoda worked, there were a handful of veterans, including some writers and editors of color. And at the *Strib* there were approximately a dozen African American journalists among the total editorial staff of about two hundred, and a handful of Asian and Latino journalists.

The relatively sanguine attitude toward race—both within the two news organizations and in terms of their coverage of racial issues—was a double-edged sword, by my estimation. The working environments at the *Strib* and *PiPress* were civil, and productive—and yet an absence of aggression sometimes left the editorial staffs flat-footed when breaking news developments called for a high level of energy and expertise on race-related issues.

In-house political discussions around race or class at the *Star Tribune* were infrequent, rarely reaching the elevated pitch that I had observed in other big news organizations. Even before the Mc-Clatchy Company bought the paper in 1998, the Strib's previous owners, the Cowles family, had steadily built a respectable internship program that recruited journalists of color and sought to retain and promote them in the appropriate circumstances. But given the *Strib*'s location—in the Upper Midwest, locale of some of the coldest temperatures in the continental United States, and in a metropolitan area that until the 1980s had a population that was nearly 100 percent white—the paper wasn't exactly a popular destination for journalists of color.

For most of the twentieth century, the racial homogeneity of Minneapolis and St. Paul was reflected in the makeup of the news staffs at both papers. By 2007 the ethnic minority population had grown to 28 percent of the total metropolitan population of nearly 1.2 million residents. This growth resulted from twenty years of a steady influx of immigrants from Southeast Asia (including Vietnamese, Cambodians, and ethnic Hmong from Laos), Africa (including Somalis and Ethiopians), and Central and South America (including Guatemalans, Brazilians, Mexicans, Peruvians, and Hondurans). Census experts predicted that by end of the 2000s the Twin Cities would be one of the most ethnically diverse regions in the United States.

In the newsrooms around the Twin Cities, ethnic diversity lagged behind that of the civilian population. In 2003, minorities constituted 13.4 percent of editorial employees at the *Star Tribune*, while at the *Pioneer Press* journalists of color constituted 11 percent of newsroom workers. Five years later, minorities constituted 14.4 percent of editorial workers at the *Star Tribune* and 12.6 percent at the *Pioneer Press*, according to ASNE. And at both newspapers in 2003 and 2008, African Americans were the largest ethnic minority group.

African American journalists have worked in the newsrooms of the two largest papers since at least the 1960s, according to Erna Smith, a former Minneapolis journalist who is now a journalism professor at the University of Southern California's Annenberg School for Communication and Journalism. For the journalists of color who ventured to the Twin Cities—or the few natives who landed there—working at the *Strib* or the *PiPress* was relatively stress-free. The editorial leaders and fellow reporters were "nice"—perhaps too nice. For some journalists of color, that presented an unanticipated set of problems.

"Everyone was always nice, that was never the issue," Smith recalls of the two years she worked as a reporter in the *Star Tribune* newsroom during the early 1980s. "It was just that the editorial staff and editorial leadership, which of course was overwhelmingly white, didn't really see a need to ask questions about racial issues. . . . It just wasn't on their radar." The "Minnesota Nice" sobriquet that is the region's unofficial motto, and that signifies the polite, common-sense demeanor of much of the state's residents, also influenced the coverage of race-related news at the city's largest newsrooms.

An absence of curiosity—or skepticism—characterized the management's take on covering racial matters, according to Smith. And while that made for a relatively pleasant workplace, it didn't foster aggressive coverage of the growing number of ethnic minorities who began streaming into the Twin Cities in the late 1970s, after local Lutheran and Methodist nonprofit organizations began offering services—including housing and employment training—as part of resettlement programs for political refugees from Southeast Asia and other points overseas.

Eventually the *Star Tribune* and the *Pioneer Press* produced groundbreaking coverage of the internationalization of the metropolitan area. But compared with some other big papers located in cities that saw rapid in-migration during the late 1970s and '80s—including the *Miami Herald* and the *Los Angeles Times*—the Twin City papers were slow to develop beats and in-depth projects built around immigration.

Beginning in 2003, for example, when my husband was in charge of the metro staff, he quickly noticed a general hesitancy around the subject of race among the reporters and assignment editors he supervised. After a St. Paul man who had emigrated from Laos shot and killed six white men during a confrontation in nearby Wisconsin, the *Star Tribune* news staff initially accepted the law enforcement officers' descriptions with few questions: the gunman, Chai Soua Vang, had apparently gotten the drop on a group of eight white men who, like him, had gone to the woods in northern Wisconsin to hunt deer. As I heard the initial reports, broadcast on local television stations a day after the mid-November 2004 incident, I instantly wondered whether the Laotian man had felt threatened and had believed his life to be in danger. A sheriff in Sawyer County, where the shootings took place, said the survivors told the owner of the property where they had permission to hunt that they had "discovered" Vang occupying their deer stand and that they had "asked him to leave." During a news conference, the sheriff said the men reported that Vang had complied and was walking away with his rifle, when "suddenly he stopped, turned around," and began firing at the group of men. As I watched that news report, my skepticism radar tingled.

Initial coverage in the *Star Tribune* and the *Pioneer Press* gave ample context and background about the growing community of Hmong and Laotians in the Twin Cities (they numbered about twenty-five thousand in 2004). The newspaper reports also mentioned that in the recent past, some Hmong had reported being harassed by whites they encountered during the early days of each hunting season.

Over the next week, after officials charged Vang with the murders of six of the men, Vang's statement outlined a scenario completely different from the one described by the surviving members of the group and widely reported by Twin Cities news outlets. The thirty-six-year-old said a white man had confronted him and told him he couldn't hunt there because it was private property. As he began to leave, several other white men joined the property owner, and they began to yell racial insults at him; one of the men pointed a rifle at Vang as he walked away, and that's when Vang dropped into a crouch and fired.

A year later, Vang, a truck driver and a father of six who had immigrated to Minnesota when he was a boy, was convicted by an all-white jury and sentenced to six life terms in prison. (Minnesota does not have a death penalty.)

The story made national headlines, and much of the initial coverage followed the lead of the Twin City's two major newspapers, thereby cementing a tone that, if not exactly biased in favor of the white hunters' version of the story, was nevertheless missing a level of skepticism that might have tamped down the public's anger toward Vang. During the year between the shootings and Vang's conviction, the comments sections of local blogs and the websites of the *Star Tribune* and the *Pioneer Press* carried hundreds of angry, and sometimes viciously racist, posts by residents who blamed the Hmong community for a host of infractions. The Vang story exposed a not-so-nice side of at least some Minnesotans.

The vehemently anti-immigrant subtext of many of the commenters' posts was not in itself surprising. But I couldn't help wondering whether the level of vitriol would have been as high if the two leading news organizations had been more skeptical of the surviving deer hunters' early claims that Vang had shot at them without provocation. (Which is not to say that I condone Vang's act, only that responsible news coverage should have explored the possibility that Vang might have feared for his life and believed he was acting in self-defense when he fired on the white male deer hunters.) Hubby confided in me that discussions of this aspect had taken place in the *Strib* newsroom as the Vang story unfolded. And yet the possibility that Vang might have been acting from a genuine fear—and the possibility that his fear might have been rooted in previous bad encounters with white deer hunters—was not fully explored in the pages of the paper during the height of the story.

In 2005, both the *Star Tribune* and the *Pioneer Press* got another hard lesson in how not to cover a race-related story.

On March 21, a sixteen-year-old in Red Lake, Minnesota, swiped his grandfather's gun and used it to kill the seventy-two-year-old man and his girlfriend while they slept. Like his grandfather and his parents, Jeff Weise belonged to the Red Lake Band of the Chippewa. Located 240 miles north of the Twin Cities, the Red Lake reservation, with 5,162 residents, was home to one of the poorest populations in the state. Weise, a sophomore at the local high school, left the bodies of his grandfather and the elderly man's companion and drove to his school. There he shot fifteen people, killing seven.

As the day unfolded, reporters from the *Star Tribune* scrambled to get up to Red Lake. By the time they arrived, tribal leaders had locked down the reservation and refused entrance to all outside journalists. Neither the *Star Tribune* nor the *Pioneer Press* had Native Americans as full-time staff on their reporting teams. During the next few days, both news organizations struggled to find sources who could give them access to the details of the mass shooting and to the larger community, with little success. As a result, the initial coverage consisted almost entirely of official statements from tribal leaders and local law enforcement officials, including agents from the Twin Cities branch of the Federal Bureau of Investigation.

Even in 2009, four years after the shootings at Red Lake (the deadliest school shooting incident since the massacre at Columbine High School in Colorado earlier in the decade), the *Star Tribune* listed just one of its editorial workers as Native American. That horrific story and the two papers' initial problems getting meaningful information reminded me of why I had endeavored to cover situations like the Darlene Johnson "Norplant" story in Fresno and the Jackie Johnson suicide in South Florida. It is legitimate to question the wisdom of editorial leaders in St. Paul and Minneapolis who had managed to overlook the potential value of having skilled Native American reporters or editors on their full-time staffs.

The Twin Cities in 2003 had a broad cross section of healthy media companies and a decent number of journalists of color working in them. Twin Cities Black Journalists, the local chapter of the NABJ, was fairly active, although its gatherings did not usually carry the same urgent, circle-the-wagons vibe that I'd picked up at black journalists' events I'd attended in other cities. The ranks of Minnesota's journalists then were characterized by friendly competition between news organizations and reporters and producers; it was a collegial, efficient, and dedicated community, and eventually I settled into a routine that was more relaxed than my life in New England had been.

I kept in touch with my editors at *Africana*. Kate Tuttle and I had become friends in the three years since I launched the column. Many of our conversations in the first weeks after I'd left Boston were really more therapeutic than professional. Kate listened patiently as I described the surreal aspects of my new surroundings, and if asked, she offered advice on how I might cope. (Kate is a native of Kansas.)

I was home weekdays, and while my daughter was in kindergarten and my infant son napped in the next room, I worked on my column. Back in Cambridge, Kate and the other editors at *Africana* were making a transition of their own. Time Warner had bought the website, and after that company merged with AOL, Africana.com was placed into the arms of the giant Internet service provider. By the early spring of 2004, Kate had left *Africana*, and I had been assigned to work with an AOL employee. Her position title was not "editor"; it was "programmer."

During our first phone conversation, my programmer was unable to explain in plain language exactly what she did at the company's Black Voices website, the "channel" where *Africana* would be published. Standing in my living room in St. Paul, watching through a picture window as sparrows flitted in and out of the big blue spruce in the front yard, I listened to the young woman as she spoke from her office in Dulles, Virginia, rattling on about "site traffic flow" and "page views" and "stickiness." She didn't have any interest or acumen when it came to ideas or the themes I had been exploring; nor did she show much interest in the process of reporting and writing. Similarly, although I had been a columnist at the leading online journal of black opinion since 2000, I had no interest in the technical metrics involved in publishing the site. We spoke different languages, and I knew on that day that my time as a columnist at the site was coming to a close.

On a brittle morning in late February 2004, I bundled the baby into a blue Graco carriage and walked three blocks from our house to the commercial area of our St. Paul neighborhood, Highland Park. I had a meeting at a local eatery with an editor from the *Star Tribune*, and I felt good about it.

Mi-Ai Parrish was editor of the *Strib*'s features department. In a booth at the Daily Planet, a retro-style diner on Cleveland Avenue, we hit it off immediately; we had mutual friends elsewhere in the industry. We talked about story ideas and discussed our respective careers. Parrish had worked for a time in San Francisco too. And as the only Asian American editor at the *Star Tribune*, she shared my sense of the "double consciousness" burden that journalists of color carry within big corporate news organizations. This is to say that Parrish and I, like scores of other journalists of color working in corporate news organizations, expressed the frustrations and challenges of navigating a business in which top managers claim publicly to support diversity while day-to-day experiences often belie that claim. I also confided that I wasn't sure whether my particular journalistic specialties—writing about communities of color, or race and media, or blacks and mental health—made for a good fit at the *Star Tribune*.

Blacks represented slightly more than 11 percent—33,000—of St. Paul's 287,151 residents in 2004, and nearly 6 percent, or 69,000, of Minneapolis's 382,618 residents. The newspaper's coverage of blacks and of black-oriented topics was erratic. Other than Hubby, who as an assistant managing editor occupied a seat at the higher end of the newsroom's middle management editorial ranks, no blacks filled leadership positions at the paper.

In general, the *Star Tribune*, the leading media organization in the Twin Cities, was by my lights more a booster than a snapping watchdog. I shared this opinion in direct language that I hoped was honest without sounding unduly judgmental or resentful. Parrish listened carefully, nodding and smiling above her coffee cup. We agreed to keep talking. But as I returned the baby to the carriage and we said our goodbyes, I had a sense that I would not be writing for the *Star Tribune*.

Revenue at the paper was down, and the publisher and owners fretted about how to contain costs without hurting editorial performance. The paper's website, an emerging presence in the newsroom, was not at that time generating significant income, and many editors and reporters were nervous at the prospect of integrating the traditional newsroom with the web property.

As 2004 began, I was earning $600 per column at *Africana*, having received a $100-per-column raise early in 2003. Then in mid-spring, a personnel shakeup at AOL created a problem for me and the other *Africana* writers: while internal systems were being reconfigured, our payments stopped. The twice monthly checks did not arrive from AOL headquarters in Dulles.

At that moment, I did what I had always done in times of personal or career uncertainty—I worked. The columns continued to post every other Monday, even though the paychecks hadn't come in almost three months. I had a contract. I would uphold my end of it. In late April, after several calls from me and my literary agent, AOL worked out its technical problems, and I received by overnight express a check for four thousand dollars, representing the missed payments. It had been a scary episode, and I knew I had to start seeking other work in earnest.

The Unity: Journalists of Color Convention was scheduled take place in Washington, D.C., in July; I talked it over with my programmer at AOL, and we decided that I would attend and report on the proceedings. At Unity—a week-long conference of more than six thousand black, Latino, Asian, and Native American journalists who meet jointly every four years—I would cover the panels, workshops, and symposia for AOL's Black Voices channel, where *Africana* appeared. My side agenda included taking the opportunity to network for jobs.

At the convention I reunited with Lois Henry, a former *Fresno Bee* colleague. She had advanced to the assistant managing editor's job at the *Bakersfield Californian* in the years since I'd left the Central Valley. We'd talked by phone earlier, and she said she'd put me up in her hotel room. I had jumped at the offer; AOL said it would pay only my airfare, and I couldn't have managed the cost for the hotel room without Lois's help.

I felt free during the week of the Unity 2004 convention. It was the first time since 1998 that I'd been to D.C., and the weather god had smiled on the conventioneers: the thick humidity that typically strangles the District in late July was not on tap. I happily hoofed my way around downtown. The new D.C. Convention Center vibrated with thousands of journalists from across the United States, and I soaked up the camaraderie. Around every corner, I bumped into colleagues and friends that I had not seen for years.

Since its inaugural gathering in Atlanta in 1994, Unity has become much more than just a quadrennial meeting place for journalists of color in the United States. In recent years, as increasing numbers of black, Latino, Asian, and Native American journalists have been negatively affected by the media industry downturn, Unity has become a valuable job-search clearinghouse and training resource. It is also a source of psychological and emotional comfort. Its funding from corporate media groups, including the New York Times Company, Disney, CBS, and CNN, has been directed in recent years more toward helping its members retool their journalistic skills than toward the galas and banquets that some of the big companies had previously funded. Moreover, by 2004, workshops on digital editing programs like Final Cut Pro had surpassed workshops on "How to Cover a City Hall" or "How to Write Long-Form Narrative Journalism" as the most popular offerings at the conventions.

The 2004 presidential election was to take place in November, and both candidates, Democratic senator John Kerry of Massachusetts and President George W. Bush, were scheduled to speak. I spent time on the first day of the convention hanging out at the AOL Time Warner booth in the main exhibit hall, but it made me feel depressed: my programmer hadn't attended, and the young woman from AOL Black Voices who was assigned to the booth had no clue about my work. I let her know that I planned to cover the president's talk live, and she looked at me blankly. I borrowed a laptop from Gary Dauphin, an *Africana* editor who was at the convention, and delivered a column on President Bush's talk within hours of his appearance. It posted a few days later.

A development that took place during that week outside of the convention, and which few of us managed to cover during that week, helped change the course of the election: a conservative group funded a massive TV advertising campaign that began airing that week. The advertisements featured military veterans who said they didn't believe that Senator Kerry had been an effective leader during his service in the Vietnam War. As a young Navy lieutenant, Kerry had piloted a vessel known as a swift boat through dangerous enemy territory and helped rescue servicemen who had come under fire. But the Swift Boat Veterans for Truth, as the group of anti-Kerry veterans initially called themselves, claimed that Kerry had greatly exaggerated his actions. So when Kerry spoke to the journalists of color at the Unity '04 convention in Washington, D.C., we collectively missed a chance to closely question Kerry about the issue, effectively passing up a story that was literally developing in our midst—or at least, on the television screens in our hotel rooms.

Conversely, President Bush's halting response to a question by Mark Trahant, a Native American journalist from Seattle, about the meaning of sovereignty for Indian tribes in the twenty-first century drew loads of coverage. I was in the hall during that exchange, and like the thousand or so other journalists present, I was astounded to witness, up close and in person, the president's bumbling, stumbling attempts to answer. But it is ironic that the journalists' coverage of Kerry's calm, "presidential" address and his fluid, intelligent answers during the Q&A did little to counter the devastating blow to the senator's reputation that the swift boat ads had delivered.

On the third night of the convention, Lois and I went to dinner at a downtown restaurant that was off the convention path. As we walked to the door of the eatery, a homeless man approached. He was African American, slightly pudgy, and his outstretched hand held a paper coffee cup for collecting change.

"I see you ladies are going into this establishment for some fine dining. Well, let me give you a review," he said. And he rattled off a minute-long capsule review of the fare we would encounter at the restaurant, using language that sounded culinarily appropriate. We thanked him, gave him a couple bucks, and went into the restaurant.

The next morning, as I walked from the hotel on Thirteenth Street NW near Massachusetts Avenue to the convention center, I began to notice something that I hadn't focused on earlier in my time in D.C.: on nearly every street, in doorways and on benches, homeless men sat or lay sleeping. Many of them were black. Most of them were apparently suffering from mental illness.

When I returned to St. Paul, I wrote a postconvention column about homelessness in D.C. and elsewhere in the United States. I asked my colleagues at news organizations nationwide not to give up on covering homelessness and the welter of social, political, and cultural issues that are bound up in it. That column drew high traffic at Black Voices for weeks afterward, though I can't be sure it led any of my colleagues to take up covering homelessness full-time.

In December 2004 I learned that Hubby was in talks with the *Boston Globe*. His former partner on the city desk had been named chief of the paper's Washington, D.C., bureau. Shortly after Christmas he received an offer: Would he return to the *Globe* to become its D.C. deputy bureau chief? My reaction surprised me: a strong mixture of elation and exhaustion. The prospect of returning to the East Coast had a few prominent potential benefits—notably, giving me a greater array of options for returning to work in journalism full-time. But I also knew well the logistical complications such a move entailed— just thinking about that process made me tired.

We talked it over during the holiday weeks. I told Hubby that I was daunted by the prospect of another long-haul move, but that overall I believed it was appropriate, given our respective career needs and the isolation that had nearly smothered me.

At the start of the new year, he accepted the job. With our daughter in school and our son at an age where he could attend day care, I could at last return to work full-time once we all arrived in Washington. After he'd agreed to return to the *Boston Globe*, Hubby let me know he would have to commute between D.C. and the Twin Cities for at least a couple of months—the *Globe* said it wanted him in place in their national office in March, yet it didn't make sense to uproot our daughter from her kindergarten class in St. Paul just after the spring semester had kicked off. Realistically, even had we moved in record time, April would have been the soonest we might have relocated, *tout ensemble*, to greater D.C. I didn't want to create that level of upheaval in my daughter's life. The children and I stayed in St. Paul full-time through the end of the spring and moved to Montgomery County, Maryland, just outside D.C., on the cusp of summer in 2005. I had never lived in the Mid-Atlantic region, but I knew it to be multicultural and ethnically diverse. I also knew that Montgomery County was home to a public school district that provided high-quality academic instruction.

There was this, too: even as I appreciated the comparatively relaxed attitude toward journalism that some of the Twin Cities journalists had managed to achieve, I wanted back into the thick of a competitive, high-profile media environment. I appreciated the way that Angela Davis, Duschesne Drew, and Rhoda Fukushima had found a balance of work and personal activities that suited them—but I longed to be back in the fray of an American city where journalists had to throw elbows to get stories. The nation's capital was the center of big-picture politics and policy, and it was chockablock with news organizations, including national bureaus of some of the companies I'd worked for in the past. And the *Washington Post*, of course, was a world-class newspaper that also happened to be home to scores of former *Miami Herald* reporters and editors. I wanted very much to return to journalism as a staff member somewhere.

I figured, *It is D.C.—how hard can it be to find a job?*

SEVEN

Washington, D.C.

Class and Color in the Eye of the Storm

The storm began brewing in the Atlantic Ocean near the Bahamas, and it had been gathering strength for almost a week before reaching its peak on August 28, 2005. Overnight, Hurricane Katrina weakened slightly, though its winds clocked in at 145 miles per hour by the time it wailed ashore on the United States' Gulf Coast on August 29. Armed with several days' advance notice as to the storm's severity—its winds had been estimated to reach as high as 175 miles per hour—government officials in Gulf counties had urged residents to take precautions, including safeguarding their homes and stocking up on supplies. Residents of coastal Louisiana and Mississippi, where experts estimated the storm would be most severe, were told to evacuate inland.

I watched the coverage of the growing storm and its eventual landfall from my home in Silver Spring, Maryland. At the time, it was not evident that what appeared to be a big "weather story" might also evolve into a massive story about race, class, and media. Early reporting of the approaching storm didn't focus on the potential fallout for people of color in the Gulf Coast region, and why should it? In the moment, even my finely attuned radar for catching racial subtexts—or lack thereof—in the coverage of big breaking news stories didn't anticipate the race and media storm that Katrina ultimately wrought. Satellite images of the swirling mass of extreme weather broadcast repeatedly on national news programs in the hours before Hurricane Katrina landed didn't immediately hint at the immense devastation it ultimately visited on the more vulnerable residents in the region.

There was no lack of pre-landfall coverage, but little of what aired detailed the demographic particulars of the region and its residents: pockets of economic prosperity (primarily the tourist centers in New Orleans and the Mississippi gambling centers) contrasted with large jurisdictions that are home to a multiethnic stew of residents living at or below the poverty level, attending broken-down schools and ill served by political leadership shot through with corruption and neglectful social policies. At the same time, there is only thin precedent for news organizations providing advance coverage of a big weather story that also factors in detailed population data.

Since at least 1992, when Hurricane Andrew destroyed swaths of Dade and Broward Counties in South Florida, most major news organizations have developed rote coverage plans for the onset of hurricane season. Broadcast outlets—television, radio, and online—typically produce reports of meteorologists' predictions, including satellite images of the white, tightly coiled clouds as they swirl above the Atlantic or Pacific. Print outlets also publish meteorologists' predictions, as well as helpful features on evacuation routes, tips for securing property, and public safety agency locations and resources. Usually the electronic media toss in generous doses of "B-roll," or stock footage, and print news outlets add anecdotal mini-profiles of residents preparing for the storm. A reliable image in advance of big storms shows residents lining up at local hardware stores and supermarkets while shelves are stripped clean of staples.

In late August 2005, as Katrina bore down on the Gulf Coast, the televised coverage in the hour before the storm landed also carried an image that was uniquely compelling—shots of long lines of vehicles traveling bumper-to-bumper along the Interstate 49 corridor as thousands of residents fled in advance of the storm. I watched some of the advance coverage but didn't connect the dots that might have led to key questions: What would happen to the residents who didn't own cars or couldn't afford the gas to flee on relatively short notice? What resources were available to the poor, the elderly, children, or the infirm who couldn't get out before the storm?

During the next forty-eight hours, as the first of more than fifty levees around New Orleans began to fail, Americans nationwide connected those dots—and what emerged was a vivid tableau of questionable work by some members of the press corps, shameful government incompetence, and senseless loss of life. Looking back at the immense library of Hurricane Katrina news and the political fallout in the storm's aftermath, it is easy to spot gaps and some cultural, class, and race bias in that early coverage. And it is not a stretch to identify the storm as President Bush's cultural-political Waterloo, the event that forever doomed his standing with millions of black and Latino voters and with moderates from both major political parties.

But in real time, the development of what would become the storm's prevailing narrative—public outrage at institutional failures —took place incrementally, a slow burn.

The Outrage Narrative can be divided into two pieces: the first and largest, the federal government's appallingly slow response to the storm; and the second, the media's coverage of Hurricane Katrina and its aftermath. The federal government's incompetence by now has been shorthanded to "Heckuva job, Brownie," President Bush's infamous "compliment" to the hapless Federal Emergency Management Agency chief, Michael D. Brown. Although hundreds had perished, and despite the millions of acres of water that flooded 80 percent of New Orleans in the days after Katrina's landfall, President Bush didn't manage to visit the area until September 2, almost a week after the storm had blown through.

Brown's agency, FEMA, had failed to set up appropriate evacuation centers in New Orleans or to effectively coordinate rescue and relief efforts with Louisiana state officials. (Brown claimed it was the responsibility of Louisiana's governor, Kathleen Babineaux Blanco, to set the terms for massive disaster relief—despite a prestorm briefing from top federal officials that Bush, Brown, and other key agency officials had received several days before the storm made landfall.)

President Bush stood on the tarmac at an Alabama airport during his first poststorm visit to the region, patted the back of his FEMA chief, and spoke those immortal words, "Brownie, you're doing a heckuva job." That gesture and that sentence—combined with earlier images of President Bush looking down at the Gulf Coast from aboard Air Force One as he flew from his family's home in Crawford, Texas, back to Washington, D.C., two days after the hurricane hit—crystallized in the minds of many Americans the idea that the president and his top Republican cabinet members were allowing New Orleans to drown.

In the first forty-eight hours, meanwhile, cable and network television reporters and anchors had managed to set down in the region. They included Geraldo Rivera and Shepard Smith from the right-leaning Fox News Channel, as well as Anderson Cooper of CNN and Brian Williams of *NBC Nightly News*, both practitioners of "objective" reporting. All three of those news organizations sent images to millions of viewers worldwide that showed heartbreaking, firsthand evidence of the storm's terrible human toll: hundreds of black New Orleans residents trapped atop roofs as fetid brown water swirled around them. Cooper and Rivera reported (rather theatrically) on residents in catastrophic conditions, their reports infused with heated language questioning why the federal government was leaving so many residents "stranded."

Within the first days after the storm, the Bush administration's slow response to the tragic plight of thousands of black and poor New Orleans residents who had been stranded by the floodwaters seemed to break open a well of suspicion that had been building in some Americans: President Bush, his top administration officials, and Republicans in Congress were not merely political conservatives determined to enact policies that negatively affected blacks, Latinos, and poor people, they were flat-out racists.

On the fifth day after the levees around New Orleans were breached, the *New York Times* and other national news organizations published reports describing scenes of rampant criminal activity inside the Superdome, including violent assaults and at least one alleged rape. (Local officials had urged residents who were unable to flee before the storm landed to seek shelter in the Superdome, a sports arena located in downtown New Orleans.) The subtext was implicit—thousands of residents (most of them black), abandoned by government and desperate for relief, had resorted to "savage" behavior. Weeks passed before the *Times* published another story that corrected some of those earlier claims of violent lawlessness in the Superdome; most other news organizations that had issued the original reports didn't bother to correct them.

I'm all too aware that in the hurly-burly of covering an immense, fast-changing story with obvious life-and-death developments, journalists can let go of ethical rules that ensure accurate, balanced reporting. And in the overwhelming cascade of heartbreaking developments that barreled forth, one after the other, in the first days after Katrina hit the Gulf Coast, I was far more upset by the federal government's incompetence and foot-dragging than by journalists' lapses of judgment. I too had struggled to keep loaded language and inappropriate characterizations out of my copy during the 1992 Los Angeles riots, and at least one of my editors at my home paper then, the *Fresno Bee*, had exercised poor judgment that sprang from his personal biases. Watching the Katrina tragedy unfold from the safety of my home nearly a thousand miles north, I was much more inclined to cut some slack for my colleagues in the news industry than for government officials.

Which is not to say that I viewed the journalists on the scene, or their editors at their home organizations, as being especially smart and sensitive in terms of picking up cultural nuances or reporting adequately on the demographic particulars of the region. But eventually the professional journalists—as distinct from the "citizen journalists" who also reported from the scene—noted the big-picture implications, and that is not to be diminished.

Here is one example of the manufactured language wars that broke out during the immediate aftermath, a scrape that distracted from the big-picture race and class outrage that journalists might have focused on earlier: on-site reporters from national and regional news outlets had taken to calling the storm victims "refugees." This seemingly innocuous word took on a politically loaded cast, at least in the view of some storm victims and civil rights activists, during the heated confusion.

"They are not refugees, they are American citizens," said Rev. Al Sharpton, a veteran New York civil rights activist, during an impromptu press conference at the Houston Astrodome, where hundreds of Louisiana and Mississippi evacuees were housed in the days after the storm. His comments, echoed by Rev. Jesse Jackson and dozens of evacuees in interviews, likely spurred President Bush to also acknowledge the baggage of "otherness" that the word "refugee" carried in that context.

In a September 6 interview with the Associated Press, President Bush said, "They are Americans, and they need the help, love, and compassion of our fellow citizens." By that time, though, the message frame portraying Bush and his cabinet members as being racially insensitive and neglectful of the needs of desperately displaced black and poor people had taken hold in the minds of many Americans. Within days of the storm, incompetence and a strong whiff of racially tinged neglect were twin motifs that had come to define the official federal response to the storm's aftermath.

It didn't help, either, that on Labor Day the president's mother, former First Lady Barbara Bush, visited evacuees at the Houston Astrodome and in the midst of hundreds of hot, traumatized, bedraggled storm victims crammed side by side on shaky cots, told a reporter from a public radio program that she believed the evacuees actually had it pretty good.

"Everyone is so overwhelmed by the hospitality. And so many of the people in the arena here, you know, were underprivileged anyway, so this, this is working very well for them," Barbara Bush told a journalist from American Public Media's *Marketplace*. Her comments were also recorded by someone with a cell phone camera, and the video quickly made its way onto YouTube and national news programs.

Technological innovations such as mobile phones with cameras and digital audio recorders made it possible for storm victims to become, in effect, instant "news producers" of their experience as it unfolded. The combination of amateur video and audio instantly uploaded from Gulf Coast residents and widespread access to thousands of websites by growing numbers of Americans nationwide made the aftermath of Hurricane Katrina the first major domestic natural disaster to be "covered" in real time.

At NBC headquarters in New York, network executives had hastily put together a broadcast of a live telethon to raise money for hurricane victims, with the Red Cross as the main charity. Between news updates of the dire conditions unfolding in New Orleans and elsewhere along the Gulf Coast, celebrities filled airtime with live appeals for viewers to phone in and make donations. A strange-bedfellows lineup of boldface names from Hollywood, Broadway, pop music, and professional sports teams appeared. The telethon had a ringing sense of urgency that distinguished it from traditional marathon charity appeal programs that have aired on American airwaves since 1966, when comedian Jerry Lewis first began broadcasting Labor Day weekend telethons to raise money to combat muscular dystrophy. The Katrina telethon represented an update of that model and had the distinctly twenty-first-century advantage of new broadcasting technologies that allowed the program's producers to cut seamlessly to artists in far-flung cities nationwide.

But an unscripted moment from rapper Kanye West brought unexpected notoriety to the telethon and was a sharp reminder that the race and economic status of many of the Katrina victims had heightened the sense of frustration that many viewers felt about the federal government's response. During an on-camera appeal with actor Mike Meyers, West went off script and gave a rambling, politicized commentary on how "poor people, poor and black people" had been abandoned in New Orleans. His comments were disjointed, but his passion and frustration fairly leaped through the camera. I didn't catch West's comments live, but like millions of Americans, I saw excerpts of it repeated time and again on cable and network news broadcasts in the days after it first aired. A clip of that segment available on YouTube—which had received 466,979 views by the time I pulled it up in the fall of 2009—shows West's comments in full:

> I hate the way they portray us in the media. If you see a black family, it says they're looting. See a white family, it says they're looking for food. And you know that it's been five days because most of the people are black. And even for me to complain about it, I would be a hypocrite because I've tried to turn away from the TV, because it's too hard to watch. I've even been shopping before I've even given a donation. So now I'm calling my business manager right now to see what is the biggest amount I can give, and just to imagine if I was down there, and those are my people down there. So anybody out there that wants to do anything that we can help with the set up . . . the way America is set up to help the poor, the black people, the less well-off as slow as possible. I mean,

the Red Cross is doing everything they can. We already realize a lot of people that could help are at war right now, fighting another way, and they have given them permission to go
down and shoot us. . . . George Bush doesn't care about black
people.

West caught hell from political conservatives for the last line of
the rambling soliloquy—"George Bush doesn't care about black people." Moderate and liberal commentators in the mainstream press
and the blogosphere agreed with West's assessment, even if they took
issue with the platform and the timing. But one comment he made
earlier within that rushed soliloquy—"If you see a black family, it
says they're looting. See a white family, it says they're looking for
food"—referred to another racial trope that had emerged within the
coverage and that few disputed. To a less obvious degree, the performance of journalists during Hurricane Katrina represents part two of
the Outrage Narrative that developed following the storm.

The use of language and images by the press came up for criticism from some news consumers (and even a few media professionals) within days of the flooding of New Orleans. For example, the
international photo group Agence France-Press (AFP) and the Associated Press had each moved hundreds of photographs of storm victims making their way around the drenched city in the days after the
levees broke, with many of the images accompanied by descriptive
captions. Dozens of the images showed unnamed residents waving
towels and clothing as they sought help, slogging through the brack-
ish water, or sitting forlornly alongside the Superdome. One AFP
photograph that posted on a popular site showed a twentysomething
white man and woman wading through high water, holding what
appeared to be loaves of bread and other grocery items above their
heads. The cutline on that photo read, "Two residents wade through
chest-deep water after finding bread and soda at a local grocery story
after Hurricane Katrina." An AP photo, by contrast, showed a twentysomething black man also up to his armpits in the dark water, also
holding what appeared to be grocery items over his head. But the
caption on that picture described the subject as having "looted"
the items.

Within days, a viewer at a photo-sharing site had noticed the disparate language and posted the photos side by side with a question: "Why is one considered 'looting,' but the other residents are carrying food they 'found'?" After Richard Prince, the race and media columnist at the Maynard Institute, posted a copy of the two photographs, the claims of bias in the photo agencies' coverage spread rapidly.

But as I viewed it, it was a wash (no pun intended). For one thing, AFP and AP did not coordinate the writing of photo captions, as they are two separate companies. And in a later interview, the AP editor who had written the "looting" cutline said he believed both subjects in the two separate photographs had likely found the grocery items. He couldn't account for why he selected the word "looted."

Granted, the author of the cutline beneath the image of the black man hadn't taken time to consider the potentially negative connotation of selecting the word "looted" to describe his subject's actions. He hadn't been on the scene, he hadn't snapped the image; he was in a remote station, working feverishly to move the photo on the AP's service.

Did the author of that "looting" caption harbor subconscious racial prejudices that spilled over during the high-pressure crunch of publishing Katrina photos quickly? Perhaps. But I am inclined to give him a pass—as I was not willing to do for the city editor at the *Fresno Bee* in the early 1990s, whose comments and behavior convinced me that he held racial opinions that negatively influenced his work on the LA riot stories. In the case of the AP photo editor during Hurricane Katrina, no one produced evidence demonstrating a pattern of earlier racial bias from him.

At the same time, it is valid and appropriate to question whether the accumulation of images that portrayed poor and black residents struggling in the aftermath of the storm as engaging in criminal behavior—whether at the Superdome or in commercial districts—contributed to long-standing public perceptions of poor and black Americans as inherently inferior and violence-prone human beings. Paradoxically, even as the majority of journalists from mainstream news organizations disseminated the idea that the federal government had failed thousands of Gulf Coast residents, possibly from race and class bias, the media coverage in total helped reinforce some centuries-old negative stereotypes about poor and ethnic minorities in America.

Michael Eric Dyson, the Georgetown theologian and cultural critic, observed in his book *Come Hell or High Water: Hurricane Katrina and the Color of Disaster*, published in 2006: "Reporters' anger at the government's tragic delay leaped off the allegedly neutral pages and television screens, even as the stories also reinforced stereotypes of black behavior in exaggerated reports of looting and social anarchy."

During the onset of Hurricane Katrina and its immediate aftermath, I was preoccupied with my e-mail in-box. On Sunday, August 28, 2005, the *Washington Post*'s Outlook section published an essay I'd written on the death of John H. Johnson, the longtime publisher of *Ebony* magazine. The premise of the essay was a simple but necessary question: Is *Ebony*—a glossy founded in the 1940s during the waning days of Jim Crow segregation and devoted to providing positive, uplifting stories and images of black American life—still relevant? The coincidence of that essay appearing when it did is laced with irony: while Hurricane Katrina swamped the Gulf Coast and New Orleans, creating a thoroughly twenty-first-century lens for looking at media coverage of people of color, I'd instigated a debate on the same question but centered around the fate of a venerable publication rooted in the twentieth century.

My e-mail address had been posted at the end of the essay, which had been given the headline "What's Not on My Coffee Table." By August 30, I'd received more than seventy responses from "regular people," academics, and colleagues in the news business. Most were thoughtful and centered on the possibility that the time had passed for a black general-interest magazine that focused only on the kind of "good news" that had defined *Ebony*'s editorial mission for the majority of its life. But some wrote to say that *Ebony* magazine remained relevant largely because "white" general-interest national magazines, such as the *New Yorker*, failed to devote significant space to topics concerning blacks and other ethnic minorities in the United States. It was not evident at the time, but Hurricane Katrina would spawn an entire new universe of publications devoted to filling that void.

Writers in the blogosphere produced the most pointed questioning of the mainstream media's coverage of Hurricane Katrina. While many individual journalists from print and electronic outlets performed heroically during that week, the body of coverage of the disaster by mainstream news organizations was jumbled and scattershot in terms of their ability to report accurately and sensitively on the unique ethnic mix and historic underpinning of New Orleans's economic stratification. At the same time, I of course recognize that reporting breaking news is a jump-to proposition, even in these technology-laden times. Its most expert practitioners are conditioned to provide the "first rough draft of history," as former *Washington Post* publisher Philip Graham said. Yet it is a constant source of frustration to me that as an institution, the American media do not appear to learn important lessons from recent history when it comes to covering some stories, particularly those involving people of color or other marginalized groups. Following Hurricane Andrew in 1992, the *Miami Herald* supplemented its "routine" coverage of the disaster with dozens of sidebars on how the region's more vulnerable populations—including the elderly and non-English-speaking immigrants—fared in the aftermath. Its editors also published Spanish-language editions, via *El Nuevo Herald* staffers, filled with helpful information on shelters and public safety agencies. The *Miami Herald*'s performance following Katrina, like that of the *Times-Picayune* of New Orleans and the *Sun Herald* of Biloxi, Mississippi, earned it invaluable goodwill from South Floridians in addition to a Pulitzer Prize. (In 2006, the Pulitzer for public service journalism was awarded to two newspapers, the *Times-Picayune* and the *Sun Herald*, for the first time since the prizes' 1917 inception.)

Yet in the immediate aftermath of Katrina, when it came to nailing down the race and class storyline, the traditional news organizations appeared slow off the dime compared with independent bloggers and "citizen journalists." Online publications (both established news sites and newbie blogs) captured early the race and class nuances and political implications of the federal government's bungling on those issues, as Richard Prince noted in a series of columns in September 2005. An independent blog, for example, first reported that thousands of Latino residents displaced by the storm were reluctant to seek help from officials in the Gulf Coast for fear of deportation. Journalists from the *Washington Post* and other leading "MSM" (mainstream media) news outlets found themselves following reporting by bloggers based in the Gulf cities, who filed minute-by-minute updates on the worsening conditions for hundreds of thousands of residents.

The possibility that the federal government's dismal response to the disaster may have been influenced by the race and class of many New Orleans residents was first identified and reported by nontraditional news outlets, including websites and blogs. Reporters and editors at mainstream outlets soon caught up, with a few writers also noting that some of their colleagues in media appeared to be asleep at the race and class switch.

An early voice sounding that metamedia note came from an unlikely place: the online magazine *Slate*.

I choose the word "unlikely" carefully, but it is entirely appropriate, as *Slate* is not well known for covering race and class topics regularly or in depth.

Since its inception in 1996, the online magazine has provided smart political and cultural reporting, witty commentary, and an innovative approach to covering politics and international news in an online format—from a decidedly upper-middle-class, white perspective. Its predominantly male stable of editors and writers is nearly all white. Before Katrina, *Slate*'s media critic, Jack Shafer, hadn't shown much inclination toward calling out major news organizations for poor coverage of ethnic groups or stories involving the poor.

While *Slate* is not known as a go-to publication for race and class coverage, there are exceptions, including a thoughtful piece in 1997 by writer-turned-editor Jacob Weisberg, "Not Just Talk." Weisberg argued that contemporary political debates around race in the United States missed an important factor. "The essence of the problem is the condition of the worst-off blacks in the urban ghetto," Weisberg wrote. His essay urged the Clinton administration to do more than offer lip service to fixing the income inequality that had, over decades, trapped generations of blacks in poverty and away from education, employment opportunities, and other blacks who had made gains in both those areas. But in the main, *Slate*'s from-on-high approach to race—a perch attenuated by the publication's veritable absence of black writers—was hypothetical and academic, not urgent.

Still, *Slate* is a pioneer, the first online publication with big ambitions of comprehensive, general-interest coverage in the mold of *Time* and *Newsweek*. By late summer 2005, it had broadened its normally narrow editorial eye to focus on the Outrage Narrative of the federal government's shameful post–Hurricane Katrina performance.

Although *Slate*'s predominantly white and relatively young staff fell far short of reflecting the ethnic diversity of the national population, or even of the journalism industry, its writers and editors knew a great story when it flooded vast portions of the Gulf Coast. So it is not counterintuitive that Jack Shafer, *Slate*'s prolific and usually glib media columnist, would be the first writer from an established— albeit nontraditional—news outlet to notice that something was missing from the national media's coverage during the first few days after the storm hit.

Published on August 31, 2005, Shafer's essay is headlined "Lost in the Flood." Its lead cuts right to the quick, and the piece includes a scathing indictment of the insular, risk-averse attitude on covering race and class that prevails in many major news organizations. "What accounts for the broadcasters' timidity? I saw only a couple of black faces anchoring but didn't see any black faces reporting from New Orleans. So, it's safe to assume that the reluctance to talk about race on the air was a mostly white thing," the *Slate* media critic concluded.

Five years after Hurricane Katrina, another major story involving people of color and a natural disaster raised similar issues about the media's ability to avoid promulgating negative racial stereotypes. On January 12, 2010, a massive earthquake shook Haiti, decimating buildings in and around the island's capital city, Port-au-Prince. Within days, relief workers and journalists from around the globe descended on the crumbled city, and heartbreaking scenes of death and grief began to flood the airwaves and television screens worldwide. More than a hundred thousand people had died, many of them crushed under tons of cement after poorly constructed buildings gave way. In short order, along with admirably comprehensive reporting on the grief, fear, and desperation that gripped survivors and aid workers, some news organizations fell into the same trap that had tripped them up in the wake of Hurricane Katrina: characterizing a community that had long struggled against poverty, crime, and education deficiencies as "hopeless."

In the case of Haiti—a nation with a rich history of both political rebellion and leadership failures dating back to the colonial 1700s—a narrative involving the question of whether the nation is "cursed" took hold. It was spurred by a politically conservative American televangelist, Pat Robertson, host of the Christian Broadcasting Network program *The 700 Club*. He went on the air a few days after the 7.0 temblor struck Haiti to say that the island and its people had long ago made a "pact with the devil" to win their freedom from France.

In the blogosphere and the mainstream media, commentators immediately protested. But the brush-fire nature of the Internet sent the insidious idea rocketing around message boards and chat rooms throughout the World Wide Web. And by January 18, after President Obama had pledged to send a hundred million dollars in aid to Haiti and thousands of volunteers and professional health-care workers had arrived in Port-au-Prince, some black writers back in the United States had begun to raise questions about the press's apparent eagerness to identify Haitians as "looters" and not simply as survivors of a massive natural disaster who were desperately seeking food and water in the rubble.

Writing in TheRoot.com, Natalie Hopkinson, an African American editor and author, questioned why some journalists appeared all too willing to frame Haiti and its besieged residents as an entity that could be shorthanded as "The Horror." A photograph that dominated the front page of the *New York Times* on the Sunday after the earthquake depicted a dark-skinned boy in a red shirt, holding a plastic bag that appeared to be heavy with goods, running away from men who seemed to be in pursuit. Elsewhere in that same edition of the *Times*, a story described a group of Haitian earthquake survivors who had caught a man stealing relief supplies, beat him severely, and then doused him with gasoline and set him afire.

Hopkinson wondered, in light of the "black people loot, white people find food" debate that had erupted in the aftermath of Hurricane Katrina, whether during the interim journalists had learned to recognize cultural nuances and to avoid engaging in negative stereotypes. What will it mean in the long run, Hopkinson asked, if news readers and viewers receive coverage from Haiti that overwhelmingly leaves them with an impression that the island's residents are incapable of compassion, strength, and fair play in the midst of an epic crisis? Did vivid photographs of Haitians in severe physical and emotional distress ultimately serve to desensitize readers to their plight? Were journalists' descriptions of Haitians fighting over scant supplies of food and water somehow dehumanizing the Haitian earthquake survivors in the eyes of American readers and viewers? Hopkinson wrote:

> But what is 100 percent true is that that awful scene [the beating of a man who had hoarded relief goods] had nothing to do with the child in the red shirt whose photo was snapped as food and supplies were being given away. In general, that photo conjures an image of black anarchy, aka The Horror.
>
> Maybe most telling when it comes to parallels between Katrina and the Haiti earthquake is the debate over what to call the displaced people. In the first days following Katrina, news outlets, big and small were calling the American citizens displaced by the hurricane "refugees."
>
> I was teaching journalism to university undergraduates at the time, and one of my students vigorously defended using the word refugee in that context. When pressed for a definition of "refugee," which Webster's called "a person who flees to a foreign country or power to escape danger or persecution," he held firm. "They are refugees. I watch CNN, I know what they look like."
>
> The confusion is worth remembering in the coming months and years, when there will be actual refugees com-

ing to the United States' shores [from Haiti]. They will be brown. They will poor. They will be desperate.

Whatever we call them, the media images of them will tell a truth of their own.

Hopkinson wisely used a Socratic approach to question whether journalists, however unintentionally, might be perpetuating negative cultural stereotypes by producing wrenching images of poor, dark-skinned people—in this case Haitians—suffering amid a devastated landscape. A journalist and academic, Hopkinson is an example of a less incendiary brand of hybrid media professional to emerge in the midst of the digital media revolution: a web-savvy writer and editor who adheres to the fundamental core standards of traditional journalism but who also understands that navigating roiling Internet publishing waters requires a strong knack for speed, buzz, and conversational tone. Hopkinson's ability to carefully, quickly process and deconstruct developing themes in media coverage of race- and class-related stories and to deliver thoughtful analysis in a high-profile online setting is unfortunately the exception, not the rule.

But in the big-picture context, I viewed the coverage of the 2010 disaster in Haiti as a vast improvement over coverage of Hurricane Katrina, especially in one particular aspect. Unlike in 2005, when bloggers and local journalists in New Orleans outperformed national news organizations from the moment the levees broke, major American news organizations mobilized large teams immediately following the earthquake in Haiti. From National Public Radio (NPR) to the *Washington Post* and the *New York Times*, "legacy" news organizations dug deep—despite suffering from tight editorial budgets and staffs depleted by layoffs and buyouts. Within two days after the massive earthquake in Haiti, dozens of teams from the venerable news organizations had landed in Haiti or the nearest jumping-off point, Miami, providing comprehensive coverage of the incredibly big, complex scene unfolding on the Caribbean island.

And while TheRoot.com's Hopkinson and a few other writers quickly produced essays and opinion pieces that effectively put journalists on notice about using appropriate language and imagery, I watched the majority of the coverage and found it compelling, fair, and overwhelmingly sensitive. The truth of the matter is that Haiti's long history of strife and hardship, and America's push-me, pull-you relationship with the nation's leaders for more than a century, had sensitized journalists to the unique challenges of covering Haiti and its people, even apart from a major natural disaster. American journalists had for decades reported from Haiti, or at least reported on a long string of tumultuous developments that wracked the nation, including hurricanes, presidential coups, botched elections, political upsets, and mass arrests. As I learned during my time at the *Miami Herald*, Haiti and its people represent a complicated history and untold promise—in short, a big ball of confusion for journalists who are not themselves Haitian. With exceptions, of course—including poor choices in placement of some stories involving Haitians seeking asylum in the United States during the early 1990s—major news organizations appear to have learned the right lessons over many years of covering the island.

Less clear, though, is the answer to the question of which journalists are more likely to receive industry recognition (in the form of major awards) for their work in Haiti. In my experience, journalists of color reporting from Haiti and elsewhere in the hemisphere are not as likely as white journalists to receive accolades from the official trade organizations for their work.

A former *Miami Herald* colleague, photojournalist Patrick Farrell, received a Pulitzer Prize in 2009 for images he captured following the four back-to-back hurricanes that swamped Haiti in 2008. When I learned of Farrell's award, I was both heartened and slightly disappointed. I knew Farrell to be a genius at his work—sensitive, smart, tough, and creative. Yet I also knew that Carl Juste, a Haitian American photojournalist also on staff at the *Miami Herald*, had been delivering top-quality work from the island for more than a decade, both in the pages of the *Herald* and in a side project he had developed in the mid-2000s, the Iris PhotoCollective.

Both men raced to Haiti in January 2010, following the major earthquake, and I scanned the pages of the *Miami Herald* over the next few days to find their work. The images they produced were expansive, intimate, and heartbreaking. Juste and Farrell, along with other *Herald* photographers, produced stunning work, not at all a

surprise. But I find it troubling and arbitrary that only one of them—
the white photographer—is known as a Pulitzer Prize winner, and for
images he made in Haiti. Similarly, it is worth asking why white journalists are routinely provided the space and time to excavate dormant
civil rights atrocities and turn them into rich, contemporary stories
that garner big industry awards for excellence, while black journalists
rarely receive such latitude.

Are white journalists more qualified to investigate racial injustice
than blacks or other journalists of color? Clearly there have been
exceptions over the years, including a stunning multipart series published by the *Washington Post* in the mid-1990s, "Rosa's Story," by
award-winning veteran reporter Leon Dash, who is African American. It outlined the hard-luck life of a black woman in a distressed
Washington, D.C., neighborhood and captured with unsentimental
clarity the contradictions and hardships of at least a tiny segment of
the underclass in the nation's urban regions. Dash, it must be said,
received heavy criticism from many black readers, who accused him
of being a "race traitor" and of exploiting a poor, undereducated
woman. But as I read "Rosa's Story," Dash merely honored the glo-
rious tradition of documentary journalism—observe, verify, report.
His story received a Pulitzer Prize for explanatory journalism in
1995, a vindication of sorts for the 1980 scandal around *Post* reporter
Janet Cooke, who had returned her Pulitzer Prize. But the freedom
that Dash enjoyed—he spent a year reporting and writing the week-
long series—was very much the exception in large and midsize newsrooms during the second half of the twentieth century. As I learned in
Fresno, when I attempted to fashion a full-time beat around covering
blacks in the Central Valley, journeyman reporters who are black or
Latino usually have to prove their ability to cover such beats objectively, while white journalists are thought by editors to inherently
possess the full range of qualifications necessary to cover low-income
communities or people of color.

The terrible earthquake that leveled Port-au-Prince in January
2010 gave my beleaguered colleagues a jolt of energy and credibility
after more than two years' worth of constant bad news for the traditional news organizations. In covering the Haiti disaster, the commu-

nity of American journalists from dailies and from network and cable broadcast news outlets acquitted themselves heroically, including participating in rescues of buried victims and aiding relief workers.

The usually unruly media watchers in the blogosphere mostly praised the coverage provided by journalists who had parachuted into Haiti. But after several days of watching CNN's swashbuckling anchor, Anderson Cooper, emoting on camera nightly from Port-au-Prince, some former journalists in my social media network complained that Cooper seemed to be crossing over into showboat territory. "CNN, let us see the real heroes, the people of Haiti who have lost everything and still remain standing," Tamara Kerrill Field, a former *Miami Herald* reporter, wrote on her Facebook profile one week after the Haiti earthquake. "Anderson Cooper, you will be taking a Calgon bath at home next week." Ten days after the quake, the Society of Professional Journalists posted a statement on its website, urging journalists who were covering the disaster in Haiti to avoid "putting themselves into the story."

But as I reviewed the majority of the mainstream media's coverage of the January 2010 earthquake in Haiti, notwithstanding a small number of photos that skirted the edges of exploitation, it appeared to me that important lessons had indeed been learned from Hurricane Katrina. Print and broadcast journalists, in the main, avoided using language that was patronizing or paternalistic. A mini-narrative emerged quickly in which journalists stateside and on the island debated the use of words such as "looting" and "refugees," a sign of self-awareness that had emerged far later in the coverage of Katrina.

Moreover, as a humanitarian, I would have been outraged if Cooper and some of the other high-profile broadcast journalists who went to Haiti had declined to help the quake victims. A favorable by-product of the collapse of the traditional economic underpinnings of mainstream media in the United States is that it has created the space for journalists to show their "human side." Time will tell whether this proves to be a favorable development for readers and viewers in the long run. I suspect that editors and producers will have to decide on a case-by-case basis how much first-person subjectivity they are willing to air or publish in a purely news framework, distinct from opinion airing. Left to their own devices, most reporters, correspondents, and anchors cannot resist the opportunity to inject themselves into a dramatic story. It remains an open question whether news consumers will accept such a personalized style of reporting, consistently, from a black or Latino journalist at a major news outlet.

EIGHT

Postracial News Blues

I identify Hurricane Katrina as the signal moment in the escalation of a media metanarrative that has spread like wildfire across the news industry since the early 2000s—a storyline in which news organizations, from major television networks to nascent online publications, obsessively chart the "decline" of traditional news outlets. While journalists and editors at traditional news organizations are preoccupied—however justifiably—with the future of the industry, a new crop of digital media practitioners is emerging; many of them are combining activism with journalistic practices and winning larger and larger online audiences. Some of them are blacks, Latinos, and other people of color who express frustration with the absence of focused, action-oriented coverage of ethnic or class issues in the mainstream press.

One person who said the lackluster government and press response to Katrina spurred him to take to the Internet is a young African American political activist on the West Coast, James Rucker. Like millions of other Americans, Rucker had been taking in the coverage of Katrina and experiencing a rising well of emotions—anger, despair, and frustration. But unlike most viewers, Rucker turned his outrage into Internet action. The result was ColorOfChange.org, a decidedly noncommercial online publication founded in the months after Hurricane Katrina as a fundraising and political action vehicle.

In the years since, ColorOfChange.org has led an online movement of politically active readers to engage in a number of social justice initiatives. The site's mission—encouraging readers to take action, sign petitions, and mount protests on a host of issues—is not exclusively race-based, Rucker told me when I phoned him in the summer of 2008. But the pressing existence of big gaps in education, employment, and equal opportunity that disproportionately affect blacks, Latinos, and poor people in America means that most of the site's actions involve topics of particular relevance to those groups.

It seems that Rucker's earlier involvement in a Democratic-leaning political online group, MoveOn.org, had primed him to position ColorOfChange.org as a major player in the fast-changing landscape of "new media" or "digital media" outlets. A graduate of Stanford University, Rucker is a twenty-first-century civil rights activist—politically savvy, technologically adept, and a keen observer of the fraught relationship between the press, the public, elected officials, and corporations. Merging the political and community organizing lessons he learned at MoveOn.org with his own knowledge of media outreach, he deploys ColorOfChange.org as a vehicle where socially conscious consumers can meet each other and get involved in political activism.

For instance, Rucker had an early victory with a social justice campaign involving a case known as "Jena Six." In December 2006, a group of six African American students were suspended from their high school in rural Jena, Louisiana, and arrested by local police officers following a fight with white students. After Rucker learned of the incident, he mounted an online campaign to protest the black youngsters' sentences.

Within months, thousands of online readers had signed a petition at ColorOfChange.org, demanding that the district attorney throw out or reduce the youths' sentences. The story of the Jena Six spread from an online grassroots movement to local civil rights groups and eventually caught the attention of local and national news organizations.

Three years later, in June 2009, the district attorney agreed to a plea bargain for the black teenagers, prodded by activists and citizens nationwide who argued that the white students who had also been involved in the schoolyard fight had received racially biased favorable treatment. The ColorOfChange.org website had raised nearly three hundred thousand dollars to support the black youths' legal defense and consistently posted updates about the case long after journalists from traditional news organizations had moved along to the next story.

Similarly, ColorOfChange.org continues to raise funds and push for policies to rebuild New Orleans's hardest-hit neighborhoods, including the Lower Ninth Ward, which was home to many of the town's poor black residents. While many mainstream media outlets, including CNN and the *New York Times*, produce regular coverage of the myriad ways that New Orleans residents and officials continue to struggle in the aftermath of Hurricane Katrina, ColorOfChange.org is virtually alone in consistently advocating for grassroots activism around economic, social, and political aspects of the rebuilding.

ColorOfChange.org has also mounted campaigns against disparate sentencing policies in drug cases, incendiary commentators at Fox News (including a talk show host named Glenn Beck), and numerous instances of dubious evidence leading to the jailing of black or poor people around the nation.

For Rucker, the website represents a natural progression of independent publishing opportunities made available by the Internet. It is an organic evolution of a feature that not so long ago was the sole province of opinion writers and the large news organizations where they worked: an easily accessible platform from which to champion social causes or condemn abuses of power.

ColorOfChange.org and dozens of other politically active quasi-news websites continue to gain readers domestically and around the globe, winning the loyalty of young Americans who seek political activism as much as they do "pure" news and information. They represent the next generation of news consumers, Americans born long after the journalistic heyday that followed the Watergate story and before the first Gulf War in 1991 ushered in an era of digital journalism; individuals who are tech-savvy, culturally sophisticated, and politically aware.

And these new consumers of news are not particularly concerned that they might be missing something important by shunning their parents' preferred news sources—the *New York Times*, *Ebony* magazine, NPR, the *Los Angeles Times*, *El Nuevo Herald*, or *NBC Nightly News*. What they want, in addition to direct political action, is a way to interact with and critique those who cover and produce news and information at traditional news outlets. Activism, whether of the political, environmental, or social justice variety, is the prism through which news is viewed; websites and blogs that cover topics of interest to this "millennial" demographic gain traction by being advocates and conduits for fundraising and volunteer opportunities.

Young black Americans seeking news, information, and political consciousness raising look to independent websites and blogs such as *Jack & Jill Politics*, *What About Our Daughters*, Blackpower.com, and a slew of others that began publishing in the late 2000s. The sites provide a community built on shared interests, and regular site visitors do not seem to care that no "real journalists" are producing the blog posts or selecting which topics will be covered. For journalists of color—many of whom have surmounted incredible obstacles on the path to gaining the technical and "soft" skills required to make them viable in traditional news organizations—it is painful to watch as increasing numbers of young adults choose these online properties as their primary news sources. And a big part of that pain derives from the dawning knowledge that few web-only publications are capable of providing salaries, health benefits, and the institutional support of the legacy news organizations that are vanishing by the day.

At this point it is nearly impossible to nail down accurate numbers for precisely how many journalists of color who lost their jobs at legacy media organizations have found commensurate positions in the new frontier of digital media. But anecdotally, it is safe to say the answer is "not many."

In 2008, while a fellow at the Nation Institute, I investigated the question of how the shifting sands in mainstream media were affecting journalists of color. In the context of two competing trade conventions for media professionals of color, I plumbed both sides of what is emerging as an intriguing and possibly mutually destructive divide. On one side is the legacy group—Unity: Journalists of Color—which represents thousands of black, Latino, Asian, and Native American media workers and gathers every four years in cities around the nation. On the other is the nascent trade organization for bloggers and online media professionals, Blogging While Brown, a loose confederation of online practitioners that was founded in 2007 by Gina McCauley, an African American lawyer and blogger from

Austin, Texas, who also created the *What About Our Daughters* blog. As it happened, both Unity and Blogging While Brown had scheduled their conferences during the same July week in 2008.

I had already arranged to attend the Unity convention in Chicago, but before I went, I reported and wrote a piece detailing the itinerary and mission of both conferences, to be published in the *Nation* the week that the two groups met. In reporting the story, I sought out leaders from both organizations and quizzed them on their best assessments of what the evolution in media and journalism meant, both for journalists of color and for readers and viewers interested in coverage of historically marginalized communities and related topics.

The result revealed wariness on both sides, but also a faint recognition of shared goal and needs. Both the newbie online activists and the legacy journalists of color agreed that the time had arrived for collaboration and sharing of best practices and technical expertise. In contrast to the fast-growing clique of digital media gurus led by Jeff Jarvis and Dan Gillmor—a clique that employed a chastising, scolding tone toward legacy media organizations when prognosticating the future of the news industry—no one connected to Blogging While Brown shared ill feelings toward their legacy media counterparts, the thousands of black, Latino, and Asian journalists struggling to find stability in the uncertain terrain. Moreover, McCauley told me she had formed Blogging While Brown, in part, out of growing concern that blacks and other people of color who were attempting to establish online publications had experienced a degree of exclusion from the leading news, information, and activism blogs and websites—*Daily Kos*, *Talking Points Memo* and the *Huffington Post*. To McCauley, the same protectionist instinct that helped lead to the founding of the NABJ in the 1970s led her to form Blogging While Brown.

My reporting also revealed another interesting wrinkle: I was not alone in harboring a degree of reluctance to plunge headlong into blogging. At the Unity convention, I took an informal poll of some of my friends and colleagues—experienced journalists from traditional news organizations—who were there: Why didn't they attend the Blogging While Brown conference?

"Maybe next year I will," said Claudia Perry, an African American writer and editor at the *Star-Ledger* in Newark. A year later, Perry took a buyout from the *Star-Ledger*, where she had worked for nearly a decade. She did not attend the 2009 Blogging While Brown conference. But Perry did take classes elsewhere in HTML coding, and by late 2009 she had designed and published her own blog, *Chronic Negress*, in part as a calling card to prospective employers. As of the fall of 2010, though, Perry had not landed at a news organization (web, print, or combined) that offered a salary anywhere close to what she had earned at the *Star-Ledger*.

When I talked to them for the *Nation* article and at the Unity convention, Perry and other colleagues from legacy news organizations expressed a high degree of trepidation about writing their own blogs (publishing without an editor) and writing for relatively new online sites, such as *What About Our Daughters* or even TheRoot .com, the comparatively polished online journal under the ownership of the Washington Post Company. In addition to citing the low pay for writing at online sites, some of my colleagues said they chafed at the overt advocacy that permeated most web-only publications.

Ironic, right?

Because most of us had learned to carry any agendas lightly, we old-school journalists of color still felt uncomfortable at the prospect of completely "coming out" with any crusades, whether in print or via online sites. This reluctance, in my view, is the inevitable result— a form of battle scars—of having worked in mainstream news organizations, where black journalists were often penalized for betraying any hint of an agenda when covering race or class issues.

As I outlined it in the *Nation* article, those twin realities—the comparatively low pay at online sites and the blatant advocacy that permeates much of the blogosphere—are figuring into the slow rate of participation in web-only publications by some experienced black journalists. Those two points are significant, but do not represent the whole story of why so few talented, qualified journalists of color are finding new homes in paying jobs in the online world.

Nevertheless, like Perry, many veteran journalists of color are taking steps to enter the expanding online publishing universe, however tentatively, largely out of a sense of self-preservation.

I too made a slow but steady conversion from a writer and editor for hire to self-publishing on the web. In May 2009, I launched my own website and online column, *Amy Alexander Community Forum*. I did it for two primary reasons: to demonstrate a grasp of digital publishing and to give myself an online "brand identity." In the process, I had to learn to get over the impulse to hide behind objectivity and the veneer of a "legit" news organization. It was a large but not entirely unpleasant leap; after all, I had written op-ed essays for major news publications and online journals such as *Africana* and the online edition of the *Nation* for more than a decade. I do laugh, somewhat ruefully, when I consider that after so many years as a paid staff writer or contributor, I write at my website for free! I had no business plan in launching *Community Forum* and do not take advertising on the site. I console myself by knowing that despite the widening pool of studies, surveys, and marketing metrics produced by technology and so-called digital media experts, no one really knows how much weight consumers place on the individual journalists' "brand identities" that now crowd the World Wide Web.

At the same time, a 2008 study by the Pew Research Center's Internet and American Life Project found that the growing connection between online use and civic engagement appears to be strongest among affluent Americans, whatever their race or ethnicity. The Pew report's author concluded, "Just as in offline civic life, the well-to-do and well-educated are more likely than those less well off to participate in online political activities such as emailing a government official, signing an online petition or making a political contribution."

Notwithstanding the scores of websites that are owned and operated by people of color, the Pew study's finding raises profound questions about a subtext of the digital media revolution and its ability to draw and lock in significant numbers of people of color in the United States. If blacks, Latinos, low-income families, and other historically marginalized groups find the twenty-first-century media landscape just as exclusionary as the twentieth-century version, what will the future of mass-market online publications look like? Who will be served by online media—both the multimedia versions of legacy news organizations and the newbie activist-oriented websites?

Closer to home for me are these questions: Will owners and

proprietors of twenty-first-century digital publications see the hiring and retention of news producers of color as a top priority? Can entrepreneurial blacks, Latinos, Asians, and other ethnic minorities who are publishing online news or commentary sites build them into full-service news organizations? Will legacy media companies such as NBC (in its new partnership with Comcast) and the Washington Post Company—both of which mounted online web magazines covering African American topics in the late 2000s—continue to financially support their race-specific properties if those properties fail to turn a profit?

And given the increasingly fragmented landscape of specialty publications that are cropping up online, where can Americans of different ethnicities and class levels find accurate, meaningful information that will help them reach common ground on urgent topics? Or will the nichification of "mass" media in digital form—on computer screens, mobile devices, and television boxes that receive content via the Internet—draw us farther away from reaching racial understanding even while our population becomes majority-minority (that is, mostly nonwhite)?

By 2009, five years after Hurricane Katrina, the American media landscape had changed nearly as dramatically as the flood-ravaged geography of New Orleans. But instead of the quaint nineteenth-century bungalows that once dotted the Ninth Ward, the graveyard of American media is strewn with companies whose names once exemplified the high ideals of the contemporary Fourth Estate, even as they also carried the whiff of the nineteenth-century heyday of American newspapers. The *Seattle Post-Intelligencer* ceased print operation in 2009, converting to an online publication that primarily consisted of aggregated news from other outlets and brief local news reports. The *Rocky Mountain News* closed down altogether, while the *Tucson Citizen* also went to an online-only format. All three dailies had published continuously for more than a century.

Moreover, in cities where big regional dailies had once aspired to national and international coverage as recently as the late 1980s—Miami, Boston, Detroit, and Los Angeles—papers were barely hanging on by the end of 2010. Such former regional powerhouses as the

Miami Herald, the *Boston Globe,* and the *Detroit Free Press* had to admit by the mid-2000s that their earlier cost-cutting measures—including closing domestic and foreign bureaus, offering employee buyouts, and consolidating printing operations—had failed to offset severe revenue declines. By the end of 2008, these and many other daily papers nationwide began taking a step that had been unthinkable in the early 1990s: laying off editorial workers.

Nationwide, between June and December 2007 some 2,112 newspaper personnel were laid off, including workers in editorial, advertising, and "back-shop" departments like printing and circulation, according to data compiled by Erica Davis, author of the Paper Cuts website. A multimedia and graphics designer at the *St. Louis Post Dispatch,* Davis launched Paper Cuts in April 2008 after reading a special report in a May edition of *Editor & Publisher,* the print news industry trade publication. The article described the acceleration of job losses in newspapers nationwide.

A digital map of the United States featured on Paper Cuts shows a vivid illustration of the carnage. From Texas to Seattle to New England, South Florida, and Illinois, brightly colored "balloons" are affixed to cities where newspapers have made significant staff cuts. The entire map of the continental United States is almost blanketed with them.

For writers, editors, and photographers who had survived earlier cuts and downsizings, the editorial layoffs were deeply traumatic. The downsizing disproportionately affected journalists of color at these news organizations. At the risk of playing the unhelpful game of "who is the biggest victim," I believe that journalists of color experienced the decline of the mainstream media job market more acutely than did the larger demographic of print journalists. For starters, major newsrooms have historically employed disproportionately fewer journalists of color than whites. Data compiled by ASNE for 2007–08 showed a slight decline in the percentage of journalists at mainstream print news organizations who were black, Latino, or Asian, from 13.5 to 13.4 percent during that year, or a total decline of around 300 full-time newsroom personnel. The percentage of supervisory positions held by journalists of color also declined during that same time frame, from 11.4 percent in 2007 to 11.2 percent in 2008. Missing from the ASNE survey and other industry census accountings of the downturn is how the loss of "soft skills"—the interpersonal, "meet-and-deal" capabilities that come to reporters, editors, and photographers only after years on the job—will reshape news gathering within legacy media organizations.

On topics of race and class, especially within politics, education, and criminal justice, it has historically been journalists of color who provided necessary impetus, perspective, and checks and balances to coverage. Without those checks and balances, effective, accurate coverage of marginalized populations in America and abroad will suffer. And so far, the new publications emerging as web-only entities are not capable of supporting large editorial staffs that include significant numbers of journalists of color.

My accounting of job losses for journalists of color and all editorial media professionals across the industry is not exhaustive. By the end of 2009, closures, cuts, and layoffs continued, pointing toward a massive downshift in how news organizations staff their editorial departments. Debates on the efficacy of a range of new economic models heated up. Should legacy news organizations like the *New York Times* begin charging for access to their online daily newspapers? If so, what is the appropriate amount to charge? Would customers refuse to pay any amount? The *Wall Street Journal*, with a high-income readership, had erected a "pay wall" around much of its online content during the mid-1990s, well before most other daily newspapers, and had not suffered drastic drop-offs in readers. By the end of the decade of the 2000s, the consensus among all segments of the industry—including editorial big thinkers at traditional news organizations, tech companies, media marketing outfits, and brand new digital media companies such as Blue State Digital—was that news organizations would have to learn to live with lower profits, run tighter operations from beginning to end, and lose the costly overhead elements of their businesses, including printed products, delivery systems for the printed products (trucks, bundlers, and local distributors), and large staffs of reporters, editors, and newsroom support workers. Everyone seemed to agree that "editorial integrity" should not be compromised as the massive downturn continued.

Yet for all the self-examination that gripped journalists by the end of the decade, only a handful of media watchers framed the soul-searching in the context of journalists of color and audiences of color.

Amid a sea of words in trade journals, at media programs in colleges and universities, and in the pages of the surviving dailies by the close of 2009, a tone of doom and gloom prevailed. It derived in large part from the seemingly bottomless trajectory of the downsizing. While everybody had an opinion about what led to the drop in revenue and readership at legacy news organizations, few dared to suggest that the mainstream media's historic inability to focus on minorities might have played a role in the downturn as ethnic communities nationwide expanded. I viewed this obtuseness as an unfortunate, if predictable and natural, outcome. Few journalists of color had been assigned "media beats" during the late twentieth century, so it followed that those who tracked the decline of their own industry from perches at marquee traditional outlets were not inclined to consider the race and class implications.

There were exceptions. By the late 2000s, as the blogosphere grew from a sidekick into a primary provider of daily news for millions of Americans, signs began to emerge that the loss of "institutional memory" from newsrooms would be especially problematic in terms of how people of color and historically marginalized communities are covered. At the turn of the twenty-first century, Richard Prince at the Maynard Institute, along with my column at *Africana*, raised questions about how the digital revolution would impact coverage of blacks, Latinos, and other ethnic groups. Instinctively, we two picked up where Pamela Newkirk, the New York University journalism professor, had left off in her seminal examination of blacks and mainstream media, *Within the Veil*, published in 2000. In that book, Newkirk unpacked the nineteenth- and twentieth-century history of the black press and the slow integration of mainstream American newsrooms. She closed her examination with prescient questions about whether journalists of color would find solid footing in the nascent Internet marketplace.

By 2005 (when my column was shut down by AOL), Prince and I, along with a handful of other journalists and bloggers of color, had noticed signs that Newkirk's closing question—what would the Internet mean for journalists of color?—had somewhat understandably failed to anticipate another wrinkle. Within legacy news organizations, the rise in employment of young media professionals who had mastered the emerging digital gadgetry but not the fundamentals of sound journalism had created a troubling gap in the quality of coverage across the board.

As news organizations nationwide searched desperately for cost savings, many editorial leaders shed senior journalists whose salaries and pensions were thought to be "too high" and replaced them with novice, multimedia-savvy younger journalists who happily accepted lower pay. Newspaper unions, too, had been weakened significantly during the downturn, their leadership forced to ask editorial employees to make increasingly Solomon-like choices: take a salary cut or see your newspaper close. The pay scales that guilds had hammered out over the previous fifty years, as newspaper ownership became corporatized, fell away quickly once revenues deteriorated.

We old-school media watchers of color couldn't, in a sense, identify whether the more troubling gaps were of a generational or a cultural and race-specific variety. But as the 2000s rolled on, it became increasingly evident that news organizations struggling to trim costs had begun to hire young, inexperienced editorial workers who lacked solid journalistic skills but who came with an abundance of digital and web savvy that made them irresistible. That few of the newcomers were American-born ethnic minorities—distinct from the South Asian budding multimedia stars who seemed to pop up virtually overnight in American newsrooms—raised uncomfortable questions about the future of diversity in news organizations.

By the end of the 2000s, in newsrooms from New England to San Diego, journeyman and veteran journalists of every ethnicity were disappearing, replaced by bright-eyed youngsters who knew how to blog and edit and upload videos but who could not wheedle an important street address from a police precinct desk sergeant, finesse a school board president into disclosing sensitive budget deliberations, or wade into a crowd of street protestors and emerge with pungent, accurate, relevant quotes if their lives depended on it.

I tried to keep an open mind. But it was impossible not to suspect that the trend would result in weakened coverage of communities and topics that had long been the stepchildren—present, but often

overlooked—at many mainstream newspapers and broadcast outlets. Although in the "real world" young people showed encouraging
signs of being more comfortable with interracial contact than at any
time in American history, in news organizations tribalism carried the
day, even among new recruits.

The hints of peril were evident, by the mid-2000s, in coverage
of race and class issues by many traditional and some online publications. Embarrassing examples of boneheaded mistakes, miscalcula-
tions, and misguided editing of stories concerning people of color
or race-related topics piled up rapidly as senior journalists (including copy editors, the last line of quality control in newspapers and
magazines) fell by the wayside. At the same time, it is fair to say that
a reporter's or editor's age, time in service, or skin color does not
always guarantee that cultural nuances will be observed in coverage.
Nor will they automatically forestall mistakes from being published.
In terms of distribution of labor in the newsrooms that remain, the
question of whether workers are black, white, old, or young can be
beside the point: it is unlikely that smart, experienced reporters and
editors—or young, energetic neophytes—can successfully avoid
dumb mistakes when they are consistently asked to perform several
jobs for longer hours with fewer backstops. But this is the new reality
in most American news organizations.

Moreover, the deep cuts to many newspapers' editorial staff budgets had the collateral effect of demoralizing some of the journalists
of color who had survived buyouts. (And to be sure, it demoralized
plenty of those who remained, whatever their skin color or ethnicity.) In 2008 Ju-Don Roberts, an African American who had helped
develop the *Washington Post's* online edition and was one of the site's
top editors, left the *Post* to become executive editor of Beliefnet, a
spirituality and values-oriented website. The *Post's* online property
had become something of a political football as the paper's editorial leaders struggled to come up with a realistic balance for how resources would be allocated between the printed paper and the online
Post. Roberts's departure left the *Post's* online property without any
top editors of color.

And Jose Antonio Vargas, an up-and-coming *Post* reporter who
had gained attention by covering political bloggers, "millennial" ac-

tivists, and the high rate of HIV diagnoses among D.C. residents, jumped to the *Huffington Post*, becoming its technology editor. Vargas, who is from California, said at the time that he wanted to work for a media company that viewed the promise of the Internet the same way that he did. "Technology is anthropology," Vargas said.

Other journalists of color from the diminishing ranks of legacy organizations made note of Roberts's and Vargas's decisions to leave traditional media for the untested terrain of online-only publications. Neither Vargas nor Roberts nor editors at the online outlets where they headed disclosed the former *Post* employees' new salaries. But their decisions to take the leap were intriguing: they signaled that the journalists were likely going to earn salaries at the online outlets that, at the very least, were close enough to what they had been earning at the *Post* to make them feel comfortable.

Beginning in the fall of 2005, with the publication of my essay in the *Post*'s Outlook section on *Ebony* magazine and the fate of black-oriented print magazines, I began getting regular pickup work at news organizations in Washington. This was made possible by what I think of as a postmodern cohort to the classic old boys' network: after a decade spent working in daily newspapers, I belonged to a middle-aged black women's network that I was grateful to draw from.

By early 2006 my marriage had ended, and I suddenly faced the prospect of searching for full-time work just as the economic downturn, which for the news business had been a twenty-year steady drip, accelerated to a torrent.

One of the first people I contacted when I launched my search for work in D.C. was a Baltimore native and veteran female journalist. Since the late 1980s, Farai Chideya has worked at several national news outlets, including *Newsweek* and CNN. She is as smart a journalist as you are likely to meet. She is also a big believer in ongoing training, having come of age in mainstream, legacy news organizations (where she acquired the fundamentals of shoe-leather research, reporting, writing, and fact checking) just as digital technology was gaining ground. Chideya is also a digital media wunderkind; she founded an online news and commentary site, *Pop & Politics*, way back in the day—1996, the same year that *Slate* was born. Between the mid-1990s and the late 2000s, Chideya also wrote nonfiction books on race and media, politics, and citizen activism in the United States; in 2009 she published a novel, further extending her bona fides as a multimedia, multigenre practitioner.

Well before it became a cliché for journalists to apply the phrase to their professional reputations, Farai Chideya established her name as a brand in mass media. In the parlance of the white male digital media gurus who have lately come to dominate discussions about the future of journalism, Chideya had mastered the tricky art of "entrepreneurial journalism." And she did it long before the mid-2000s, when that idea took hold in the think tanks and J-school programs where white male digital media evangelists like Jeff Jarvis and Dan Gillmor churned out papers and blog posts chiding old-school journalists and old-line news organizations for failing to reinvent themselves as multimedia multitaskers.

When I first met Chideya, in the late 1990s, she was a correspondent at ABC News in New York and a contributing editor at *Vibe* magazine, the "hip-hop bible." She is also a graduate of Harvard. That affiliation likely accrued in her favor as Chideya began making her way in national news organizations, where many top producing and editing chairs are filled by Ivy League graduates.

And yet none of that—not her sparkling personality, her genuine and compassionate outlook on life, her rigorous, expansive intellect, highly tuned journalistic skills, or vast network of big-time contacts in media and the academy—kept Chideya from losing a high-profile journalism job in the late 2000s.

So much for the stubborn myth that persisted among some white male journalists I worked with during the 1980s and '90s: news organizations were thought to be politically correct and obsessed with affirmative action policies that "unfairly" protected blacks, women, and other non-white-male journalists.

Late in 2008, Chideya lost her job after the news program she had hosted for almost three years, National Public Radio's *News & Notes*, was canceled. Like other journalists of color in my network, I felt the loss of that program acutely. Its cancellation was not unexpected, though the timing stunk: NPR announced the closing of *News & Notes* not long after Barack Obama was elected president.

Worse, editorial leaders at NPR's main office decided, mere days before Obama's historic inauguration, that they would not pay to send any *News & Notes* staffers to the District to cover the event. (The program was produced at NPR's West Coast operation in Culver City, California.)

For Chideya, that decision was incomprehensible—and it led her to leave the program before it had officially ceased production. Watching these unhappy developments from a distance—and having worked at NPR myself for several months on the launch team of another "multicultural" talk program, *Tell Me More*—I shared Chideya's sadness and frustration. If NPR, a well-funded leading news organization with a reputation (deserved or not) for producing liberal-leaning coverage, could not support a daily program aimed at "nontraditional"—a.k.a. minority—audiences, who could?

NPR is supported by a combination of public donations, funding from member stations (which is also public donation money), some government assistance (through the Corporation for Public Broadcasting), private corporate donations, and support from the likes of the Knight Foundation and other big nonprofits. It was not immune to the downturn of the economy that accelerated late in 2007. NPR is also not immune to a cultural blind spot that is common in some large American news organizations. It is a myopia that allows CEOs, publishers, and top newsroom leaders to cut staff and projects aimed at audiences of color in spite of the increasing numbers of ethnic people living in the United States.

Chideya, adept at the internecine personal politics within the news industry, at first said very little in public about the closure of *News & Notes*. Other voices lamented its passing in public, primarily in the comments section at Richard Prince's online column, "Journal-isms." Prince, the Jack Webb of race and media issues, also noted that the shuttering of NPR's *News & Notes* had taken place barely three years after the company stopped airing its only earlier black-oriented national talk program, *The Tavis Smiley Show*.

In 2003 NPR had formed an alliance with the African American Public Radio Consortium (AAPRC), a collection of stations at historically black colleges and universities located in the Mid-Atlantic, Southeast, and Southwest regions of the United States. The goal of the alliance was to draw on the editorial and technical expertise and financial resources of NPR in order to develop high-quality news and information programming aimed at black listeners. The first host of a program birthed by this partnership was Tavis Smiley, a former host at Black Entertainment Television and a regular contributor to a popular black commercial radio talk show, *The Tom Joyner Morning Show*.

Smiley had been named host of the inaugural collaborative program between NPR and the AAPRC at the urging of some top officials within the consortium. Smiley's program had all the hallmarks of any nationally syndicated NPR news and information show: expertly produced interviews with guests from the top tiers of national politics, education, and entertainment discussing the issues of the day during an hour-long program. However, when Smiley's contract came up for renewal in 2004, a fissure was revealed: Smiley said he wanted NPR to spend more money to promote and market *The Tavis Smiley Show*, while NPR officials said they spent as much to market the program as they did on any other nationally syndicated program—that is, very little.

In the end, Tavis Smiley walked away from his show at NPR. He later gave an interview to an online publication in which he accused NPR of "not being serious" about mounting programs that appeal to black listeners. It was a messy, unfortunate public breakup. At the time, I believed that both Smiley and NPR had probably somehow failed to keep the bigger picture—building and keeping audiences among people of color—as the top priority.

For his part, Smiley did return to public radio a few years later, on Public Radio International (PRI), a smaller, publicly funded and corporate-underwritten network that produces high-quality programming. (Although PRI's programs air on some NPR stations, it does not have a long string of top-rated affiliate stations, such as WBEZ in Chicago and KQED in San Francisco. As a result, the programs produced by PRI are heard on far fewer stations than programs produced by NPR itself.)

When I profiled Smiley for the *Nation* in the fall of 2006, I mentioned his unhappy departure from NPR. But I played it straight down the middle, outlining his and the network's positions without their comment, since neither Smiley nor anyone at NPR would speak any further on the record about what had taken place. I did, though, raise a larger question about how much NPR was willing to commit to investing in multicultural programming over the long haul.

By the end of the decade, Smiley had emerged as a high-profile, self-described "journalist-activist." He hosted not only a weekly program for PRI but a nightly half-hour television talk show based at KCET in Los Angeles and syndicated in PBS markets nationwide. He had authored several books on his own life and on civic and political engagement for black Americans. And he had mounted a series of annual summits called "State of the Black Union" in cities coast to coast, drawing top academics, politicians, writers, and activists to lengthy discussion panels aimed at examining class and race issues and helping black Americans chart a positive path.

Yet however messy and painful Smiley's departure from NPR may have been for him or the network, it didn't deter the AAPRC. Its putative leader, Loretta Rucker, told me in the spring of 2007 that the end of NPR's relationship with Tavis Smiley had been a "learning experience," both for the network and for Smiley. The entire situation raised important questions about NPR's ability to turn the corner from programming aimed squarely at well-educated middle-class listeners in urban regions—the network's focus since its inception in the early 1970s—to programming that also appeals to "nontraditional" audiences: people of color, rural residents, and audiences that are not necessarily earning six figures, or even five figures.

Rucker and the other representatives of the AAPRC did not give up on NPR, though. She told the network executives that the station managers she represented still hungered for smart, well-reported news and information of the kind produced at NPR—and that it would be to their benefit, in the long run, to continue producing programming that suited the audiences within the consortium's markets, since NPR's own market research showed that older, loyal listeners—and donors—were not being replaced by large numbers of new listeners (and potential donors).

News & Notes was born from the remnants of Tavis Smiley's NPR program and began airing in 2005 on a handful of affiliate stations. (By contrast, NPR's oldest and most popular daily news programs,

All Things Considered and *Morning Edition*, air on several hundred public radio stations nationwide.) The first host of *News & Notes* was veteran television broadcaster Ed Gordon, an erudite news anchor who had worked at *NBC Nightly News* and other national outlets. Farai Chideya was the program's top correspondent and occasional fill-in host. After Gordon left the program in 2006, citing logistical matters (he lived in New York to be near his young daughter, but the program was produced in Los Angeles and Washington, D.C.), Chideya became the full-time host of *News & Notes*.

In 2005, at Chideya's suggestion, I began writing and recording on-air commentaries on the program. (This is an example of how the old boys' network looks when modified for black women journalists.) Not long after I relocated from Minnesota to suburban Washington, D.C., I had contacted Chideya to sound her out about work prospects in the region. In response, Chideya suggested to her producer colleagues at NPR that with regular commentaries—what amount to op-ed essays—I might bring a degree of depth and perspective to round out the interviews and reports that were the bread and butter of the *News & Notes* editorial content. I was about to learn to repurpose the skills I'd developed writing op-eds and race and media opinion columns into commentaries for air at NPR.

On my first visit to the network's headquarters in Washington, D.C., in September 2005, I was slightly nervous but confident in my ability to read aloud the inaugural essay that I'd written and submitted to a *News & Notes* producer via e-mail. I wasn't especially concerned about translating my writing style to a radio essay, in large part because Chideya had talked me through the most important basic steps—follow the format of an op-ed piece; make your ideas clear, logical, and compelling; keep it brief; then read the essay aloud to see if it comes in at roughly three minutes in length. Plus I had studied theater arts in high school and college, and I had listened to enough NPR programming over the years (reports, interviews and commentaries) to have a good idea of what was required.

That first essay aired on *News & Notes* in mid-September, a few weeks after Hurricane Katrina upended the Gulf Coast. Its focus was on the possibility that funds for disaster relief and economic recovery might not be equally distributed, with poor and black residents coming up short. Drawing on what I had witnessed during the aftermath of the Loma Prieta earthquake in Northern California in 1989—when middle-class neighborhoods in San Francisco were inundated with relief supplies and resources, while poorer communities received less—I encouraged journalists covering the aftermath of Katrina to keep a close eye on the disbursement of relief money and other resources.

That essay led to another, and many more over the next several months. The essays didn't pay much—$250 each—but combined with frequent book reviews and the occasional essay for the *Washington Post*, I was at least earning some income and getting to know the media landscape in the District.

Indeed, the first essay that I published in the *Post*, on *Ebony* magazine, resulted in a connection that surprised me: an e-mail from Michel Martin, an ABC News correspondent based in Washington. She wrote that she'd appreciated my discussion of *Ebony* and the fate of black, mass-market print magazines. I replied that I admired her work at *Nightline*, where she had delivered interesting reports on a range of topics for more than a decade. We stayed in touch, and in November 2005 we met for lunch.

At that time, Martin asked whether I might be interested in working with her at some point in the near future; she was cagey, but hinted that she might be leaving ABC for NPR. As we sat in the swank dining room of a downtown D.C. restaurant, Georgia Brown's, she seemed pretty confident that it would happen. I told her that I absolutely wanted to be involved.

Michel is a native New Yorker, the daughter of working-class parents; she is a few years older than I am. She is down-to-earth and expert in the language and byways of postmodern, black women sistafriends. She also has a robust intellect, having attended a prestigious New England prep school, St. Paul's, on scholarship and graduated from Harvard. She is both wicked "book smart" and "people smart"—if also tough as nails. Her husband, William "Billy" Martin, is a prominent defense attorney in Washington. He and Michel constitute a classic D.C. power couple. I hadn't asked for it, but Michel took on the role of mentor, and we talked by phone and e-mailed frequently between late 2005 and early 2007. I was grateful for her insights.

So it was that in January 2007, Michel Martin and her top producer, a black woman who had worked with her at ABC News, invited me to work as an editor on the program they planned to launch at NPR. (Michel had left ABC in 2006.) It was a full-time, temporary assignment. No health benefits were offered, but the pay was quite generous.

I was to report to NPR on February 21 for at least six full weeks of work. During that time, my hours would move from a standard 9 a.m. to 6 p.m. shift to a pilot schedule of early morning to early afternoon hours. That early morning start time raised a big question for me around child care, since my son's day-care center didn't open until 7 a.m. and my daughter's elementary school opened two hours later. But I didn't ask the producer for more details when I got the call; I was too relieved and grateful for the offer of full-time work that would last at least six weeks.

After I received that phone call, I sat down at the small kitchen table in my rented house. Crossing my arms atop the table and resting my head on my forearms, I looked out the window into the backyard and breathed deeply. The "divorce house" I had been renting since my marriage cracked up was small but clean. It was located close to the children's elementary school and day-care center in Silver Spring, and it had just enough space for the three of us. Since mid-2006, I had been consumed with the challenge of scratching enough money together each month to pay our lease and other expenses. Until my divorce was final, I would receive no financial support from my former husband. But following that call from NPR, I could at least breathe easier for as long as the job lasted.

When I turned up for my first day of work in late February 2007, I joined a skeleton staff of three producers, a director, two production assistants, and two engineers. I wasn't sure how to actually edit an entire broadcast. But the program's godmother, the veteran NPR producer of *Talk of the Nation*, Sue Goodwin, taught me the process and assured me that I'd be fine.

In truth, though, I was also rusty in one important area: the basic workplace socialization skills that are crucial in a small team environment, most especially at a highly ritualized place like NPR. I had been starved for regular, adult workplace contact for years, and was now gorging on the attentive ears of my new coworkers. I didn't want to sound like some of the old-timers I had worked with in San Francisco and Fresno—salty veteran journalists whose best years were behind them; gnarled and grizzled men and women with whiskey voices who had told their best stories so often that they had the patness of a candidate's stump speech. But my new coworkers looked at me with genuine admiration and told me they'd been impressed and a bit intimidated when I joined Michel's team. "You are a great writer, Amy," an assistant producer told me. "I couldn't believe it when they told us the other day you'd be joining us soon—I was like, 'Oh my God, really? Amy Alexander is going to be working with us?!'"

I didn't know if she was just flattering me or what. But it made me feel good.

We spent long editorial meetings brainstorming and hatching the editorial vision for the new program. Michel and operatives from the AAPRC had sold NPR's top executives on a one- or two-hour daily talk program that would be unlike anything else on their network: a smart, meaty, accessible news and information program covering multicultural issues. *News & Notes* was airing in a few dozen markets nationwide, but the consortium wanted to continue pressing NPR to build more programming that might appeal to listeners at its string of small stations at historically black colleges and universities.

"We want to take the news of the day and come at it from our own perspective," Michel said in one of our first editorial meetings. "None of the usual guests, experts, or angles on the news of the day— and we will *own* any big story about people of color." Michel made it clear to me that she'd invited me in for three main reasons: my ability to generate quality, high-concept ideas; my writing and editing skills; and my Rolodex.

In an editorial meeting early in March, Sue Goodwin told us that NPR had committed to launching the new, as yet unnamed program in late April. (Following focus group meetings and marketing research by NPR, it was ultimately named *Tell Me More*.) The executives expected us to produce twenty-five to thirty pilot programs—a frighteningly large amount of hour-long programs, even if they would never be heard by the public. (We ultimately produced half that many test broadcasts before *Tell Me More* went live.) The fruits of our editorial meetings—including the development of regular, standing segments on religion, the economy, and culture—were strung together little by little between late February and late April. Many of the interviews and other segments that we cobbled together for those pilots were posted at the NPR website, where readers were asked to weigh in on the content and general tone of the material. The producers and production assistants, known as PAs, took the names of potential guests that we'd all come up with in morning editorial meetings and began contacting them for preinterviews.

Tell Me More would be carried initially on all of the public radio stations within the consortium, about thirty, with larger stations nationwide expected to add the program over time. We were not informed about the costs of launching, but based on what we overheard Michel, the executive producer, and Sue discussing from time to time, we knew the pressure was on. NPR had produced a "black-oriented" talk program only twice before: *News & Notes* in 2005 and the ill-fated Tavis Smiley program in 2003.

By the time I started on Michel Martin's team, some employees occasionally made oblique references to how the Tavis Smiley situation had played out. It was said that the executive leadership at NPR saw African Americans, Latinos, and other nontraditional audiences as exotic and outré, not as loyal listeners and potential donors to be cultivated long-term. This attitude sounded like the twenty-first-century version of the insincere, window-dressing lip service that Frank McCulloch had described years earlier in San Francisco and that I had experienced, to varying degrees, at other news organizations where I'd worked.

I began to listen to the big programs on NPR more critically and to think of how the people of color that I knew around the country interacted—or didn't—with NPR. Most of my neighbors and colleagues listened to NPR programming at least occasionally, and we occupied similar rungs on the socioeconomic ladder—college graduates with incomes of more than eighty thousand dollars annually. (At least, that *was* my income bracket before the end of my marriage.) On the other hand, no one in my immediate family regularly listened to NPR or their local public radio stations, nor did the friends and classmates that I'd grown up with in San Francisco and still kept in touch with. That represented a small mystery since they too were college educated and earned middle-class incomes—some in teaching jobs, some by working at government agencies, and some in corporate jobs in the Bay Area or elsewhere around the nation. But to the majority of my age cohorts who were not journalists or working in media-related fields, NPR programming held little interest.

I didn't know enough about marketing science as it related to news broadcasting to parse out the exact reason for that. My longtime friends were all intelligent, they worked hard, and they kept up with what was going on in the world, mostly by watching television news and reading newspapers. They consumed what seemed to me to be a healthy diet of news. Yet among the dozen former high school or college classmates that I stayed in touch with, only two—who were white—reported that they regularly listened to programming on KQED, the NPR member station in San Francisco. Another college classmate, Maria Elena Camposeco, regularly listened to NPR—but she is a former newspaper journalist and a self-described "news junkie." And even she sometimes made jokes about how "white bread" the NPR reports she listened to were.

I began to look more closely at the demographics of the staff members I encountered at NPR in Washington. In the editorial ranks, I noticed a dearth of black men in staff positions across the programs. I'd heard rumblings for years that some black male correspondents had a tough time succeeding on NPR's marquee programs and on its national and international desks.

At the same time, NPR boasted at least one high-profile black male journalist in its roster: Juan Williams, a veteran Washington writer and editor. Since 1997, Williams had floated in and out of NPR. He delivered news analysis on the network's marquee programs, including *Weekend Edition*, and sometimes served as a substitute host of programs. Williams was the highest-profile African American male on the air at NPR, and we newcomers viewed him as something of an "untouchable" when we met him during the winter of 2007. He stopped in at our offices at NPR one morning several weeks before the Michel Martin program launched, and he struck me and the other team members as friendly, approachable, and comfortable in his own skin.

Williams had worked for many years at the *Washington Post* and had authored one of the most important nonfiction books of the mid-twentieth century, *Eyes on the Prize*, the companion edition to the groundbreaking PBS series on the civil rights movement. He regularly keynoted big cultural and media events around D.C. and also provided analysis at another big broadcast news company—Fox News. Williams was not a full-time employee at NPR or at Fox, and it seemed to me that he had managed to leverage his profile as a leading journalist specializing in covering or analyzing political and social issues into lucrative arrangements with two top news organizations.

All the same, Williams, notwithstanding his seemingly protected status as a top D.C. journalist with gigs at two major national news outlets, found himself at the red-hot center of the escalating war between news consumers' expectations for what news organizations are supposed to accomplish and news companies' efforts to stay competitive in a mass media landscape increasingly defined by highly partisan reporting and commentary offered at websites and on blogs. During the 2000s, even some cable news outlets had begun airing partisan coverage.

After more than a decade at NPR, Williams was fired from his role as a contributing news analyst in the fall of 2010. Top editors at NPR let Williams go after he appeared on the Fox News Channel and admitted that he sometimes felt fear whenever he saw Muslims board commercial airliners. When word of his firing emerged in news-oriented blogs—and after Williams appeared on a Fox News program and described the firing by NPR—the episode quickly escalated, drawing coverage by the *New York Times*, the *Washington Post*, and other high-profile news organizations. In a flash, Williams had become a symbol of the public's increasing anger toward the national media in general and—for consumers who held conservative political viewpoints—the "liberal pinheads" at NPR in particular.

For those of us living and working in the hothouse media environment of the Beltway—and particularly for those who were aware that NPR had a history of failing to hire and retain talented black male journalists—it was a strange and sad development. Williams may indeed have played out his time at NPR, but the management's decision to fire him for something he'd said on another network, not on NPR's air, gave the impression that it cared more about its image as a liberal-leaning news organization than it did about maintaining clearly stated ethical standards and applying them fairly among all employees and contributors. Granted, Williams had earlier in the decade been told by NPR's managers not to allow the Fox Network to identify him as an NPR news analyst while he made appearances on their air. But still, his firing—which took place during a single phone conversation from a top news editor at NPR—came off, at least to me, as cold, ruthless, and undignified. And after Williams gave interviews on other national news programs—including a top NPR-produced talk show, *The Diane Rehm Show*—and described feeling confused and betrayed by the network's leadership, media watchers, including Richard Prince, observed that NPR's firing of Williams had only added to its reputation as insensitive to audiences of color and to racial and ideological diversity among its employees.

And truth be told, even before that Juan Williams blowup in 2010, I gleaned that NPR could indeed benefit from a stronger focus on building a news staff that was more diverse in terms of race, economic background, and political ideology. The top editors and department heads that I encountered in 2006 and 2007 were more alike than different in terms of their class, values, and social affiliations. Most of the NPR staffers that I encountered had attended top-tier colleges, came from middle- or upper-income families, and lived in parts of the District or suburban D.C. that were borderline swanky—Chevy Chase, Bethesda, Shepherd Park, or the quickly gentrifying neighborhoods in Northwest D.C. Those affiliations are not intrinsically problematic. But the onset of groupthink and a propensity for being closed-minded to opposing viewpoints and experiences are inevitable byproducts of any large organization in which the majority of participants hail from similar backgrounds.

"NPR is expert at hiring itself," a veteran editor and producer, Audrey Wynn, told me in 2006. Wynn, who is African American, had spent more than twenty years at NPR before being encouraged to take a buyout during one of the rounds of cost-cutting the network made in 2007 and 2008. It didn't seem to matter that Wynn was one of only four experienced blacks in editorial management at that time.

The standard-bearer NPR national news programs—*Morning Edition* and *All Things Considered*—had between them one host who was a person of color, the veteran journalist Michele Norris, a cohost at *All Things Considered* since 2002. And interestingly, in spite of her high-profile standing at NPR and long track record of consistently delivering tough, fair interviews, Norris too was at the center of a 2010 incident that raised questions about NPR's commitment to ethnic diversity.

The network had participated in the creation of an official history of NPR, a book published in the fall of 2010, in which veteran staff producers and hosts discussed life inside the network. Norris had been on a sabbatical for several months early in 2010 while she worked on a book of her own. She had been asked to contribute an essay to the NPR book, which was organized as a chronological history of the network, but had to demur owing to the production of her own memoir. When *This Is NPR* was published in November 2010, it emerged that not only had Norris not contributed an essay to the volume, but she was not mentioned anywhere in it. For that matter, neither were Juan Williams, Tavis Smiley, Farai Chideya, or the AAPRC, according to Eric Deggans, media writer at the *St. Petersburg Times*. An NPR spokeswoman told Deggans that leaving Norris out of the history was "an inexcusable mistake," adding that they hoped to "rectify" the omission in subsequent editions.

Such episodes raise important questions about NPR. Namely, how can NPR hope to grow, from within, more original programming that appeals to black and other ethnic audiences if they don't have black reporters, producers, and editors with the experience and ranking to help drive coverage that would best appeal to those audiences? Can their editorial leadership, which is made up primarily of white, upper-middle-class journalists, improve the culture of the organization so that racial, class, and ideological diversity becomes not just a distant goal but a way of life?

Given that the network's own demographic research showed signs that it needed to reach out to new audiences, it seemed to me that the alliance with the AAPRC—along with a Texas-based syndicated NPR program aimed at Latinos, *Latino USA*, hosted by Maria Hinojosa—just made good sense.

But while I worked at NPR full-time, I couldn't afford to ponder for long all the nuances of personnel issues. I needed to focus every ounce of energy I could muster on learning the ins and outs of radio journalism. The process was fun, if intense and surpassingly stressful. On most late afternoons I returned to Silver Spring following a ten-hour workday, and only after having dinner with my children, helping them with homework, and putting them to bed did I realize that my stomach muscles had been clenched virtually all day.

I left NPR in September 2007, wrung out from the combined stress of my domestic situation and the grueling requirements of editing and producing a daily hour-long talk program. I had learned how to produce high-quality radio, though, and made contributions to *Tell Me More* that helped the program expand from the thirty or so stations in the AAPRC to sixty or more stations by late 2010. I had connected the program to the *Washington Post*'s Sunday magazine, an idea that had been a big hit with Michel Martin, NPR, and the D.C. member station that aired *Tell Me More*, WAMU-FM. By the time of the program's launch on April 30, 2007, I had moved from editing to full-time producing on the show. It had occurred to me, during the early planning meetings for the new show, that in order to fill five hours per week of original programming—with each of those hours requiring between four and six guests, on average—we would need a good plan for standing segments in which the content and "talkers" were virtually guaranteed to be high quality.

I was friends with the deputy editor of the Sunday *Washington Post Magazine*—a former *Miami Herald* editor, Sydney Trent—and pitched to her the idea that on Mondays, once or twice a month, writers or columnists from the magazine should come to studio 4B at NPR in Washington, where *Tell Me More* was recorded, to be interviewed by Martin about their stories. Additionally, I developed a segment called "Magazine Mavens," in which Martin would regularly interview top editors at women's or lifestyle magazines.

It had been exhilarating and fun to hear those guests, and others that I personally booked, being interviewed on *Tell Me More*. But the breakneck pace of the work was grinding me down, and I hardly saw my children at all. I missed being able to write long form, too, and had tabled work on this book in order to earn income while my divorce made its way through the court system.

I was fortunate to be offered a year-long fellowship at the Nation Institute to begin in the new year; I eagerly accepted. And for 2008, the Alfred Knobler Fellowship allowed me to resume work on this book and to write about the cultural and political issues that swirled throughout the American electorate during the historic presidential race of that year.

Near the end of 2008, even as the entire nation was riveted by the unlikely presidential candidacy of a black freshman Democratic senator from Illinois, Barack Obama, my alma mater, *News & Notes*, was losing ground at NPR. Or at least that is how the network framed its decision to end the program. Despite having drawn a solid, if relatively small, base of loyal listeners, *News & Notes*, during its nearly five-year run, was not picked up by enough key NPR member stations in big markets, the network said. In the major markets where it was carried, including San Francisco and Chicago, it had been relegated to unpopular time slots.

The relationship between NPR and its member stations is a source of frustration to many of those who work for the network at its Washington, D.C., headquarters. During the months I'd spent producing and editing *Tell Me More*, I had numerous conversations with producers and technical people who did not understand why NPR's top executives do not simply order station managers in local markets to air certain national programs. The member stations exist in a tight, sometimes hostile, codependent relationship with NPR: their listeners make donations in the form of memberships, and the stations in turn pay fees to NPR in order to "buy" programs produced by NPR, including *Morning Edition* and *All Things Considered*. The official position from NPR executives is that they can only "offer" programs to local stations, not force station managers to air them. Slightly more than 40 percent of NPR's annual overhead costs are paid by fees from member stations—fees that are made possible by contributions from "listeners like you" around the nation.

As I view it, though, member stations would not garner donations from local listeners without the marquee programs produced out of Washington, so it seems to me that the network has the ultimate upper hand. Yet in the case of new programming designed to grow nontraditional audiences (ethnic minorities), NPR's leadership appears all too willing to allow local station managers to remain within their comfort zones rather than strongly encouraging them to give ethnic-themed programs breathing room to grow audiences. Thus when local stations claim they cannot make a go of a program like *News & Notes* and either dump it from their lineups or bury it in obscure time slots, NPR executives cite the program's low ratings as justification for ending it—without acknowledging the role that their own benign neglect played in the program's slow growth.

In key markets, including Chicago, New York, and Los Angeles, local station managers failed to recognize the potential for appealing to audiences of color in their markets and just did not bother to pick up *News & Notes* or *Tell Me More*, or they aired the shows but declined to grant them time slots where they would be most likely to succeed—either late morning rush hour, after the *Morning Edition* broadcast, or early afternoon rush, leading into *All Things Considered*.

So even as NPR acknowledges a common-sense need to grow its audiences, it appears to be hamstrung when it comes to devoting its full brain power and considerable endowment (estimated at more than $150 million, even after the stock market downturn of 2008) to producing and widely airing high-quality programming aimed at growing ethnic communities in the United States. Many of us who watched the slow demise of *News & Notes* thought it all looked very predictable.

News & Notes was canceled for "budgetary reasons," according to NPR's president and CEO, a former *New York Times* online executive, Vivian Schiller. In fairness, Schiller has said she wants to make NPR's programming and staff truly reflect the changing demographics in America—although she stumbled badly with the inept handling of Juan Williams's firing in 2010. During a talk at the National Press Club early in 2009, Schiller was asked about the closing of *News & Notes* and whether it meant that she—like her predecessor, former CEO Ken Stern—intended to continue paying only "lip service" to diversity in NPR's programming and staff hiring. She vehemently protested and said her preference was to be "inclusive" across all programming, not just produce specific programs with ethnic themes or staffs. In late 2009 the network announced the creation of a new position, vice president of diversity. And it hired Keith Woods, a veteran black journalist and media educator at the Poynter Institute, for the job.

I did not expect Farai Chideya to go public with her opinions of what had happened to *News & Notes*, but early in 2009 she did. As I followed Chideya's comments, a picture emerged of a disillusioned professional who appeared to be coming to the conclusion that mainstream news organizations—yes, NPR is mainstream—are still not prepared to acknowledge the value of courting ethnic audiences or to see the bottom-line value and long-term survival advantages to be gained by appealing to people of color.

First, Chideya spoke on the record to a New York blogger and Hunter College English professor, Eisa Ulen:

> The company said the issue was economic. But while the company is running in the red, there were other shows that cost more per listener than we did. If they cut based on that basis, I don't know that we would have been cut.
>
> Of course, both of the LA-based shows (us and *Day to Day*) [another relatively new daily news magazine, which NPR produced in partnership with *Slate* magazine] got the axe. That was very controversial, because America is growing faster in population in the West than the East. You also have a different role of the Latino American and Asian American populations in the West. Foundations and individuals poured a lot of money into building the NPR West Facility, and now there is no need for a full-fledged NPR facility. So was the decision geographic? It seems likely that there was a move to consolidate resources in the East. Was that wise? Time will tell.

Richard Prince, the race and media online columnist, published portions of Chideya's interview with the blogger. But Jim Romenesko and other front-line mainstream media writers, including Jack Shafer at *Slate*, failed to so much as mention the critique from Chideya.

Later, Chideya published a thoughtful essay that plumbed the larger themes around race and media in America during this new, economically and demographically turbulent century. In June 2009, she posted it at the website she had founded, *Pop & Politics*, under the headline "The Journey of the Journalist, Part One—Why Is 'Saving Journalism' Not Enough?" She wrote:

> Rebuilding is great. But is it enough? What if we put the profit back in media? What if you can build new media empires that make the owners rich or the foundation heads lauded; the employees comfortable; and the consumers reasonably satisfied? What then? Do we in the business breathe with relief, pay off our credit card bills, and settle in for another round of who-gets-the-corner-office? . . . But judging from my personal on- and off-the-record discussions with for- and non-profit media businesses, as well as interactions at an endless numbers of "whither this/whither that" panels and conferences (and looking at the demographics of who's in the room) . . . we're not ready to face our biggest demon. That demon is exclusion: the way many Americans are cut out of media production and consumption, and the way many of us in the business are sanguine about it.
>
> We in the media are not "the people," nor do we represent them as fully as we often claim to. "Citizen journalism," as we now call it, may be valuable and produced by non-traditional journalists. But most of the people who create it are still more educated, more technologically skilled, and more likely to be white than the demographics of the overall U.S. population.

At the beginning of 2010, Chideya could be heard guest-hosting local talk programs at WNYC, an NPR station in New York. The ideas and arguments she put forth in "The Journey of the Journalist" resonated with me, even if they failed to earn much attention amid the widening cacophony of mainstream discourse taking place on the Internet and in legacy news organizations about the future health of the news industry. To date, the most influential authors of the first rough draft of *this* history—the epic transformation of American mass media—fit a familiar demographic profile: that of the white men who have always defined Serious Journalism in the United States. To use a coldly dispassionate term that has come to define the uncertain fate of journalism in America: Is this model sustainable?

I intend to keep covering the many aspects and tributaries that will, over time, make it possible to answer that question. What I do not expect, though, is that I will be paid a decent amount to do so.

I have worked fairly consistently during the past twenty-five years in a business that is excessively hard on one's soul—on the souls of black women especially. The criteria for success have changed dramatically since the 1980s, when I first became a reporter at daily newspapers. As I am writing this, late in 2010, it appears that the definition of journalism—and consequently the key characteristics, skills, and traits that make up a "successful" journalist—will continue to evolve at a shockingly fast pace. The great reporters' knack for meeting and dealing with sources and contacts from all walks of life was highly prized by news editors in my earliest days in newspapers. Now, that ephemeral, crucial skill set has slipped down the list of what most editors look for when considering job candidates. How this development—along with the overall shrinking of editorial staffs—will play out in the coming years for audiences interested in accurate, thoughtful reporting on communities of color can be surmised, if not known absolutely.

By the end of 2010, more than fifteen thousand professional journalists had been turned out of traditional news organizations nationwide, with no end in sight. At the same time, a quiet hiring boom was underway in some traditional media organizations and at new online-only outlets: young, relatively inexperienced journalists who had no fear of gadgetry were being brought on at salaries much lower than even the entry-level rates that big news organizations offered until the late 1990s. As some daily papers closed their print operations and laid off or bought out hundreds of veteran journalists, they quietly welcomed small numbers of novice "content producers" who had grown up with digital technology. The leading news industry trade group, ASNE, struggled to keep its doors open and laid off most of its staff; it did, though, retain as a contractor the editor Bobbie Bowman, who had spearheaded the group's annual survey of minority hiring and retention. Anecdotally, however, it seemed by the end of 2009 that my cohorts in traditional media—seasoned journalists of color—had seen their numbers shrink dramatically from once-powerful news organizations, while the small spurts of hiring at these remaining news organizations did not include many young journalists of color.

The prospect of a daily newspaper that published only online once seemed crazily farfetched. Yet in Seattle in 2009, the Hearst-owned *Post-Intelligencer* began publishing exclusively online, immediately after the owners shut down its 146-year-old print version. The reconstituted staff, those left to produce the online version of the *P-I*, numbered around twenty-five journalists, down from more than two hundred who had produced the "dead tree" printed daily. By my unofficial survey, ethnic minorities filled only a few of those twenty-five positions.

The severe shrinking raises important questions, on many levels, about the future of our American democracy and the role of the media in protecting the public's interests. To me, the most important questions in that context center on our swiftly changing race and class demographics: As America's cities and suburbs grow increasingly multiethnic, will the smaller, more digitally focused newsrooms of the future remain stubbornly monochromatic (that is, white), as well as middle- and upper-middle-class, as they've been in the recent past? And if that happens, what will it mean for the way Americans view themselves?

The self-made, working-class reporter has about as much cachet these days as a flight attendant. The crusading, ink-stained scribe is, of course, a lumpy cliché. But at the center of that cliché was a belief in the journalist as the citizens' surrogate, a historian-cum-watchdog who stayed hot on the case of the latest affront to egalitarianism. Anyone who stayed in the business longer than a New York minute inevitably got hit with enough cold water to wash the romantic twinkle out of her eyes. And yes, journalists are not unique or more privileged than other American workers who've seen their workplaces vanish in midstride. As the 2000s wound down and Americans elected the nation's first black president, a small number of high-profile mainstream journalists began raising questions about what the loss of the *Front Page*–style journalist might mean for our body politic.

Dana Priest, for example, gave a poignant talk at a leading university that had given her a journalism award in 2007. A national security correspondent at the *Washington Post*, Priest, who is white, is an expert at a brand of intimate, deep-dish reporting that relies as much on the ability to get sources to open up as it does on the ability to mine documents and decipher arcane government rules and regulations. At the pinnacle of her career, following publication of a Pulitzer Prize–winning investigative series on official neglect at Walter Reed Army Medical Center in Washington, D.C., Priest delivered a talk at Columbia University that might have been given by Farai Chideya or any number of other high-performing journalists of color who have been upended by the massive evolution in the news business. Its most pointed message centered on the need for journalists to continue honing their ability to meet and deal with other humans. Even amid the rise of technology and the speed-of-light communication delivery systems that now augment the news business, journalists simply can't afford to lose sight of the Real People who depend on the press to force accountability from our government, corporations and institutions. The Real People whom journalists cover are not merely "consumers"; they are also sources who can help guide an inquiring reporter to the heart of a story.

Priest said, in part:

> You must learn to develop your eyes and ears. And your sense of people. An important part of this is discarding your prejudices and stereotypes about everything. Be patient. Take time. . . .

Find people you can work with on the inside who you don't ever intend to quote. Have them help you find other people, other sources, other scraps of information. Burrow into the bureaucracy, find the secretaries, the clerks, the mid-level managers, the former managers . . . not all Washington journalists choose to work those circles. Take risks. Be bold.

The emotional-intelligence muscles that Priest urged those Columbia students to develop have often allowed journalists of every ethnicity to uncover important news. I argue that those muscles have been especially valuable to legacy news organizations when flexed by journalists of color, even if that flexing sometimes created tense moments in newsrooms. Now, though, I do not know how mainstream news organizations will successfully cover the growing majority-minority U.S. population when they operate with fewer of those particular muscles or with their strength considerably diminished.

At the same time, it is important to try to keep things in historical perspective. Contemporary journalists aren't the first and won't be the last class of American workers to feel abandoned as technological advancements push large-scale changes across global industries. Our work will become more streamlined and efficient. But in a business that depends so heavily on humans—in all their messy unpredictability—to get the story right, it is troubling to consider what exactly that streamlining process might leave by the wayside.

I wonder: Is the kind of journalist trained in the tradition of shoe-leather reporting, rigorous fact checking, and the careful cultivation of official sources, contacts, and regular people on the street a dying breed? And when it comes to old-school journalists of color, well, we were rare birds to begin with. Only after the tumultuous 1960s and the publication of the Kerner Commission's report on the urban riots of that era did big news outfits begin hiring blacks and Latinos in measurable numbers. Now our ranks are shrinking faster and more dramatically than those of white journalists amid the massive downsizing that is taking place in mainstream media. In 2008 ASNE reported that about three hundred journalists of color lost their jobs during the previous year, representing roughly 12 percent of those dismissed, while they constituted, in total, just 5 percent of newsroom employees. In July 2008, as the rate of layoffs increased across the news industry, leaders at the National Association of Black Journalists went so far as to issue an open letter to newspaper publishers declaring that "NABJ will hold you accountable if you do not consider diversity in your hiring and, particularly, firing practices." The layoffs continued through the end of the decade, suggesting that fewer journalists of color will be in a position to accumulate the experience needed to perform high-level reporting at a time when the percentage of people of color in the United States is increasing.

My résumé now contains the names of nearly as many web-only news organizations as it does print-only publications. This is, from at least one angle, a happy development: it allows me to stay current. But the universe of web publications so far is thin on the checks and balances—the armies of assignment, line, and copy editors—that ensure quality control of content in most traditional print publications. The last lines of defense are small indeed at even the most popular online publications, including the ethnic-themed sites owned by large corporate news companies such as NBC and the *Washington Post*. At small, independent web magazines, they are in many cases nonexistent, raising questions about the healthfulness of the diet that news readers consume at the online upstarts.

At the same time, because it mirrors the hundred-year tradition of black and other ethnic community publications in America, the web will, I like to believe, eventually prove beneficial as fertile territory for new voices and perspectives. In 2000, for example, the Pacific News Service, a progressive, nonprofit media group, launched New America Media. Nearly a decade later, New America is the umbrella organization for more than three thousand ethnic publications, online and in print, stretching around the globe. The organization's website says it reaches some 57 million adults, mostly from ethnic communities, and that its publications collectively represent the "fastest growing sector" of America's news media industry. New America Media aggregates news from other ethnic news organizations and does not produce much in the way of original reporting. But its wide footprint on the web indicates that a full-service news and information online publication aimed at ethnic minorities may be viable—culturally and economically—in the years to come.

In that context, it is intriguing to consider that the two parallel universes that have long existed in print—exemplified, for example, by the likes of a black newspaper like the *Chicago Defender* as counterpoint to the *Chicago Tribune*—may become the norm in the web world too. I've had the good fortune to write for "white" web-only publications and for "black" web organizations. I'm not yet certain whether that bifurcation can or should continue. Nor am I yet convinced that publications and media groups like TheRoot.com and New America Media can sustain large numbers of well-trained journalists of color. It is a bitter but entirely accurate truism among black journalists: write for the "black press" and you will fight the good fight all the way to the poorhouse.

Now, slightly more than a decade after web-only publications began to penetrate American media markets in earnest, my best assessment is that for all their welcomed analysis of black-oriented issues, the growing universe of smart, black-focused websites cannot fill one significant void that is widening by the day: the empty space once occupied by scores of smart, experienced journalists of color at places tasked, first and foremost, with reporting the news every day. Not commenting on it. Not ranting about it. Reporting it.

The "niching" of web-only publications, furthermore—the accelerating growth of online publications aimed at narrower and narrower topics, from national security from a conservative perspective to international affairs from a liberal view—makes me worry that journalists who sign on at these sites will be speeding up the demise of media literacy among consumers, rather than helping consumers strengthen the vital critical reading and thinking skills required to achieve a healthy democracy. The "old media" model of one-stop shopping, where readers might graze through "objectively" reported stories on sports, lifestyle, international, national, and local news, was not perfect. But it trained readers to expect a range of coverage and analysis—not simply coverage and analysis that reinforced their existing beliefs.

My first dozen years in journalism were exciting, frustrating, harrowing, and for the most part satisfying, in that I accomplished my early, somewhat naive mission of bringing light to people and experiences that didn't often get decent airing in the mainstream press.

I didn't set out to be an Explainer of Blackness within "establish-ment" media, yet I recognized after working in mainstream news-rooms for many years that I had a responsibility to provide such coverage. And in the main, I engaged in creative, influential work that had the benefit of providing financial support, health care, and a degree of respectability. (The "respectability" part seems especially quaint right about now.)

At the same time, there are hints that at least some gatekeepers at the large-scale news organizations that remain are catching on to the potential drawbacks of allowing racial inclusion to fall off the table. The current narrative of old-media-morphing-to-new-media is be-ing duly chronicled in journalism trade publications and by news or-ganizations themselves, in vivid, occasionally overwrought language. It is a worthy, if self-referential, storyline, and it is being told by some of the very journalists who are experiencing wrenching losses at their own workplaces.

The White House press corps, historically a bastion of white males, now contains dozens of journalists of color and women, many of whom were assigned there in direct response to the election of Barack Obama in November 2008. The assignment editors and producers at CNN, ABC, *Politico*, CBS, and other major news or-ganizations made a pragmatic decision with clear racial and cultural implications: put black journalists on the job of providing daily cov-erage of our newly elected black president in the hope of maximizing access. It was a cynical development, no doubt, especially since most legacy news organizations have for decades employed at least a few veteran journalists in D.C. who were qualified to cover the White House but had been routinely passed over for the spot.

As President Obama's first term got underway early in 2009, a small army of black reporters covered the White House and ma-jor federal agencies in the new administration. Their ascendance was bittersweet, since the Obama administration's arrival coincided with the downward spiral of legacy news organizations that once provided the nation with its daily intake of national and presidential news. And only one of the popular digital media publications with a White House correspondent, *Politico*, saw fit to assign an African American correspondent to the beat.

The *Huffington Post*, an increasingly influential—if politically partisan—online publication, sent a young white male blogger to cover the White House, earning the distinction of becoming the first "paperless" publication in American history to earn an official White House correspondent's credential. Some media writers, particularly at large publications in the Northeast, made much of that development. But what caught my attention was the fact that the *Huffington Post* had selected a relatively untested young white reporter to cover the Obama administration while overlooking dozens of seasoned black, Latino, and Asian journalists who would gladly have taken the assignment.

Mini-scandals around language, identity, and racial sensitivity emerged during Obama's first two years in office, and journalists across the spectrum of news organizations and web upstarts grappled with how (or even whether) they should report on what appeared to be increasingly racist rhetoric from some political activists. By the time of the midterm elections in 2010, the Tea Party movement— a loose conglomeration of local political activists, voters, and new politicians that leaned to the right—held rallies and spewed invective that carried the strong hint of racial animus toward the nation's first black president. (And the Fox News Channel, which airs reporting and opinion programming with a decidedly conservative bent, gave hours of airtime to activists and political candidates who questioned President Obama's American citizenship—a not-so-veiled way of casting doubt on the legitimacy of America's first black president.)

The network is also home to a talk show host, Glenn Beck, who early in 2010 told another Fox News journalist that he believed President Obama "hates white people." Beck later retracted that comment, but his daily hour-long program on Fox regularly inveighed against what he described as Obama's "socialist" programs and attempts to use policy to strip Americans of their civil rights and their wealth. And by the end of 2010, Fox News had welcomed a new full-time employee to its lineup of on-air talent: Juan Williams.

By the end of 2010, several black journalists, including Eugene Robinson of the *Washington Post*, Gwen Ifill of PBS, and Michele Norris of NPR, had published nonfiction books that examined the state of race relations, and I sense they were spurred, in part, by

the general ratcheting up of racial anxiety across the nation. Historically, of course, journalists of all ethnicities have published nonfiction
books, usually on topics that grew from a story they'd reported. But
President Obama's election gave rise to kitchen-table talk and professional punditry surrounding the question of whether America had
at last reached a "postracial" standing, a cultural and political place
where racism had been defeated. The "postracial" commentary was
largely academic, in my view, especially as the severe downturn that
gripped the U.S. economy beginning in late 2007 revealed that job-
lessness for black Americans—double the rate of unemployment for
whites, as of late 2010—is a solid indication that racial discrimination, however subtle, is far from dead.

More pointedly, the increasingly large number of vocal citizens
who have thrown in with Tea Party groups and who engage in public
rallies and loud rhetoric that bear the distinct whiff of racial divi-
siveness indicates that racism likely drives much of the anger that
undergirds the protests. The Tea Party members primarily claim to
be in favor of fiscally conservative government policies rather than
being focused on race, gender, or other social issues; and based on
news reports in 2009 and 2010, it appears that at least a few blacks be-
long to the group. Yet owing to professional ethical dictates as much
as to their shrinking ranks, and perhaps because producers don't consider them, black journalists are rarely shown on national political
talk programs discussing the undercurrent of racial anxiety that exists
within the Tea Party movement. It is too bad, since blacks and other
journalists of color, especially those who have experience covering
cultural politics, might actually help American audiences understand
what is really happening on the political scene—not merely engage
in the kind of mudslinging and eye gouging that tends to characterize
political analysis on some national news outlets.

As for the journalists of color who were assigned to the White
House beat following Obama's election, it will be interesting to
see whether that trend continues after the Obama administration
departs.

When I stepped off the treadmill of daily journalism in the late
1990s to try my hand at independent journalism and to build a family,
I assumed I'd get back on. These days, largely because of the pres-

ence and influence of my two children, whose web lives I bird-dog voraciously, I am as much a highly attuned media consumer as I am a journalist. I see the evidence every day of other professionals selectively remaking their professional identities, carefully editing out the between-the-lines details of their lives and careers to fit the changing landscape. As a skilled journalist, I am as well equipped to analyze and suss out these changes for myself as I am to interpret them for others. I still have faith in the news business—however flawed, however panicked it has become.

I just know that all the retrenchment and remaking in the business must include a commitment to meeting the immense race and class shift that is also taking place.

For as long as I reasonably can manage it, I want my byline to be on the first draft of *this* part of our American history, the moment when the narrative of our nation came to truly convey the great promise of all its residents.

The idea for *Uncovering Race* was born in Cambridge, Massachusetts, in 2000, when I first began writing about race and media in the United States. Its development was made possible by many, beginning with three key editors at the late, lamented website Africana.com: Kate Tuttle, Phillipe Wamba (now deceased), and Henry Louis Gates Jr. Thanks to them and to the entire *Africana* team.

Helene Atwan, director at Beacon Press, agreed that the theme of the column I wrote for five years at *Africana*—race and media—was a great topic for a book. I cannot thank Helene enough for supporting this book through its unexpectedly complicated development. Also at Beacon Press, Allison Trzop, Cris Rodrigues, Pamela MacColl, and the entire editorial and production team showed a level of steadfastness, goodwill, and professional expertise that is a precious thing in the publishing world.

The Nation Institute, and the *Nation* magazine too, helped make this book possible with a year-long fellowship. Major thanks to Katrina vanden Heuvel, editor and publisher of the *Nation*, and to Betsy Reed, Karen Rothmyer, Richard Kim, Gary Younge, and Chris Hayes of the *Nation*, as well as to Taya Kitman, Hamilton Fish, Joe Conason, and Pamela Newkirk of the Nation Institute.

This work was also supported by friends, colleagues, and family members from coast to coast. Thanks to my children, Grace and Joseph, for their patience. Thanks also to my brother and sister, Eric and Gladys Fermon; to my mom, Hazel; to my niece, Chante Simmons Hersey, and her husband, Mark Hersey; and to Erna Smith, Lois Henry, Larry Fields, Anthony Duignan-Cabrera, Robert Moll, Maria Elena Camposeco, Mary Schmich, Sam and Stacy Diaz, Claudia Perry, Sydney Trent, Sharon Tabak-Bisk, Jennifer Longmire-Wright, Phillip Dixon, Lynne Duke, Sheryl McCarthy, Len Hollie, Nancy Lawrence Hill and Kirby Lawrence Hill, Vanessa Williams, Amy Langfield, Ron Nixon, Sabrina Thomas, Alicia Shepard, Patricia Thomas, Lynette Clemetson, Terence Samuel, Donna Britt, Kevin Merida, Evita Leonard Smedley, Marjorie Valbrun, Jabari Asim, Audrey Wynn, and Natalie Hopkinson.

Finally, I have to express gratitude to the teachers and child-care experts who helped me balance my family's needs with my work: Lisa Coppollino, director of the Rockville Day Care Association in Silver Spring, Maryland, and Principal Sarah Sirgo and the staff at Woodlin Elementary School in Silver Spring. I am extremely grateful for their dedication, integrity, and compassion.

Printed in the United States
By Bookmasters